Adobe Photoshop® 5.0

Classroom in a Book

Adobe

Contents

Masks and Channels

Lesson 5

Photo Retouching

Lesson 6

Basic Pen Tool Techniques

Advanced Layer Techniques

Optimizing Images for Web Publication

Creating Animated Images

Introduction

Adobe® Photoshop® is a powerful application for color painting, photo retouching, and image editing. You'll find that Photoshop excels as an art production tool, whether you are a graphics producer who needs to merge and edit color images, a photographer who wants to retouch proofs, or a graphic designer who is creating original or composite artwork, collages, or photo montages for print or on the Web.

About Classroom in a Book

Adobe Photoshop 5.0 Classroom in a Book® is part of the official training series for Adobe graphics and publishing software developed by experts at Adobe Systems. The lessons are designed to let you learn at your own pace. If you're new to Adobe Photoshop, you'll learn the fundamental concepts and features you'll need to master the program. If you've been using Adobe Photoshop for a while, you'll find Classroom in a Book teaches many advanced features, including tips and techniques for using the latest version of Adobe Photoshop.

Although each lesson provides step-by-step instructions for creating a specific project, there's room for exploration and experimentation. You can follow the book from start to finish or do only the lessons that correspond to your interests and needs. Each lesson concludes with a review section summarizing what you've covered.

Lessons for Adobe ImageReady 1.0

Lessons for Adobe ImageReady™ 1.0 are included in this Classroom in a Book. Adobe ImageReady is an application for preparing graphics for the World Wide Web, CD-ROM, or other multimedia. With Adobe ImageReady you can compress images, editing interactively to select the best balance of file size and image quality. ImageReady also provides a fast and simple way to create animated GIFs. You can create and edit images directly in ImageReady, but the program is ideal for working with images created in Adobe Photoshop.

Prerequisites

Before beginning to use *Adobe Photoshop 5.0 Classroom in a Book,* you should have a working knowledge of your computer and its operating system. Make sure you know how to use the mouse and standard menus and commands and also how to open, save, and close files. If you need to review these techniques, see the printed or online documentation included with your system.

Checking system requirements

Before you begin using *Adobe Photoshop 5.0 Classroom in a Book*, make sure that your system is set up correctly and that you've installed the required software and hardware.

Windows system requirements

You need the following components:

- An Intel® Pentium®-class or faster processor.
- Windows® 95 (or later), or Intel-based Windows NT® version 4.0 or later.
- At least 32 megabytes (MB) of random-access memory (RAM).
- A hard drive with at least 60 MB of free space. You'll need additional disk space if you work with very large image files.
- An 8-bit (256-color) display adapter card.
- A CD-ROM drive.
- A sound card (required to use the Adobe Photoshop Tour and Training CD-ROM).

For the best performance, Adobe Systems recommends the following hardware and software:

- 64 MB or more of RAM.
- A 24-bit (millions of colors) video display card.
- A PostScript® printer.

Adobe Photoshop and Adobe ImageReady performance improves with more RAM, faster CPUs, and faster and larger hard disk drives. Multiprocessor systems and systems with Intel's MMX technology can also speed performance.

For the latest system requirements, see the Read Me file.

Mac OS system requirements

You need the following components:

• An Apple Power Macintosh computer.

• At least 32 megabytes (MB) of random-access memory (RAM).

• Mac OS version 7.5 or later.

• A color monitor with an 8-bit (256-color) or better video display card.

• A hard drive with at least 60 MB of free space. You'll need additional disk space if you work with very large image files.

• A CD-ROM drive.

For the best performance, Adobe Systems recommends the following hardware and software:

• Mac OS version 8.1 or later.

• At least 64 MB of RAM.

• A 24-bit (millions of colors) video display card.

• A PostScript printer.

Adobe Photoshop and Adobe ImageReady performance improves with more RAM, faster CPUs, and faster and larger hard disk drives. Multiprocessor systems can also speed performance.

For the latest system requirements, see the Read Me file.

Installing the program

You must purchase the Adobe Photoshop or Adobe ImageReady software separately. For complete instructions on installing the software, see the Introduction to the *Adobe Photoshop 5.0 User Guide* or the *Adobe ImageReady 1.0 User Guide*.

Copying the Classroom in a Book files

The Classroom in a Book CD-ROM includes folders containing all the electronic files for the lessons. Each lesson has its own folder. You must install these folders on your hard drive to use the files for the lessons. To save room on your drive, you can install the folders for each lesson as you need them.

To install the Classroom in a Book files for Windows:

1 Insert the Adobe Photoshop Classroom in a Book CD-ROM into your CD-ROM drive.

2 Create a subdirectory on your hard drive and name it **PS5_CIB**.

3 Copy the Lessons folder into the PS5_CIB subdirectory.

To install the Classroom in a Book folders for Mac OS:

1 Create a folder on your hard drive and name it **Adobe Photoshop CIB**.

2 Drag the Lessons folder from the CD-ROM into the Adobe Photoshop CIB folder.

Restoring default preferences

The Preferences file controls how palettes and command settings appear on your screen when you open the Adobe Photoshop or Adobe ImageReady program. Each time you quit Photoshop or ImageReady, the position of the palettes and certain command settings are recorded in the preferences file.

To ensure that the tools and palettes function exactly as described in each lesson, rename or delete the preferences file before you begin each lesson. Rename the file if you want to save and reuse a set of preferences.

To quickly locate and delete the Photoshop Preferences file, create a shortcut (Windows) or an alias (Mac OS) for the Preferences folder.

To restore default Photoshop preferences in Windows:

1 Exit the Adobe Photoshop program.

2 Delete the Adobe Photoshop 5 Prefs file in the Photoshop5\Adobe Photoshop Settings directory.

To restore default Photoshop preferences in Mac OS:

1 Quit the Adobe Photoshop program.

2 Locate the Adobe Photoshop 5 Prefs file in the Adobe Photoshop 5.0\Adobe Photoshop Settings folder.

If you can't find the file, choose Find from the desktop File menu, enter **Adobe Photoshop 5 Prefs** in the text box, and click Find.

Note: If you still can't find the file, you probably haven't started Adobe Photoshop for the first time yet. The preferences file is created when you start the program.

3 Drag the Adobe Photoshop 5 Prefs file to the Trash.

4 Choose Special > Empty Trash.

Important: If you want to save the current settings, rename the Adobe Photoshop 5 Prefs file rather than throwing it away. When you are ready to restore the settings, change the name back to Adobe Photoshop 5 Prefs, and make sure that the file is located in the Photoshop5\Adobe Photoshop Settings directory (Windows) or the Adobe Photoshop 5.0\Adobe Photoshop Settings folder (Mac OS).

To restore default ImageReady preferences:

Do one of the following:

• In Windows, use the Registry Editor to restore ImageReady preferences to their default settings. See the online documentation accompanying Registry Editor for information.

• In Mac OS, open the Preferences folder in the System Folder and rename the Adobe ImageReady 1.0 Prefs file, or drag the file to the Trash.

Calibrating your monitor

Calibration is the process of adjusting a monitor and Photoshop settings to compensate for factors that affect how colors appear on-screen and in print. Calibrating your monitor is essential for accurate color reproduction and should be the first step in working in Photoshop.

For information on how to calibrate a monitor, see Lesson 13, "Ensuring and Printing Accurate Color," in this book.

Additional resources

Adobe Photoshop 5.0 Classroom in a Book is not meant to replace documentation that comes with the program. Only the commands and options used in the lessons are explained in this book. For comprehensive information about program features, refer to these resources:

• The User Guide. Included with the Adobe Photoshop or Adobe ImageReady software, the User Guide contains a complete description of all features. For your convenience, you will find excerpts from these guides, including the Quick Tours for both programs, in this Classroom in a Book.

• The Tour Movie, available on the application CD-ROM.

• The Quick Reference Card, a useful companion as you work through the lessons.

• Online Help, an online version of the User Guide and Quick Reference Card, which you can view by choosing Help > Contents. (For more information, see Lesson 1, "Getting to Know the Work Area.")

• The Adobe Web site, which you can view by choosing File > Adobe Online if you have a connection to the World Wide Web.

Adobe certification

The Adobe certification program offers end users, instructors, and training centers the opportunity to demonstrate their product proficiency and promote their software skills as Adobe Certified Experts, Adobe Certified Instructors, or Adobe Authorized Learning Providers. Visit the U.S. web site at http://www.adobe.com to learn how you can become certified.

Tour

A Quick Tour of Adobe Photoshop

This interactive tour of Adobe Photoshop, excerpted from the Adobe Photoshop User Guide, provides an overview of key features of the program. A movie version of the tour is also available on the Photoshop 5.0 CD. More detailed instructions on how to use the features in this tour are provided in individual lessons throughout this book.

Projects in Adobe Photoshop can begin in a variety of ways. Most projects start with a scanned image, stock digital art, or artwork created with a drawing program, such as Adobe Illustrator®. Some images can also be created from scratch within Adobe Photoshop. For this tour, you'll use files that were created from all of these sources.

1 Start Adobe Photoshop.

2 Choose File > Open, and open the files Tour.psd, CD.psd, and Horn.psd, located in the Tour folder. Arrange the windows so that you can work with them easily.

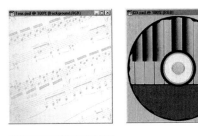

Selecting

In Adobe Photoshop, you modify part of an image by first selecting that area. You'll begin the tour by making selections in images using the selection tools. (If you make a mistake at any point in the tour, simply choose Edit > Undo, and try again.)

First, you'll make a simple selection, and drag an image from one file to another.

1 Click the title bar of the CD.psd window to make it active.

2 Hold down the mouse button on the rectangular marquee tool (⬚) in the toolbox, and drag to the elliptical marquee tool (◯). Click in the upper left corner of the image's gray background, and begin dragging diagonally. Then hold down Shift to change the elliptical selection to a circular selection, and drag to the bottom right corner of the image.

3 When the selection border matches the outside edge of the CD, release the mouse button and then release Shift.

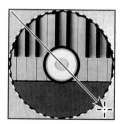

4 Select the move tool (►₊) in the toolbox, position it within the selection border, and drag the CD onto the Tour.psd window. The CD is now part of that file.

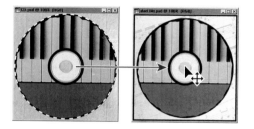

Now you'll resize the CD.

5 Choose Edit > Free Transform. Move the pointer onto one of the corner handles. Hold down Shift, and drag a corner handle to shrink the CD to about three-fourths its current size. Holding down Shift constrains the image's proportions as you resize it.

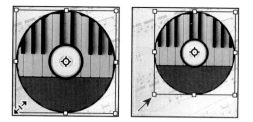

6 Move the pointer outside the selection handles, and drag clockwise to rotate the CD about 30°. Press Enter (Windows) or Return (Mac OS) to apply the transformation to the CD.

Note: You can also use the Numeric Transform dialog box to transform a selection using specific numeric values.

Next, you'll make a selection with the magic wand tool, which selects areas based on how similar they are in color.

7 Select the magic wand tool (✳); then click the title bar of the Horn.psd window to make it active.

8 Click the white background in the upper right corner of the image to select it. Notice that not all the white background was selected.

9 Choose Select > Similar to add the rest of the background to the selection. You've now selected everything except the horn.

10 Choose Select > Inverse. The Inverse command selects everything that wasn't selected—in this case, the horn.

11 Hold down Control (Windows) or Command (Mac OS), position the pointer within the selection marquee, and drag the horn onto the Tour.psd window. (Holding down Control/Command temporarily changes the current tool to the move tool.) Move the horn to the bottom left corner of the image.

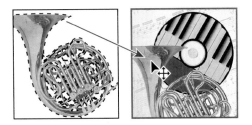

12 Choose File > Save As. Select a folder in which to save the file, enter the filename Work01.psd, and click Save.

13 Close the CD.psd and Horn.psd files.

Layers

Photoshop lets you organize artwork on separate transparent layers so that you can easily construct composite images and experiment with various effects.

1 If the Layers palette is not visible on your screen, choose Window > Show Layers. Click the minimize/maximize box (Windows) or resize box (Mac OS) at the top of the Layers palette to expand the palette.

Notice that this file has several layers, each named and with a *thumbnail*, or miniature representation, of the image on that layer. Photoshop automatically created separate layers for the CD image (Layer 1) and horn image (Layer 2) when you brought them into the Tour file. In addition, the background and the Notes layer were already in the file.

From the Layers palette you can display or hide layers in the image.

2 Click the eye icon column to the far left of the Notes layer to display the layer. Then try clicking the eye icon for Layer 2 to hide the layer, and again to redisplay it.

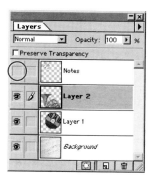

By changing the order of layers, you can restack images in the artwork.

3 Drag Layer 2 (the horn layer) until it's between Layer 1 (the CD layer) and the background on the Layers palette. Release the mouse button to set Layer 2 in its new position. The horn now appears behind the CD in the artwork.

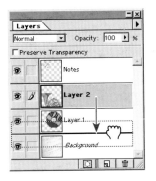

4 Click Layer 1 in the Layers palette to make it the active layer. The layer is highlighted and a paintbrush icon appears next to the layer thumbnail, indicating that your changes now will affect artwork only on that layer.

5 Select the move tool (✥). Then drag the CD to the top right corner of the artwork. Because the CD is on its own layer, you can move it separately from artwork on other layers.

Now you'll adjust the opacity of Layer 1.

6 Select Layer 1 in the Layers palette, and drag the opacity slider to 40%. You can now see other layers through the CD.

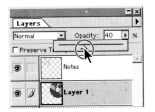

By specifying *blending modes*, you can determine how one layer interacts with another.

7 Choose Multiply from the mode menu at the top left of the Layers palette. Notice how the CD blends with the layers below it.

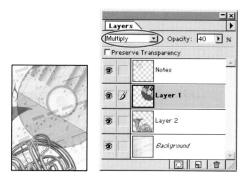

Now you're ready to create and manipulate some text. You will create the text with the type tool, which places the text on its own type layer. You will then edit the text and apply special effects to its layer.

8 Select the type tool (T), and click the image in the upper right corner.

9 Choose a font from the Font menu in the Type Tool dialog box, and enter a point size in the Size and Leading boxes (we used 22-point Lucida Sans Bold with 43-point leading). At the far right of the dialog box, select the right alignment option.

10 Type "MEZZO PIANO" in two lines in the large text box at the bottom of the dialog box.

11 Click the color box on the left side of the dialog box, select a color from the color picker, and click OK.

12 Then select "PIANO," and enter a larger point size in the Size box.

13 With the Type Tool dialog box still displayed, move the pointer into the image area. Notice that the pointer temporarily changes to the move tool. You can now reposition the text.

14 When the text looks the way you want it, click OK in the dialog box. The text is automatically placed in the Layers palette on a new type layer, marked with a T icon.

You can enhance any layer by adding a shadow, glow, bevel, or emboss special effect from the program's assortment of layer effects. You can also apply a combination of layer effects to the same layer. Here you'll apply the Drop Shadow and Bevel and Emboss layer effects to the type.

15 Make sure that the MEZZO PIANO type layer is active. Then choose Layer > Effects > Drop Shadow.

16 In the dialog box, change the opacity to 60% and set the angle to 150°.

17 Now choose Bevel and Emboss from the menu at the top of the dialog box.

18 In the new dialog box, click Apply. Then change the opacity for both Highlight and Shadow to 50%, select Inner Bevel for Style, set Blur to 2 pixels, and click OK. The drop shadow and bevel and emboss effects are now applied to the type.

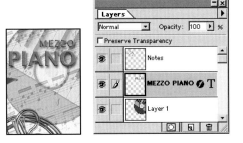

Photoshop makes it easy to change text on a type layer and ensures that any layer effects applied will automatically track changes made to the layer. You can see how this works by changing the wording of your text.

19 Double-click the T icon on the Mezzo Piano layer in the Layers palette. In the Type Tool dialog box, select the word "PIANO" and change it to "FORTE." Notice how the layer effects are applied to the new word.

20 If you like, try applying other layer effects to the text. When you have finished, click OK.

21 Choose File > Save.

Filters

To quickly add special effects to your artwork, you can choose from a wide variety of filters. In this part of the tour, you'll apply some filters to transform the background.

1 Click the background in the Layers palette to make it active.

2 Choose Filter > Distort > Wave. In the dialog box, set Number of Generators to 3, Maximum Wavelength to 350, Minimum Amplitude to 1, and Maximum Amplitude to 20. Click OK.

3 Choose Filter > Brush Strokes > Angled Strokes, and click OK to accept the default settings.

4 Then choose Filter > Fade Angled Strokes. In the dialog box, set the opacity to 50%, select Multiply for the mode, and click OK.

Explore some additional filters if you like.

Painting

With the Photoshop painting tools, you can add color to your artwork using preset swatches, colors you create, or colors you sample from existing art. Now you'll paint part of the background using the paintbrush tool.

1 Double-click the paintbrush tool (✐), and make sure that the opacity in the Paintbrush Options palette is set to 100%.

Note: Each tool in Photoshop has its own Options palette, which you can display by double-clicking the tool in the toolbox.

2 Choose Window > Show Brushes, and click the 35-pixel brush from the bottom row of the Brushes palette.

Now you'll paint arcs of four different colors over the bell of the French horn. The first color is white, which you'll select through the toolbox color selection box. This box sets the foreground color, the color you paint with, and the background color, the color used when you erase part of an image. The default colors are black for foreground and white for background.

3 Click the Switch Colors icon (↳) in the upper right corner of the color selection box to make the foregound color white.

4 Paint a white arc over the bell of the French horn.

You can use the eyedropper tool to select additional colors by sampling (copying) them from artwork in the image. You'll use a keyboard shortcut to access the eyedropper when selecting colors for the next three arcs.

5 Hold down Alt (Windows) or Option (Mac OS) to temporarily change from the paintbrush tool to the eyedropper tool (✐). Then click a yellow note in the image. The foreground color in the color selection box switches to the same yellow as in the note, indicating that you can now paint with this color.

6 Release the Alt/Option key, change the opacity in the Options palette to 80%, and paint a yellow arc just above the first white arc.

7 Now hold down Alt/Option, and click a red note to change the foreground color to red. Release the Alt/Option key, change the opacity in the Options palette to 60%, and paint a red arc above the yellow arc.

8 Repeat the process but this time sample the foreground color from a green note, change the opacity to 40%, and paint a green arc.

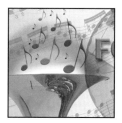

Next you'll use the History palette to remove the paint you just applied. The History palette records changes you make to the image and lets you step back through recent changes. Using this palette, you can return to an earlier version of the image and continue working from that point.

9 To display the History palette, choose Window > Show History.

10 Click Fade Angled Strokes in the history list. The image reverts to the way it looked right after you applied the Fade Angled Strokes filter.

You can now continue working from this version of the image. All changes past Fade Angled Strokes will be deleted, and new changes will be recorded in their place.

Next you'll try out a gradient fill to "paint" or blend between two colors on the background of the image.

11 Choose Window > Show Swatches, and click a blue swatch to set your foreground color. Then double-click the linear gradient tool ( ), and in the Gradient Tool Options palette choose Foreground to Transparent for the gradient, 30% for the opacity, and Multiply for the mode.

12 Drag the gradient tool from the top left to the bottom right corner of the background to set the beginning and end of the gradient.

13 Choose File > Save.

Retouching

Adobe Photoshop provides a full range of tools for retouching images, including dodge and burn tools, as well as features for adjusting color, tone, contrast, hue, and saturation. You'll use a few of these tools to do some basic color correction and editing on an image.

1 Click Layer 2 in the Layers palette to make it active.

2 To set the basic contrast and tonal range between the highlights and shadows in the horn, choose Image > Adjust > Levels.

3 In the dialog box, select the Preview option and then drag the left and right triangles inward to where the first spikes of the dark and light ends of the histogram's color range begin.

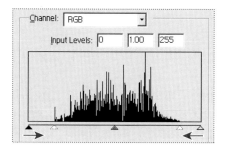

4 Click OK to apply the changes and extend the tonal range of the image.

Notice that the midtones in the horn are still not right; they need to be more red. To correct the color, you'll use the Color Balance command.

5 Choose Image > Adjust > Color Balance. A dialog box appears for adjusting the mixture of colors in the image.

6 Select the Preview option in the dialog box, drag the top slider away from Cyan toward Red, and click OK. The horn turns more red.

Now you'll remove a scratch on the horn with the rubber stamp tool. This tool lets you sample part of an image and then paint with a copy of the sampled area.

7 Double-click the rubber stamp tool (🖃) to display its Options palette, and select the Aligned option. Then choose a small feathered brush in the second row of the Brushes palette.

8 Place the rubber stamp tool over the horn next to the scratch. Hold down Alt (Windows) or Option (Mac OS), and click to sample this area. Release the Alt/Option key. Then drag the rubber stamp tool to paint over the scratch.

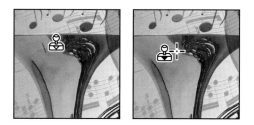

9 Choose File > Save.

Actions

The Actions palette lets you combine a set of commands into a single command or *action* and then execute the action on a single file or multiple files within a folder. With the Actions palette, you can record, play, edit, and delete commands to easily automate common techniques.

Adobe Photoshop offers some ready-made actions you can run on a file or set of files. You'll use one of these actions to add a vignette effect to the image. But first, to get the best results from the vignette, you'll flatten the file's layers into one layer. Then you'll make a selection to set the vignette's border.

1 Choose Layer > Flatten Image.

2 Hold down the mouse button on the elliptical marquee tool, and drag to the rectangular marquee tool. Then click approximately 1/8-inch in from the upper left corner of the image, and drag diagonally to 1/8-inch in from the lower right corner.

You can now apply the vignette action.

3 To display the Actions palette, choose Window > Show Actions.

4 In the Actions palette, open the Default Actions folder by clicking the folder arrow. Then select Vignette (selection) by clicking its name.

5 Click the Play button (▷) at the bottom of the palette.

6 In Mac OS, accept the default feather radius of 5 pixels in the Feather Selection dialog box, and click OK.

The action is then run on the image, creating the vignette.

7 When the action is complete, choose Layer > Flatten Image, and in the dialog box click OK to discard the hidden layers.

Saving the file

Because you may want to return to a version of the file with all its layers intact, you can use the Save As command to save the flattened file with a new name.

Choose File > Save As. Select a folder in which to save the file, enter a new filename, and click Save.

Note that you can save files in various formats, depending on how you plan to use the file. For example, you can save a file in JPEG format for display on the World Wide Web.

For more information on file formats, see "Saving and Exporting Images" in online Help or Chapter 14 in the Adobe Photoshop User Guide.

Congratulations, you've finished the tour.

For an illustration of the finished artwork, see the color signature.

Lesson 1

Getting to Know the Work Area

As you work with Adobe Photoshop, you'll discover that there is often more than one way to accomplish the same task. To make the best use of Adobe Photoshop's extensive editing capabilities, you first must learn to navigate the work area. The work area consists of the image window, the toolbox, and the default set of floating palettes, which are used repeatedly during the editing process.

In this introduction to the work area, you'll learn how to do the following:

- Open an Adobe Photoshop file.
- Select tools from the toolbox.
- Use viewing options to enlarge and reduce the display of an image.
- Work with palettes.
- Use online Help.

Starting the Adobe Photoshop program

When you start Adobe Photoshop, the menu bar, the toolbox, and four palette groups appear on the screen.

1 So that you can see the program's default settings, delete the Adobe Photoshop Preferences file to restore the program's default palettes and command settings. For step-by-step instructions on how to delete the preferences file, see "Restoring default preferences" on page 4.

2 Double-click the Adobe Photoshop icon to start the Adobe Photoshop program.

Opening files

Adobe Photoshop works with bitmapped, digitized images (that is, continuous-tone images that have been converted into a series of small squares, or picture elements, called *pixels*). You can create original artwork in Adobe Photoshop, or you can get images into the program by scanning a photograph, a slide, or a graphic; by capturing a video image; or by importing artwork created in drawing programs. You can also import previously digitized images—such as those produced by a digital camera or by the Kodak PhotoCD process.

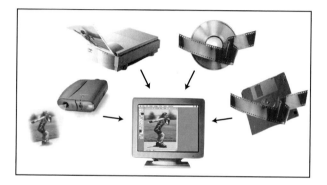

For more information on the kinds of files you can use with Adobe Photoshop, see "Getting Images into Photoshop" in online Help or Chapter 3 of the Adobe Photoshop User Guide.

1 Choose File > Open. Locate and open the Lesson01 folder. Then select Start01.psd, and click Open.

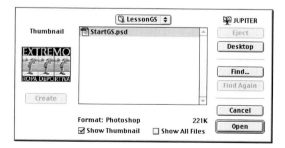

Note: The Classroom in a Book files are stored in individual lesson folders within the Photoshop CIB folder.

2 Choose File > Save As, type the name **Work01.psd**, and click Save.

Using the Photoshop tools

The toolbox contains selection tools, painting and editing tools, foreground and background color selection boxes, and viewing tools. This section introduces the toolbox and shows you how to select tools. As you work through the lessons, you'll learn more about each tool's specific function.

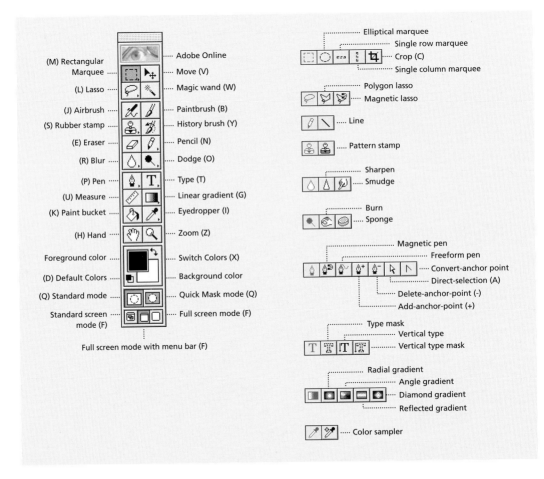

For an illustration of the toolbox, see figure 1-1 in the color signature.

1 To select a tool, you can either click the tool in the toolbox or you can press the tool's keyboard shortcut. For example, you can press M to select the marquee tool from the keyboard. Selected tools remain active until you click a different tool.

2 If you don't know the keyboard shortcut for a tool, position the mouse over the tool until its name and shortcut are displayed. (All keyboard shortcuts are also listed in the Quick Reference section of online Help. You'll learn to use online Help later in this lesson.)

3 Some of the tools in the toolbox display a small triangle at the bottom right corner, indicating the presence of additional hidden tools.

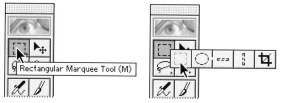

Name and shortcut displayed   Hidden tools

Select hidden tools in any of the following ways:

• Click and hold down the mouse button on a tool that has additional hidden tools. Then drag to the desired tool, and release the mouse button.

• Hold down Alt (Windows) or Option (Mac OS), and click the tool in the toolbox. Each click selects the next hidden tool in the hidden tool sequence.

• Press Shift + the tool's keyboard shortcut repeatedly until the tool you want is selected.

Note: *When you click a viewing tool to change the screen display of an image, you must return to the Standard screen mode to see the default work area displayed.*

*Standard
screen mode*

Viewing images

You can view your image at any magnification level from 0.198% to 1600%. Adobe Photoshop displays the percentage of an image's actual size in the title bar. When you use any of the viewing tools and commands, you effect the *display* of the image, not the image's dimensions or file size.

Using the View menu

To enlarge or reduce the view of an image using the View menu, do one of the following:

- Choose View > Zoom In to enlarge the display of the Work01 image.

- Choose View > Zoom Out to reduce the view of the Work01 image.

Each time you choose a Zoom command, the view of the image and the surrounding window are resized. The percentage at which the image is viewed is displayed in the Title bar and at the bottom left corner of the Adobe Photoshop window.

View percentage

You can also use the View menu to fit an image to your screen.

1 Choose View > Fit on Screen. The size of the image and the size of your monitor determine how large the image appears on-screen.

2 Double-click the zoom tool in the toolbox to return to a 100% view.

Using the zoom tool

In addition to the View commands, you can use the zoom tool to magnify and reduce the view of an image.

1 Click the zoom tool (🔍) in the toolbox to select the tool, and move the tool pointer onto the Work01 image. Notice that a plus sign appears at the center of the zoom tool.

2 Position the zoom tool over one of the skaters in the Work01 image, and click. The image is magnified to a 200% view.

3 With the zoom tool selected and positioned in the image area, hold down Alt (Windows) or Option (Mac OS). A minus sign appears at the center of the zoom tool (🔍).

4 Click once; the view of the image is reduced to a 100% view.

You can also drag a marquee with the zoom tool to magnify a specific area of an image.

5 Drag a marquee around the head of one of the skaters using the zoom tool.

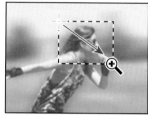

Area selected *Resulting view*

The percentage at which the area is magnified is determined by the size of the marquee you draw with the zoom tool. (The smaller the marquee you draw, the larger the level of magnification.)

Note: *You can draw a marquee with the zoom-in tool to enlarge the view of an image, but you cannot draw a marquee with the zoom-out tool to reduce the view of an image.*

You can use the zoom tool to quickly return to a 100% view, regardless of the current magnification level.

6 Double-click the zoom tool in the toolbox to return the Work01 file to a 100% view.

Because the zoom tool is used frequently during the editing process to enlarge and reduce the view of an image, you can select it from the keyboard at any time without deselecting the active tool.

7 To select the zoom tool from the keyboard, hold down spacebar+Ctrl (Windows) or spacebar+Command (Mac OS). Zoom in on the desired area, and then release the keys.

8 To select the zoom-out tool from the keyboard, hold down spacebar+Ctrl+Alt (Windows) or spacebar+Command+Option (Mac OS). Click the desired area to reduce the view of the image, and then release the keys.

Scrolling an image

You use the hand tool to scroll through an image that does not fit in the active window. If the image fits in the active window, the hand tool has no effect when you drag it in the image window.

1 Resize the image window to make it smaller than the image.

2 Click the hand tool in the toolbox. Then drag in the image window to bring another skater into view. As you drag, the image moves with the hand.

3 Like the zoom tool, you can select the hand tool from the keyboard without deselecting the active tool.

4 First, click any tool but the hand tool in the toolbox.

5 Hold down the spacebar to select the hand tool from the keyboard. Drag to reposition the image. Then release the spacebar.

6 Double-click the zoom tool in the toolbox to return the Work01 image to a 100% view.

Using the Navigator palette

The Navigator palette lets you scroll an image at different magnification levels without scrolling or resizing an image in the image window.

1 Make sure that the Navigator palette is at the front of the palette group. (If necessary, click the Navigator palette tab, or choose Show Navigator from the Window menu.)

2 In the Navigator palette, drag the slider to the right to about 200% to magnify the view of the skater. As you drag the slider to increase the level of magnification, the red outline in the Navigator window decreases in size.

3 In the Navigator palette, position the pointer inside the red outline. The pointer becomes a hand.

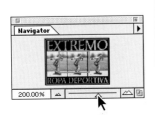

Dragging slider to 200%   *200% view of image*   *View in Navigator palette*

4 Drag the hand to scroll to different parts of the image.

You can also drag a marquee in the Navigator palette to identify the area of the image you want to view.

5 With the pointer still positioned in the Navigator palette, hold down Ctrl (Windows) or Command (Mac OS), and drag a marquee over an area of the image. The smaller the marquee you draw, the greater the magnification level in the image window.

Using the Info bar

The Info bar is positioned at the lower left corner of the application window (Windows) or of the image window (Mac OS) and provides information about a file's size, resolution, view, and placement on the printed page.

Info bar

1 To change the view of an image using the Info bar, drag over the number with the percentage sign at the far left corner of the Info bar.

2 Type the percentage at which you want the image displayed (you don't have to type the percent symbol). Then press Enter (Windows) or Return (Mac OS).

3 Double-click the zoom tool in the toolbox to return the file to a 100% view.

Working with palettes

Palettes help you monitor and modify images. By default, they appear in stacked groups. To show or hide a palette as you work, choose the appropriate Window > Show or Window > Hide command. Show displays the selected palette at the front of its group; Hide conceals the entire group.

Changing the palette display

You can reorganize your work space in various ways. Experiment with several techniques:

• To hide or display all open palettes and the toolbox, press Tab. To hide or display the palettes only, press Shift+Tab.

• To make a palette appear at the front of its group, click the palette's tab.

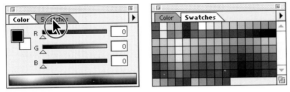

Click the Swatches tab to move it to the front.

• To move an entire palette group, drag its title bar.

• To rearrange or separate a palette group, drag a palette's tab. Dragging a palette outside of an existing group creates a new group.

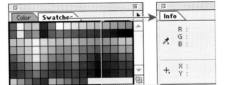

Palettes are grouped.　　　　*Click the palette tab, and drag the palette to separate from group.*

• To move a palette to another group, drag the palette's tab to that group.

• To display a palette menu, position the pointer on the triangle in the upper right corner of the palette, and hold down the mouse button.

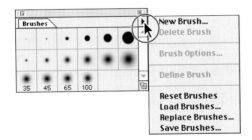

• To change the height of a palette (except the Color, Options, or Info palette), drag its lower right corner. To return the palette to default size, click the minimize/maximize box (Windows) or the resize box (Mac OS) in the right of the title bar. (A second click collapses the palette group.)

Click to collapse or expand palette.
A. Windows B. Mac OS

• To collapse a group to palette titles only, Alt-click the minimize/maximize box (Windows) or Option-click the resize box (Mac OS). Or double-click a palette's tab. You can still access the menu of a collapsed palette.

Setting the positions of palettes and dialog boxes

The positions of all open palettes and moveable dialog boxes are saved by default when you exit the program. Alternatively, you can always start with default palette positions or restore default positions at any time:

• To reset palettes to the default positions, choose File > Preferences > General. Click Reset Palette Locations to Defaults.

• To start always with the preset palette and dialog box positions, choose File > Preferences > General. Deselect Save Palette Locations. The change takes effect the next time you start Adobe Photoshop.

Using context-sensitive menus

In addition to the menus at the top of your screen, context-sensitive menus display commands relevant to the active tool, selection, or palette.

To display context-sensitive menus, position the pointer over the image or over an item in a palette list. Then click with the right mouse button (Windows) or press Control and hold down the mouse button (Mac OS).

Here we've used the eyedropper tool. The Sample Size options are displayed in the tool's context-sensitive menu. (You access these same options by double-clicking the tool to display its Options palette.)

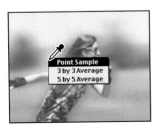

Using online Help

For complete information about using palettes and tools, you can use online Help. Online Help includes all of the information from the *Adobe Photoshop 5.0 User Guide*, plus keyboard shortcuts and some additional information. All of the illustrations in online Help are in color. In addition, online Help includes full-color galleries of examples that are not included in the printed User Guide.

Online Help is easy to use, because you can look for topics in several ways:

- Scanning a table of contents.
- Searching for key words.
- Using an index.
- Jumping from topic to topic using related topic links.

First you'll try looking for a topic using the Contents screen.

1 Display online Help:

- In Windows, press F1 to display the Help Contents menu, choose Help > Contents, or choose another topic from the Help menu.
- In Mac OS, choose Help > Help Contents.

The Adobe Photoshop 5.0 Help Contents screen appears.

💡 *In Windows, you can also use context-sensitive Help. Press Shift + F1 (a question mark appears next to the pointer), and choose a command or click in a palette to display the appropriate Help topic. Or with a dialog box open, press F1 to display the Help topic for that dialog box.*

2 Click Contents at the upper left of the Help screen to display the Contents menu.

3 Drag the scroll bar or click the arrows to navigate through the contents. The contents are organized in a hierarchy of topics, much like the chapters of a book. Each book icon represents a chapter of information in Help.

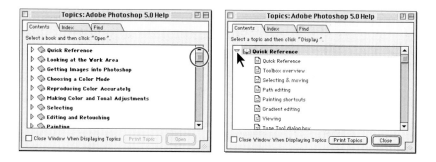

4 Position the pointer on the Quick Reference book, and click to display its contents.

5 Locate the Toolbox overview topic, and double-click to display it. An illustration of the toolbox and toolbar shortcut information appear.

The online Help system is interactive. You can click any red underlined text, called a *link*, to jump to another topic. The pointer icon indicates links and appears when you move the mouse pointer over a link or a hot spot.

6 Position the pointer over a tool in the toolbox, and click. The tool topic appears. At the top of the tool topic, click Next to display the next topic. You can continue to click Next or Previous to display the individual tool topics. You can also click Print to print the topic.

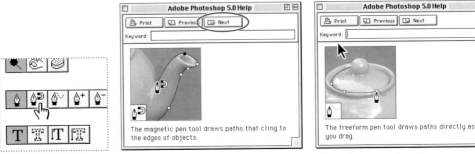

Click on a tool.   *The tool topic appears.*   *Show the next tool topic.*

7 When you have finished browsing the topics, click the Close box to close the topic and return to the toolbox overview.

Using keywords, links, and the index

If you can't find the topic you are interested in by scanning the Contents page, then you can try searching using a keyword.

1 Move the pointer to the Keyword text box, and begin typing **Correcting mistakes**. Notice that as soon as you type "cor," the entire phrase appears in the text box. Press Enter or Return to go to that topic.

2 Read through the topic, and if desired, click some of the links to go to the related topics. When you have finished browsing, click the Close box to close the topic window.

You can also search for a topic using the index.

3 In the Topics window, click Index to display index entries. These entries appear alphabetically by topic and subtopic, like the index of a book.

4 In the text box under the instructions in step 1, type the word **background**. Notice that entries for "background" appear as you begin typing. Add an **s** to the entry to change it to **backgrounds**. Then find the subentry "adding" and select it. (You may have to double-click "backgrounds" to display the subentries.)

5 Click Display to display the entry.

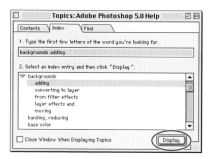

Using the online galleries

As you work with the Help system, you will find full-color galleries of examples associated with several topics. Some of these galleries are not included in the printed User Guide. Throughout online Help, you will find full-color illustrations of various Photoshop features.

1 In the online Help Topics window, click the Find tab. In the empty text box under step 1, type the word **gallery**. Notice that you can refine your search by choosing an option from the pop-up menus to the left. Click Search.

2 In the list that appears, select "Photoshop Filter Sample Gallery," and click Display. (You can also double-click the entry to display it.)

3 Click one of the links to display the filter topic. Use the Next and Previous buttons to browse the topic.

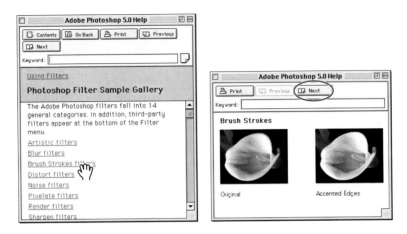

Try looking at another gallery.

4 Click the Find tab again and type **blending**. In the list that appears, select one of the following:

• Click "Selecting a blending mode," and then click Display.

• Double-click "Specifying layer blending modes" to display the topic. (You may have to scroll to find the topic.) Then click Display.

5 In the topic that appears, click the mode names to see examples of the effects.

6 When you have finished, click the Close box to close the topic. Then click the Help Close box to exit Help.

Using Adobe online services

Another way to get information on Adobe Photoshop or on related Adobe products is to use the Adobe online services. If you have an Internet connection and a Web browser installed on your system, you can access the U. S. Adobe Systems Web site (at http://www.adobe.com) for information on services, products, and tips pertaining to Photoshop.

1 If you have an Internet connection, choose File > Adobe Online, or click the icon at the top of the toolbox. The first time you do this, click Refresh, and download the latest version of Welcome to Adobe Online. Then you can click a topic to go to the Adobe Web site.

You can easily find information specifically on Photoshop—including tips and techniques, galleries of artwork by Adobe designers and artists around the world, the latest product information, and troubleshooting and technical information. Or you can learn about other Adobe products and news.

2 When you have finished browsing the Adobe page, close the browser and exit it.

You're ready to begin learning how to begin creating and editing images.

Review questions

1 Describe two ways to change your view of an image.

2 How do you select tools in Photoshop?

3 Describe two ways to get more information about the Photoshop program.

4 Describe two ways to create images in Photoshop.

Review answers

1 You can select commands from the View menu to zoom in or out of an image, or fit it to your screen; you can also use the zoom tools in the toolbox and click or drag over an image to enlarge or reduce the view. In addition, you can use keyboard shortcuts to magnify or reduce the display of an image. You can also use the Navigator palette to scroll an image or change its magnification without using the image window.

2 To select a tool, you can either click the tool in the toolbox or you can press the tool's keyboard shortcut. For example, you can press M to select the marquee tool from the keyboard. Selected tools remain active until you click a different tool.

3 Adobe Photoshop contains online Help, with all the information in the *Adobe Photoshop User Guide*, plus keyboard shortcuts and some additional information and full-color illustrations. Photoshop also has context-sensitive help about tools and commands and online services including a link to the Adobe Systems home page for additional information on services, products, and tips pertaining to Photoshop.

4 You can create original artwork in Adobe Photoshop, or you can get images into the program by scanning a photograph, a slide, or a graphic; by capturing a video image; or by importing artwork created in drawing programs. You can also import previously digitized images—such as those produced by a digital camera or by the Kodak PhotoCD process.

Lesson 2

Working with Selections

Learning how to select areas of an image is of primary importance when working with Adobe Photoshop—you must first select what you want to affect. Once you've made a selection, only the area within a selection can be edited. Areas outside the selection are protected from change.

In this lesson, you'll learn how to do the following:

• Use the marquee, lasso, and magic wand tools to select parts of an image in various ways.

• Reposition a selection marquee.

• Deselect a selection.

• Move and duplicate a selection.

• Constrain the movement of a selection.

• Adjust a selection with the arrow keys.

• Add to and subtract from selections.

• Rotate, scale, and transform a selection.

• Combine selection tools.

• Crop an image.

Tool overview

In Adobe Photoshop, you can make selections based on size, shape, and color using four basic sets of tools—the marquee, lasso, magic wand, and pen tools. In addition, you can use a fifth tool, the move tool, to reposition the selections you create.

Note: In this lesson, you will use just the marquee, lasso, magic wand, and move tools; for more information on the pen tools, see Lesson 7, "Basic Pen Tool Techniques."

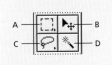

A. *Marquee tool*
B. *Move tool*
C. *Lasso tool*
D. *Magic wand tool*

The marquee and lasso tool icons contain hidden tools, which you can select by holding down the mouse button on the toolbox icon and dragging to the desired tool in the pop-up menu.

The *rectangular marquee tool* (⬚) lets you select a rectangular area in an image. The *elliptical marquee tool* (◯) lets you select elliptical areas. The *single row and single column marquee tools* (⋯) (▯) let you select a 1-pixel-high row and 1-pixel-wide column. You can also use the *crop tool* (⛏) to crop an image.

The *lasso tool* (◠) lets you make a freehand selection around an area. The *polygon lasso tool* (◹) lets you make a straight-line selection around an area. The *magnetic lasso tool* (◈) lets you draw a freehand border that snaps to the edges of an area.

The *magic wand tool* (✎) lets you select parts of an image based on the similarity in color of adjacent pixels. This tool is useful for selecting odd-shaped areas without having to trace a complex outline using the lasso tool.

Getting started

Before beginning this lesson, delete the Adobe Photoshop Preferences file to restore the program's default settings. For step-by-step instructions, see "Restoring default preferences" on page 4. Then restart the Photoshop program.

Now you'll open the finished art file for this lesson to see what you'll create.

1 Choose File > Open. Locate and open the Lesson02 folder; then select End02.psd and click Open. An image of a face, constructed using various types of fruits and vegetables, is displayed.

2 If you like, choose View > Zoom Out to make the image smaller and leave it on your screen as you work. If you don't want to leave the image open, choose File > Close.

Now open the start file to begin the lesson.

3 Choose File > Open. Locate and open the Lesson02 folder, select Start02.psd, and click Open.

4 Choose File > Save As, type the name **Work02.psd**, and click Save.

Selecting with the rectangular marquee tool

You'll start by practicing selection techniques using the rectangular marquee tool.

1 Click the rectangle marquee tool ([ ]) in the toolbox.

2 Drag it diagonally from the top left to the bottom right corner of the melon to create a rectangular selection.

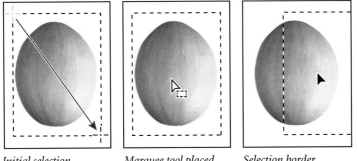

Initial selection   *Marquee tool placed within selection*   *Selection border repositioned*

You can move a selection border after you've created it by positioning the tool within the selection and dragging. Notice this technique changes the location of just the selection border; it does not affect the size or shape of the selection.

3 Place the marquee tool anywhere inside the selection surrounding the melon. The pointer becomes an arrow with a small selection icon next to it.

4 Drag to reposition the border around the melon.

Note: Repositioning techniques for selection borders work with any of the marquee, lasso, and magic wand tools.

If you are still not happy with the selection after repositioning it, you can deselect it and redraw it.

5 Deselect the selection by using either of these methods:

• Choose Select > Deselect.

• Click anywhere in the window outside the selection border.

6 Reselect the melon using the rectangle marquee tool.

 ♀ *To back up one action at any point in the lesson, choose Edit > Undo.*

Selecting with the elliptical marquee tool

Next you'll use the elliptical marquee tool to select eyes for the face. Note that in most cases, making a new selection replaces the existing selection.

1 Select the zoom tool (🔍), and click twice on the blueberry to zoom in to a 300% view.

2 Hold down the mouse button on the rectangular marquee tool, and drag to the elliptical marquee tool (◯).

3 Move the pointer over the blueberry, and drag it diagonally from the top left to the bottom right edge of the blueberry to create a selection. Do not release the mouse button.

Repositioning a selection border while creating it

If a selection border isn't placed exactly where you want it, you can adjust its position and size while creating it.

1 Still holding down the mouse button, hold down the spacebar, and drag the selection. The border moves as you drag.

2 Release the spacebar (but not the mouse button), and drag again. Notice that when you drag without the spacebar, the size and shape of the selection changes, but its point of origin does not.

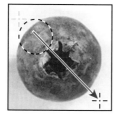 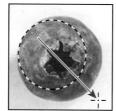

Incorrect point of origin   *Corrected point of origin*   *Adjusted border*
(Click and drag)   *(Spacebar depressed)*   *(Spacebar released)*

3 When the selection border is positioned and sized correctly, release the mouse button.

Selecting from a center point

Sometimes it's easier to make elliptical or rectangular selections by drawing a selection from the center point of the object to the outside edge. Using this method, you'll reselect the blueberry.

1 Choose Select > Deselect.

2 Position the marquee tool at the approximate center of the blueberry.

3 Click and begin dragging. Then without releasing the mouse button, hold down Alt (Windows) or Option (Mac OS), and continue dragging the selection to the blueberry's outer edge. Notice that the selection is centered over its starting point.

4 When you have the entire blueberry selected, release first the mouse button and then Alt/Option.

If necessary, adjust the selection border using one of the methods you learned earlier.

Moving a selection

Now you'll use the move tool to move the blueberry onto the carrot slice to create an eye for the face. Then you'll duplicate and move the selection to make a second eye.

1 Make sure that the blueberry is selected. Then click the move tool (▸₊), and position the pointer within the blueberry's selection. The pointer becomes an arrow with a pair of scissors to indicate that dragging the selection will cut it from its present location and move it to the new location.

2 Drag the blueberry onto the carrot slice.

 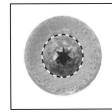

Move tool placed within blueberry selection

Blueberry moved onto carrot slice

3 Choose Select > Deselect.

4 Choose File > Save.

Moving and duplicating simultaneously

Next you'll move and duplicate a selection simultaneously.

1 Choose View > Fit on Screen to resize the document to fit on your screen.

2 Select the elliptical marquee tool.

3 Drag a selection around the carrot slice containing the blueberry. If necessary, adjust the selection border using one of the methods you learned earlier.

4 Click the move tool, then hold down Alt (Windows) or Option (Mac OS), and position the pointer within the selection. The pointer becomes a double arrow, which indicates that a duplicate will be made when you move the selection.

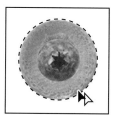

5 Continue holding down Alt/Option, and drag a duplicate of the eye onto the left side of the melon face. Release the mouse button and Alt/Option, but do not deselect the eye.

Holding down Shift when you move a selection constrains the movement horizontally or vertically. Using this technique, you'll drag a copy of the left eye to the right side of the face so that the two eyes are level.

6 Hold down Shift+Alt (Windows) or Shift+Option (Mac OS), and drag a copy of the eye to the right side of the face.

7 Choose File > Save.

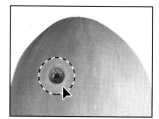
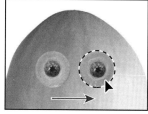

Eye moved onto left side of face   *Duplicate of eye moved with Shift+Alt/Option*

Moving with a keyboard shortcut

Next you'll select the kiwi fruit for the melon's mouth and then move it onto the melon using a keyboard shortcut. The shortcut allows you to temporarily access the move tool instead of selecting it from the toolbox.

1 Select the elliptical marquee tool from the toolbox.

2 Drag a selection around the kiwi fruit using one of the methods you learned earlier.

3 With the marquee tool still selected, hold down Control (Windows) or Command (Mac OS), and position the pointer within the selection. A pair of scissors appears with the pointer to indicate the selection will be cut from its current location.

4 Drag the kiwi mouth onto the face. Do not deselect.

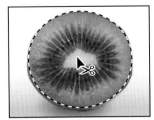 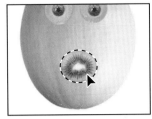

Selection to be cut   *Selection moved onto melon*

Moving with the arrow keys

You can make minor adjustments to the position of a selection using the arrow keys, which allow you to nudge the selection 1 pixel or 10 pixels at a time.

Note: The arrow keys adjust the position of a selection only if you've already moved the selection or if you have the move tool selected. If you try the arrow keys on a selection that has not yet been moved, they will adjust the selection border, not the part of the image that is selected.

1 Press the up arrow (⬆) key a few times to move the mouth upward. Notice that each time you press the arrow key, the mouth moves in 1-pixel increments. Experiment with the other arrow keys to see how they affect the selection.

Sometimes the border around a selected area can distract you as you make adjustments. You can hide the edges of a selection temporarily without actually deselecting and then display the selection border once you've completed the adjustments.

2 Choose View > Hide Edges. The selection border around the mouth disappears.

3 Now hold down Shift, and press an arrow key. Notice that the selection moves in 10-pixel increments.

4 Use the arrow keys to nudge the mouth until it is positioned where you want it. Then choose View > Show Edges.

5 Choose File > Save.

> ### Copying selections or layers
>
> *You can use the move tool to copy selections as you drag them within or between Photoshop images. Or you can copy and move selections using the Copy, Copy Merged, Cut, and Paste commands. Dragging with the move tool saves memory because the Clipboard is not used as it is with the Copy, Copy Merged, Cut, and Paste commands.*
>
> *Keep in mind that when a selection or layer is pasted between images with different resolutions, the pasted data retains its pixel dimensions. This can make the pasted portion appear out of proportion to the new image. Use the Image Size command to make the source and destination images the same resolution before copying and pasting.*
>
> *Photoshop includes two copy and two paste commands:*
>
> *• The Copy command copies the selected area on the active layer.*
>
> *• The Copy Merged command makes a merged copy of all the visible layers in the selected area.*
>
> *• The Paste command pastes a cut or copied selection into another part of the image or into another image as a new layer.*
>
> *• The Paste Into command pastes a cut or copied selection inside another selection in the same image or different image. The source selection is pasted onto a new layer, and the destination selection border is converted into a layer mask.*
>
> –From the Adobe Photoshop User Guide, Chapter 8

Selecting with the magic wand

The magic wand tool lets you select adjacent pixels in an image based on their similarity in color. You'll use the magic wand tool to select the pear tomato, which you'll use as a nose for the face.

1 Double-click the magic wand tool ( ) in the toolbox to select the tool and display its Options palette. Notice that the Options palette has moved to the front of the Info/Navigator/Options palette group.

Note: Most tools in the toolbox come with their own Options palettes, which allow you to change the way the tools work.

In the Magic Wand Options palette, the Tolerance setting controls how many similar tones of a color are selected when you click an area. The default value is 32, indicating that 32 similar lighter tones and 32 similar darker tones will be selected.

2 For Tolerance, enter **50** to increase the number of shades that will be selected.

3 Click the magic wand tool anywhere within the pear tomato. Most of it will be selected.

4 To select the remaining area of the pear tomato, hold down Shift, and click the unselected areas. Notice that a plus sign appears with the magic wand pointer indicating that you're adding to the current selection.

Initial selection   *Adding to selection*   *Complete selection*
(Shift key depressed)

5 When the pear tomato is completely selected, hold down Control (Windows) or Command (Mac OS), position the pointer within the selection, and drag the tomato nose onto the melon face.

6 Choose Select > Deselect.

7 Choose File > Save.

Selecting with the lasso tool

You can use the lasso tool to make selections that require both freehand and straight lines. You'll select a bow tie for the face using the lasso tool this way. It takes a bit of practice to use the lasso tool to alternate between straight-line and freehand selections—if you make a mistake while you're selecting the bow tie, simply deselect and start again.

1 Select the zoom tool, and click twice on the bow tie pasta to enlarge its view to 300%.

2 Select the lasso tool (⌐). Starting at the top left corner of the bow tie pasta, drag to the right to create a freehand outline across the curves at the top of the bow tie. Continue holding down the mouse button.

3 To select the right edge of the bow tie, hold down Alt (Windows) or Option (Mac OS), release the mouse button, and then begin outlining with short, straight lines by clicking along the edge. (Notice that the pointer changes from the lasso icon to the polygon lasso icon.) When you reach the bottom right corner of the bow tie, do not release the mouse button.

Freehand outline with lasso tool *Straight-line outline with polygon lasso tool* *Completed selection (outline crosses starting point)*

4 Release Alt/Option, and drag to the left to create a freehand outline across the bottom of the bow tie. (The pointer returns to the lasso icon.)

5 Hold down Alt/Option again, and click the mouse button along the left edge of the bow tie to draw straight lines.

6 To complete the selection, make sure that the last straight line crosses the start of the selection, release Alt/Option, and then release the mouse button.

7 Choose View > Fit on Screen to resize the document to fit on your screen.

8 Hold down Control (Windows) or Command (Mac OS), and drag the bow tie selection to the bottom of the melon face.

9 Choose File > Save.

Adding and subtracting selections

Holding down Shift while you are selecting an area adds to the current selection. Holding down Alt (Windows) or Option (Mac OS) subtracts from the selection. You'll now use these techniques with the lasso tool to perfect a rough selection of the mushroom image. The mushroom will become a hat for the melon face.

1 Select the zoom tool, and click twice on the mushroom to enlarge its view to 300%.

2 Select the lasso tool, and drag a rough outline around the mushroom (include some of the area outside the mushroom and some of the stem).

3 Hold down Shift. A plus sign appears with the lasso tool pointer.

4 Drag the lasso tool around an area you want to add to the selection. Then release the mouse button. The area is added to the current selection.

Initial selection *Adding to selection* *Result*
(Shift key depressed)

Note: If you release the mouse button while drawing a selection with the lasso tool, the selection closes itself by drawing a straight line between the starting point and the point where you release the mouse. To create a more precise border, end the selection by crossing the starting point.

Next, you'll remove, or subtract, part of the selection.

5 Hold down Alt (Windows) or Option (Mac OS). A minus sign appears with the lasso tool pointer.

6 Drag the lasso tool around an area you want to remove from the selection. Then repeat the process until you've finished removing all the unwanted parts of the selection.

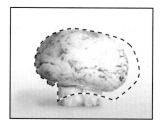

Selection

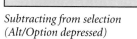

Subtracting from selection (Alt/Option depressed)

Result

7 Choose View > Fit on Screen.

8 To move the mushroom hat onto the melon head, hold down Alt+Control (Windows) or Option+Command (Mac OS), and drag a copy of the mushroom to the top of the melon.

9 Choose File > Save.

Selecting with the magnetic lasso

You can use the magnetic lasso tool to make freehand selections of areas with high-contrast edges. When you draw with the magnetic lasso, the border automatically snaps to the edge you are tracing. You can also control the direction of the tool's path by clicking the mouse to place occasional fastening points in the selection border.

You'll now make an ear for the melon face by using the magnetic lasso to select the red part of the grapefruit slice.

1 Select the zoom tool, and click the grapefruit slice to zoom in to a 200% view.

2 Hold down the mouse button on the lasso tool in the toolbox, and drag to the magnetic lasso tool (🅿) to select it.

3 Now click once at the lower left corner of the red flesh of the grapefruit slice, release the mouse button, and begin tracing the outline of the flesh by dragging to the right over the curved upper edge. Notice that the tool snaps to the edge and automatically puts in fastening points.

If you think the tool is not following the edge closely enough (in low-contrast areas), you can place your own fastening point in the border by clicking the mouse button. You can add as many fastening points as you feel necessary. You can also remove fastening points and back up in the path by pressing Delete and moving the mouse back to the last remaining fastening point.

4 When you reach the lower right corner of the grapefruit flesh, double-click the mouse button, which signals the magnetic lasso tool to return to the starting point and close the selection. Notice that the tool automatically follows the remaining edge of the flesh as it completes the border.

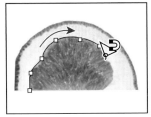 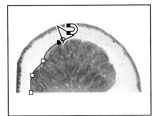 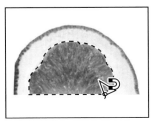

Laying down fastening points   *Removing fastening points*   *Double-clicking at corner to close path*

You can now move the selected part of the grapefruit next to the melon.

5 Double-click the hand tool (🖐) to fit the image on-screen.

6 Click the move tool, and drag the grapefruit ear to the middle of the left side of the melon face. Do not deselect.

7 Choose File > Save.

Softening the edges of a selection

Photoshop offers two ways to smooth the hard edges of a selection.

Anti-aliasing smooths the jagged edges of a selection by softening the color transition between edge pixels and background pixels. Since only the edge pixels change, no detail is lost. Anti-aliasing is useful when cutting, copying, and pasting selections to create composite images. Anti-aliasing is available for the lasso, polygon lasso, magnetic lasso, elliptical marquee, and magic wand tools. (Double-click the tool to display its Options palette.) You must specify this option before using these tools. Once a selection is made, you cannot add anti-aliasing.

Feathering blurs edges by building a transition boundary between the selection and its surrounding pixels. This blurring can cause some loss of detail at the edge of the selection. You can define feathering for the marquee, lasso, polygon lasso, or magnetic lasso tool as you use the tool, or you can add feathering to an existing selection. Feathering effects become apparent when you move, cut, or copy the selection.

• To use anti-aliasing, double-click the marquee, lasso, polygon lasso, or magnetic lasso tool to display its Options palette. Then select Anti-aliased in the Options palette for the selected tool.

• To define a feathered edge for a selection tool, double-click the marquee, lasso, polygon lasso, or magnetic lasso tool to display its Options palette. Then enter a Feather value in the Options palette. This value defines the width of the feathered edge and can range from 1 to 250 pixels.

• To define a feathered edge for an existing selection, choose Select > Feather. Then enter a value for the Feather Radius, and click OK.

–From the Adobe Photoshop User Guide, Chapter 7

Transforming a selection

Next you'll use the Free Transform command to rotate and scale the melon's left ear, and then you'll duplicate and flip a copy to create a right ear.

1 Choose Edit > Free Transform. A bounding box appears around the ear selection.

2 To rotate the ear, position the pointer outside a corner handle until you see a double-headed arrow, and then drag in the direction you want the ear to rotate. Notice that the ear rotates around the selection's center point (✧).

3 To scale the ear, position the pointer directly on one of the corner handles, and drag to reduce the size of the ear. To scale the ear proportionately, hold down Shift as you drag.

4 To reposition the ear, place your pointer within the bounding box, but not on the center point, and drag. (If you place the pointer on the center point and drag, you will move the center point.)

🛈 For more information on working with the center point in a transformation, see "Editing and Retouching" in online Help or Chapter 8 in the Adobe Photoshop User Guide.

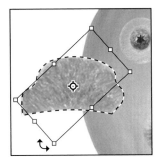
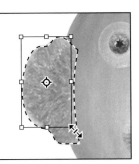
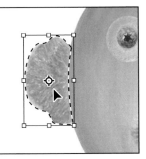

Dragging outside border to rotate ear

Dragging on corner to scale ear

Dragging within border to reposition ear

💡 *If you don't like the results of a Free Transform, press Esc and start over.*

5 When you have the ear positioned correctly, press Enter (Windows) or Return (Mac OS) to apply the transformation. The ear remains selected.

You will now move a copy of the ear to the right side of the face, flip the ear horizontally, and fine-tune its placement.

6 Position the pointer within the ear selection, hold down Shift+Alt (Windows) or Shift+Option (Mac OS), and drag a copy of the ear to the right side of the face.

7 Choose Edit > Transform > Flip Horizontal.

8 If necessary, place the pointer within the selection, and drag to reposition it next to the melon face.

9 If necessary, choose Edit > Free Transform, rotate the ear to fit the right side of the face, and press Enter (Windows) or Return (Mac OS) to complete the transformation.

10 Choose File > Save.

Combining selection tools

As you already know, the magic wand tool makes selections based on color. If an object you want to select is on a solid-colored background, it can be much easier to select the object and the background and then use the magic wand tool to subtract the background color, leaving the desired object selected.

You'll see how this works by using the rectangular marquee tool and the magic wand tool to select radish eyebrows for the face.

1 Hold down the mouse button on the elliptical marquee tool, and drag to the rectangular marquee tool.

2 Drag a selection around the radishes. Notice that some of the white background is included in the selection.

At this point, the radishes and the white background area are selected. You'll subtract the white area from the selection, resulting in only the radishes being selected.

3 Click the magic wand tool in the toolbox; then hold down Alt (Windows) or Option (Mac OS). A minus sign appears with the magic wand pointer.

4 Click anywhere in the white area surrounding the radishes. Now only the radishes are selected.

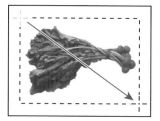  

Initial selection   *Subtracting from selection with*   *Result*
                       Alt/Option magic wand

5 To duplicate and move the radish eyebrow to the melon face, hold down Alt+Control (Windows) or Option+Command (Mac OS), and drag the radish above the left eye on the melon face. Do not deselect.

Left eyebrow placed with Alt+Control/Option+ Command

Right eyebrow placed with Shift+Alt+Control/ Shift+Option+Command

Right eyebrow flipped horizontally

6 Hold down Shift+Alt+Control/Shift+Option+Command, position the pointer within the selection, and drag to duplicate and reposition another eyebrow above the right eye.

7 Choose Edit > Transform > Flip Horizontal to adjust the right eyebrow. If you like, reposition the eyebrow using any of the methods you've learned.

8 Choose File > Save.

Cropping the completed image

To complete the artwork, you'll crop the image to a final size.

1 Choose the crop tool (🔲) from the toolbox. The crop tool is located in the hidden tools palette under the marquee tool.

2 Move the pointer into the image window, and drag diagonally from the top left to the bottom right corner of the completed artwork to create a crop marquee.

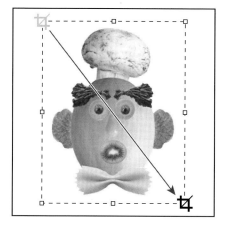

3 If you need to reposition the crop marquee, position the pointer anywhere inside the marquee and drag.

4 If you want to resize the marquee, drag a handle.

5 When the marquee is positioned where you want it, press Enter (Windows) or Return (Mac OS) to crop the image.

6 Choose File > Save.

The fruit-and-vegetable face is complete.

For an illustration of the finished artwork in this lesson, see the color signature.

Review questions

1 Once you've made a selection, what area of the image can be edited?

2 How do you add to and subtract from a selection?

3 How can you move a selection while you're drawing it?

4 When drawing a selection with the lasso tool, how should you finish drawing the selection to ensure that the selection is the shape you want?

5 How does the magic wand tool determine which areas of an image to select? What is tolerance, and how does it affect a selection?

Review answers

1 Only the area within the selection can be edited.

2 To add to a selection, hold down Shift and then drag or click the active selection tool on the area you want to add to the selection. To subtract from a selection, hold down Alt (Windows) or Option (Mac OS), and then drag or click the active selection tool on the area you want to remove from the selection.

3 Without releasing the mouse button, hold down the spacebar, and drag to reposition the selection.

4 To make sure that the selection is the shape you want, end the selection by dragging across the starting point of the selection. If you start and stop the selection at different points, Photoshop draws a straight line between the start point of the selection and the end point of the selection.

5 The magic wand selects adjacent pixels based on their similarity in color. The Tolerance setting determines how many shades of color the magic wand will select. The higher the tolerance setting, the more shades the magic wand selects.

Lesson 3

Layer Basics

Adobe Photoshop lets you isolate different parts of an image on layers. Each layer can then be edited as discrete artwork, allowing unlimited flexibility in composing and revising an image.

In this lesson, you'll learn how to do the following:

- Organize your artwork on layers.
- Create a new layer.
- View and hide layers.
- Select layers.
- Remove artwork on layers.
- Reorder layers to change the placement of artwork in the image.
- Apply modes to layers to vary the effect of artwork on the layer.
- Link layers to affect them simultaneously.
- Apply a gradient to a layer.
- Add text and layer effects to a layer.
- Save a copy of the file with the layers flattened.

Organizing artwork on layers

Every Adobe Photoshop image contains one or more *layers*. Every new file is created with a *background,* which can be converted to a layer. You can view and manipulate layers in Photoshop with the Layers palette.

All new layers in an image are transparent until you add artwork (pixel values). Working with layers in Photoshop is analogous to placing portions of a drawing on sheets of acetate: Individual sheets of acetate may be edited, repositioned, and deleted without affecting the other sheets, and when the sheets are stacked, the entire drawing is visible.

Getting started

Before beginning this lesson, delete the Adobe Photoshop Preferences file to restore the program's default settings. For step-by-step instructions, see "Restoring default preferences" on page 4. Then restart the Photoshop program.

Now you'll open the finished art file to see what you'll create.

1 Choose File > Open. Locate and open the Lesson03 folder; then select End03.psd and click Open. A collage of business images is displayed.

2 If you like, choose View > Zoom Out to make the image smaller, and leave it on your screen as you work. If you don't want to leave the image open, choose File > Close.

Now, you'll open the start file and work with the image as you learn about the Layers palette and layer options.

3 Choose File > Open. Locate and open the Lesson03 folder, select Start03.psd, and click Open.

4 Choose File > Save As, type the name **Work03.psd**, and click Save.

Creating and viewing layers

To begin, you'll create a new layer in the Work03.psd file by bringing in an image from another file.

1 Choose File > Open. Locate and open the Lesson03 folder. Then select Clock.psd from the list of files.

Clock image in Clock.psd   *Clock image moved into Work03.psd*

2 Select the move tool (⊹). Then hold down Shift, click the image in Clock.psd, and drag it into the Work03.psd file on top of the image of the keyboard. (Holding down Shift when dragging artwork into a new file centers the art on the new file's image.) The clock now appears on its own layer, Layer 1, in the Work03.psd file's Layers palette.

Note: If the Layers palette is not visible on your screen, choose Window > Show Layers. If you want to expand the Layers palette, click the minimize/maximize box (Windows) or resize box (Mac OS) at the top of the palette.

3 Close the Clock.psd file.

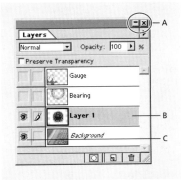

A. *Minimize/maximize or resize box*
B. *New layer (clock image) added to palette*
C. *Show/hide column*

You can use the Layers palette in a Photoshop file to hide, view, reposition, delete, rename, and merge layers. The Layers palette displays all layers with the layer name and a thumbnail of the layer's image that is automatically updated as you edit the layer.

You will now use the Layers palette Options dialog box to rename Layer 1 with a more descriptive name.

4 In the Layers palette, double-click Layer 1.

5 In the Layer Options dialog box, type the name **Clock,** and click OK. Layer 1 is now renamed Clock in the Layers palette.

The Layers palette shows that Work03.psd contains three layers in addition to the Clock layer, some of which are visible and some of which are hidden. The eye icon (👁) to the far left of a layer name in the palette indicates that the layer is visible. You can hide or show a layer by clicking this icon.

6 Click the eye icon next to the Clock layer to hide the clock. Click again to redisplay it.

Creating a layered image

Adobe Photoshop lets you create up to 100 layers in an image, each with its own blending mode and opacity. However, the amount of memory in your system may put a lower limit on the number of layers possible in a single image. Newly added layers appear above the selected layer in the Layers palette. You can add layers to an image in a variety of ways:

• By creating new layers or turning selections into layers.

• By converting a background to a regular layer or adding a background to an image.

• By pasting selections into the image.

• By creating type using the horizontal type tool or vertical type tool.

–From the Adobe Photoshop User Guide, Chapter 11

Selecting and removing artwork on a layer

Notice that when you moved the clock image onto the keyboard in Work03.psd, you also moved the white area surrounding the clock. This opaque area blocks out part of the keyboard image, since the clock layer sits on top of the keyboard, or background.

You'll now remove the white area from around the clock image on the Clock layer.

1 Make sure that the Clock layer is selected. To select the layer, click the layer name in the Layers palette. The layer is highlighted, and a paintbrush icon appears to the left of the layer name, indicating the layer is active.

2 To make the opaque areas on this layer more obvious, hide the keyboard by clicking the eye icon in the Layers palette to the left of the background name. The keyboard image disappears, and the clock appears against a checkerboard background. The checkerboard indicates transparent areas on the active layer.

3 Now select the magic wand tool (✎), click the white area surrounding the clock to select it, and press Delete to delete the selection. Notice that the checkerboard fills in where the white area had been, indicating this area is now also transparent.

4 Choose Select > Deselect.

5 Turn the background back on by clicking the eye icon column next to its name. The keyboard image now shows through where the white area on the Clock layer was removed.

Opaque white area selected   *Opaque area removed*   *Background turned on*

Rearranging layers

In Photoshop, the order in which the layers of an image are organized is called the *stacking order*. The stacking order of layers determines how the image is viewed—you can change the order to make certain parts of the image appear in front of or behind other layers.

Next you'll rearrange layers in the Work03.psd file so that the clock image moves in front of the other images in the file.

1 Make the Gauge and Bearing layers visible by clicking the eye icon column next to their layer names. Notice that the clock image is partly covered up by the other images in the file.

Making all layers visible   *Result*

2 Click the Clock layer in the Layers palette, and drag upward to position it at the top of the palette. When you see a thick black line above the Gauge layer, release the mouse button. The Clock layer moves to the top of the palette's stacking order, and the clock image appears in front of the other images.

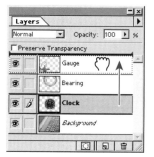

Repositioning Clock layer

Result

Changing the opacity and mode of a layer

The clock image now blocks out any images that lie on layers below it. You can reduce the opacity of the clock layer, which allows other layers to show through it. You can also apply different blending modes to the layer, which affect how the clock image blends with the layers below it.

1 With the Clock layer still active, click the arrow next to the Opacity text box in the Layers palette and drag the slider to 50%. The clock becomes partially transparent, and you can see the layers underneath. Note that the change in opacity affects only the image areas on the Clock layer.

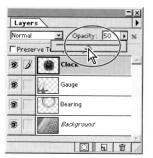

Changing opacity

Result

2 Next try applying some blending modes to the Clock layer. Choose Difference and then Darken from the mode menu (to the left of the Opacity text box), and notice the effect on the clock image. Then select the Screen mode, which is the mode we used for our example, and change the opacity to 90%.

Changing mode and opacity   Result

3 Choose File > Save.

🔲 For more information on blending modes, see "Painting" in online Help or Chapter 9 in the Adobe Photoshop User Guide.

Specifying layer options

The layer options let you change a layer's name and opacity and control how the pixels in the layer blend with the layers underneath. It's important to remember that the opacity and blending modes chosen for a specific layer interact with the opacity and mode settings for the tools you use to paint and edit the pixels on the layer.

For example, suppose you are working on a layer that uses the Dissolve mode and an opacity of 50%. If you paint on this layer using the paintbrush tool set to Normal mode with an opacity of 100%, the paint will appear in Dissolve mode with a 50% opacity because this is the maximum the layer can display. On the other hand, suppose you are working on a layer created using Normal mode and 100% opacity. If you use the eraser tool with an opacity of 50%, only 50% of the paint will disappear as you erase.

–From the Adobe Photoshop User Guide, Chapter 11

🌑 For an illustration of some layer mode effects, see figure 3-1 in the color signature.

Linking layers

An efficient way to work with layers is to link two or more of them together. By linking layers, you can move and transform them simultaneously, thereby maintaining their alignment to each other.

You'll now move the clock image away from the bearing image; link the two layers; and then reposition, scale, and rotate them together.

1 Select the move tool, and drag the clock to the bottom right corner of the collage so that just the top half of the clock face is visible.

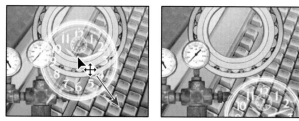

Dragging clock image   *Result*

2 With the Clock layer active in the Layers palette, click the small box to the right of the eye icon for the Bearing layer. Notice that a link icon appears in the box, indicating that the Bearing layer is linked to the Clock layer. (The active or selected layer does not display a link icon when you create linked layers.)

3 Position the move tool in the image window, and drag toward the top margin of the image. Notice that the clock and bearing images move simultaneously.

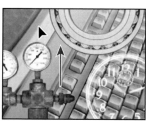

Linking Clock layer to   *Moving layers simultaneously*
Bearing layer

Now you'll try scaling and rotating the linked layers by using the Free Transform command.

4 Choose Edit > Free Transform. A transformation bounding box appears around the clock face.

5 To rotate the clock, position the pointer outside one of the handles until you see a double-headed arrow, drag the face clockwise, and release the mouse button. Notice the bearing rotates as well.

6 Hold down Shift, drag on a handle of the bounding box, and scale the clock and bearing to a smaller size.

Rotating clock and bearing   Scaling clock and bearing   Repositioning clock and bearing

7 If necessary, position the pointer inside the bounding box, and drag to reposition the two images.

8 Press Enter (Windows) or Return (Mac OS) to apply the transformation changes.

Adding a gradient to a layer

Next you'll create a new layer and add a gradient effect to it. You can add a layer to a file with the New Layer command, which creates a transparent layer with no artwork on it. If you then add a special effect to the layer, such as a gradient, the effect is applied to any layers stacked below the new layer.

1 In the Layers palette, click the background to make it active.

2 Choose New Layer from the Layers palette menu.

3 In the New Layer dialog box, type the name **Gradient**, and click OK. The Gradient layer appears above the background in the Layers palette.

You can now apply a gradient to the new layer. A gradient is a gradual transition between one or more colors. In Photoshop, you control the type of transition using the gradient tool.

4 Double-click the linear gradient tool ( ) in the toolbox to select the tool and its Options palette.

5 In the Options palette, choose Foreground to Transparent for the type of Gradient.

Gradient Options palette   *Swatches palette*

6 Click the Swatches palette tab to bring it to the front of its palette group, and select a shade of purple that appeals to you.

7 With the Gradient layer active in the Layers palette, drag the gradient tool from the right to the left margin of the image.

The gradient extends over the width of the layer, starting with purple and gradually blending to transparent, and affects the look of the keyboard on the layer below it. Because the gradient partially obscures the keyboard, you'll now lighten the effect by changing the Gradient layer's opacity.

8 In the Layers palette, change the opacity for the Gradient layer to 60%. The full keyboard shows through the gradient.

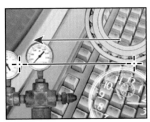

Dragging gradient tool
(right to left)

Gradient at 100% opacity

Gradient at 60% opacity

Adding text

Now you're ready to create and manipulate some type. You'll create text with the type tool, which places the text on its own type layer. You'll then edit the text and apply a special effect to that layer.

1 In the Layers palette, click the Clock layer to make it active.

2 Select the type tool (**T**), and click the image in the upper left corner.

3 Click the color box on the Type Tool dialog box, select a beige color from the color picker, and click OK.

4 Choose a font from the Font menu in the dialog box, and enter a point size in the Size text box (we used 70-point Helvetica Neue Condensed Heavy).

5 Type **Z2000** in the large text box at the bottom of the dialog box. The text is automatically placed on a new layer in the upper left corner of the image where you clicked.

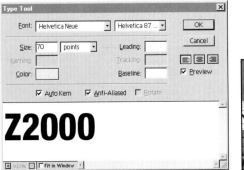

6 Move the cursor into the image area, where the cursor temporarily changes to the move tool, and reposition the text.

7 When the text is placed where you want it, click OK. Notice that the Layers palette now includes a layer named *Z2000* with a T icon next to the name, indicating it is a type layer.

Adding a layer effect

You can enhance a layer by adding a shadow, glow, bevel, or emboss special effect from the program's collection of automated layer effects. These effects are easy to apply and link directly to the layer you specify.

You'll now apply a bevel and emboss layer effect to the type.

1 With the Z2000 type layer still active, choose Layer > Effects > Bevel and Emboss.

2 In the Effects dialog box, change the opacity for Highlight to 20%. Then click the Highlight color box, select a color from the color picker (we chose a light blue), and click OK.

3 Next change the opacity for Shadow to 40%. Click the Shadow color box, select a color from the color picker (we chose black), and click OK.

4 Select Emboss from the Style menu, and click OK to apply the layer effect to the type.

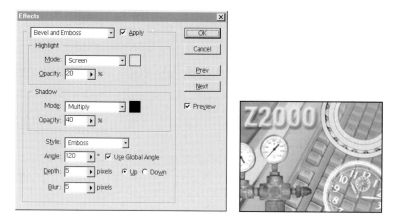

Layer effects are automatically applied to changes you make to a layer. You can edit the text and watch how the layer effect tracks the change.

5 Double-click the Z2000 type layer in the Layers palette.

6 In the Type Tool dialog box, select "Z2000" and change it to "Z999."

7 Reselect the new text, enter a larger point size in the Size text box (we used 90 points), and click OK. Note that the layer effect is applied to the text both as you type the new word and when you change to the larger font size.

8 Choose File > Save.

Using layer effects

Photoshop has numerous different effects that you can apply in any combination to a layer.

• The Drop Shadow effect lets you add a shadow that falls behind the contents on the layer.

• The Inner Shadow effect lets you add a shadow that falls just inside the edges of the layer contents, giving the layer a recessed appearance.

• The Outer Glow and Inner Glow effects let you add glows that emanate from the outside or inside edges of the layer contents.

• The Bevel and Emboss effect lets you add various combinations of highlights and shadows to a layer.

When you apply a layer effect, an "f" icon appears to the right of the layer's name in the Layers palette. Layer effects are linked to the layer contents. When you move or edit the contents on the layer, the effects are modified correspondingly. Layer effects are especially useful for enhancing type layers.

Note: You cannot apply layer effects to a background.

–From the Adobe Photoshop User Guide, Chapter 11

Flattening and saving files

When you have edited all the layers in your image, you can make a copy of the file with the layers flattened. Flattening a file's layers merges them into a single background, thus greatly reducing the file size. Note that you shouldn't flatten an image until you are certain you're satisfied with all your design decisions. In most cases, you will also want to retain a copy of the file with its layers intact, in case you later need to change a layer.

To save a flattened version of the file, you will use the Save a Copy command.

1 Choose File > Save a Copy.

2 In the dialog box, type the name **Flat03.psd**, and select the Flatten Image option.

3 Click Save. The Save a Copy command saves a flattened version of the file while leaving the original file and all its layers intact.

Your collage of business images is now complete. For an illustration of the finished artwork in this lesson, see the color signature.

Review questions

1 What is the advantage of using layers?

2 How do you hide or show individual layers?

3 How can you make artwork on one layer appear in front of artwork on another layer?

4 How can you adjust multiple layers simultaneously?

5 When you've completed your artwork, what can you do to a file to minimize its size?

Review answers

1 Layers allow you to edit different parts of an image as discrete objects.

2 The eye icon to the far left of the layer name in the Layers palette indicates that a layer is visible. You can hide or show a layer by clicking this icon.

3 You can make artwork on one layer appear in front of artwork on another layer by dragging the layer name in the Layers palette or by using the Layer > Arrange > Bring to Front command.

4 You can link the layers you want to adjust by clicking the square box to the left of the Layer name in the Layers palette.

5 You can flatten the image, which merges all the layers onto a single background.

Lesson 4

Painting and Editing

Adobe Photoshop lets you create original artwork or retouch existing artwork in lots of different ways. You can select from many painting tools and fill commands that let you add and manipulate color.

In this lesson, you'll learn how to do the following:

• Use the painting tools to create original artwork and to apply various painting effects to existing artwork.

• Understand the relationship between a painting tool, its Options palette, and its brush size.

• Select paint colors from the Color palette, the Swatches palette, and the Adobe Photoshop Color Picker.

• Select options for the painting tools to enhance the behavior of the tools.

Getting started

Before beginning this lesson, delete the Adobe Photoshop Preferences file to restore the program's default settings. For step-by-step instructions, see "Restoring default preferences" on page 4. Then restart the Photoshop program.

Now you'll open the finished artwork, to get an idea of what you'll create.

1 Choose File > Open. Locate and open the Lesson04 folder, select End04.psd, and click Open.

For an illustration of the finished artwork in this lesson, see the color signature.

2 To make the image smaller so that you can leave the finished example on-screen as you work, choose View > Zoom Out. Or close the file by choosing File > Close.

You'll also open a black-and-white line drawing of the coyote, which you'll color using painting tools and their options.

3 Choose File > Open. Locate and open the Lesson04 folder, select Start04.psd, and click Open.

4 Choose File > Save As, enter the name **Work04.psd**, and click Save.

Painting and filling images with color

In this lesson, you'll explore many ways to add and manipulate color in an image.

In Adobe Photoshop, the paintbrush, airbrush, and pencil tools generally are referred to as the painting tools. The paint bucket tool and the gradient tools also add pixels to an image. In addition, you can use a wide variety of editing and retouching tools and various commands and filters for making changes to existing colors in an image and applying special effects.

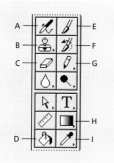

A. *Airbrush* B. *Rubber stamp*
C. *Eraser* D. *Paint bucket*
E. *Paintbrush* F. *History brush*
G. *Pencil* H. *Gradient*
I. *Eyedropper*

You'll start simply by experimenting with the painting tools.

1 To get an idea of how easy it is to paint in Photoshop, click any of the painting tools in the toolbox to select the tool.

2 Click or drag in the image to paint.

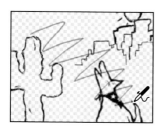

Notice that your paint strokes are black, the default *foreground color.*

Photoshop uses the foreground color to paint, to fill selections, and as the beginning color for gradient fills. The *background color* (white, by default) appears when you delete pixels in a transparent area of color, and as the ending color for gradient fills. Think of the background color as the canvas behind a painting—when you remove paint, the canvas shows through.

The current foreground and background colors are shown in the *color selection boxes* in the toolbox.

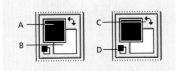

A. Foreground color B. Background color
C. Switch colors D. Default colors

3 Position the pointer over the color bar in the Colors palette (the pointer becomes the eyedropper tool), and click to select another color.

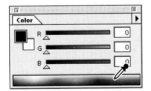

In Photoshop, you can choose the foreground and background colors in many ways. In addition to using the color bar and Colors palette, you can also use the color picker, the eyedropper tool, or the Swatches palette. You'll learn about the painting colors and selecting them later in this lesson.

4 Now double-click a different painting tool in the toolbox to select it and display its options.

Simply clicking any tool in the toolbox selects the tool. Double-clicking the tool displays its Options palette. In addition, the Brushes palette displays a set of brushes for the various painting and editing tools. So when you paint or edit, typically you select a color. Then you select a tool and specify its options and brush, always using the tool's Options palette and Brushes palette. You'll try out different options as you work through this painting and editing lesson.

Selected tool   Options palette   *Current brush size*

5 Change the opacity of the paint by entering a different value in the Opacity text box in the Options palette, and select a different sized brush in the Brushes palette.

You can choose how painting and editing tools apply and alter color in many ways:

• Display the tool pointer as a brush of a specific size and a specific shape.

• Change the size and shape of the brush.

• Control the distance between brush strokes or the angle of a brush stroke.

• Change the opacity of the color a tool will apply.

• Change the color a tool will apply. (You can even paint with patterns or with previous versions of the image.)

• Make paint fade out as you paint with a tool.

• Create all kinds of special effects by changing how the color applied by the tool blends with other pixels in the image.

6 If you have a small screen and you want to make it easier to work with the palettes and select color, you can click the Brushes palette tab and drag the palette to another location on-screen. This separates the palette from the Color/Swatches/Brushes palette group so that it stays visible as you work.

7 Try out the painting tool and settings in the image, clicking or dragging to apply paint.

When you've finished experimenting with the painting tools, you'll delete your work so far. You'll use the History palette to remove the paint you just applied so that you can restore the image to how it looked when you first opened it.

8 To display the History palette, choose Window > Show History.

The History palette records changes you make to an image and lets you step back through recent changes. Unlike the Undo command, which undoes only the last performed operation, the History palette lets you undo a series of tool operations or commands, called states. Each state is listed with the name of the tool or command used to change the image. Using this palette, you can return to an earlier version of the drawing and continue working from that point.

The list shows that several changes to the drawing have already been recorded, ending with the most recent changes. By default, a snapshot of the initial state of the image appears at the top of the palette.

9 Click the snapshot at the top of the History palette list. Photoshop displays the state of the image when you first opened it and before you painted it. The subsequent open and painting states in the History palette are dimmed.

You can still select any of these states to have Photoshop redisplay your work up to that point in the image, and to continue editing the image from that state.

10 Select any of the painting states in the History palette, and watch the effect on the image.

As soon as you start working in the image again, any states beneath the selected state in the History palette are deleted. For now, you'll continue to work from the state when you first opened the image.

11 Click the snapshot again in the History palette to select that state.

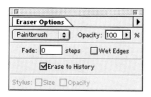

The image reverts to the way it looked when you first opened it. All states but the snapshot at the top of the History palette are dimmed. Continuing your work from this point will clear all painting from the image.

Another way to reverse all changes made to the image since it was last saved is to use the File > Revert command or to use the eraser tool (✐) with the Erase to History option selected.

While the History palette allows you to undo tool operations and commands, it does not reset tool options. To return to the program's default tool options, you must use the Reset All Tools command.

12 In the currently displayed tool Options palette, click the arrow to the right of the palette name and select Reset All Tools from the pop-up menu. You are now ready to proceed with the lesson.

As you work with the painting tools to create the drawing, keep in mind that you don't have to select the "right" colors or exactly replicate the drawing. As you just saw, it's easy to undo your work.

About the History palette

The History palette lets you jump to any recent state of the image created during the current working session. Each time you apply a change to an image, the new state of that image is added to the palette. For example, if you select, paint, and rotate part of an image, each of those states is listed separately in the palette. You can then select any of these states, and the image will revert to how it looked when that change was first applied. You can then work from that state. The following guidelines can help you with the History palette:

• Program-wide changes, such as changes to palettes, color settings, actions, and preferences, are not changes to a particular image and so are not added to the History palette.

• By default, the History palette lists the previous 20 states. Older states are automatically deleted to free more memory for Photoshop. To keep a particular state throughout your work session, make a snapshot of the state.

• Once you close and reopen the document, all states and snapshots from the last working session are cleared from the palette.

• By default, a snapshot of the initial state of the document is displayed at the top of the palette.

• States are added from the top down. That is, the oldest state is at the top of the list, the most recent one at the bottom.

• Each state is listed with the name of the tool or command used to change the image.

• By default, selecting a state dims those below. This way you can easily see which changes will be discarded if you continue working from the selected state.

• By default, selecting a state and then changing the image eliminates all states that come after.

• If you select a state and then change the image, eliminating the states that came after, you can use the Undo command to undo the last change and restore the eliminated states.

• By default, deleting a state deletes that state and those that came after it. If you choose the Allow Non-Linear History option, deleting a state deletes just that state.

–From the Adobe Photoshop User Guide, Chapter 6

Setting up a painting or editing tool

Before you start painting the coyote with the paintbrush tool, first you'll make some decisions about how you want the tool to apply color. You'll soon be able to select options for the painting and editing tools effortlessly as you switch between the array of tools.

The painting and editing tools all work in a similar way, so once you've set up one tool, you'll know generally how to set up any of the other painting and editing tools. You select a color that the tool will apply, set the tool pointer display if desired, and then select the tool's brush size and any options.

Any time you're deciding which painting tool to use, consider their differing effects:

• The paintbrush tool ( ) creates soft strokes of color.

• The airbrush tool ( ) applies gradual tones to an image, simulating traditional airbrush techniques. The edges of the stroke are more diffused than those created with the paintbrush tool. The pressure setting for the airbrush tool determines how quickly the spray of paint is applied.

• The pencil tool ( ) creates hard-edge freehand lines.

Selecting foreground and background colors

To begin, you'll select a painting color. You can easily select another color as you paint.

1 Click the Swatches palette tab to bring the palette to the front of its group. (If the palette is not visible, choose Window > Show Swatches.)

The Swatches palette contains 122 color swatches from the default Photoshop palette. To select a foreground color, click the desired swatch. When you click a color swatch, the new color appears in the foreground color selection box in the toolbox.

2 Click a brown swatch that appeals to you; the foreground box in the toolbox is updated to reflect the change.

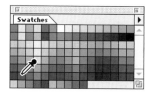

Setting the tool pointer to display as a brush

Each tool has a *hot spot*, the point from which the tool's action begins. By default, when you select a tool and move it into the image window, the pointer becomes an icon of the tool in the toolbox.

For painting tools, it's helpful to change their display so that you can see the actual size of the painting tool in pixels.

1 Choose File > Preferences > General to open the Preferences dialog box.

The Preferences dialog box contains eight groups of settings that apply to different aspects of the program.

2 Choose Display & Cursors from the pop-up menu at the top of the Preferences dialog box. You can also click the Next or Previous button to get the desired preferences section.

3 In the Painting Cursors section of the dialog box, click Brush Size.

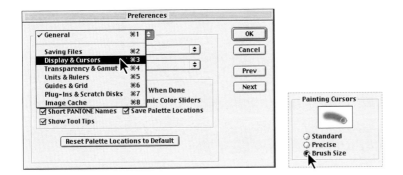

4 Click OK.

The brush size pointer remains in effect until you reset it in the preferences or delete the preferences file. Position the paintbrush tool in the window again; the pointer displays the paintbrush by its size in pixels.

Note: *Caplock, if set, will override the Brush Size option.*

Using the Brushes palette

Now you'll choose a medium-sized brush for your painting. The brush sizes and shapes available for painting and editing appear in the Brushes palette. Brush settings are retained for each painting or editing tool.

1 Select the paintbrush tool ( ) in the toolbox.

2 To display the Brushes palette, choose Window > Show Brushes. You can click the Brushes palette tab any time to bring the palette to the front of its group. The default brush size for the paintbrush tool is highlighted.

3 Click a medium-sized brush in the middle row.

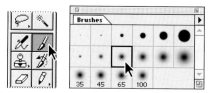

Paintbrush tool and medium-sized brush selected

Using the Options palette

You'll specify an opacity setting for the paintbrush tool to determine the transparency of brush strokes—the lower the value, the more transparent the paint. This is only one of the options you can specify for a painting or editing tool by using its Options palette. You'll learn about other options later.

1 Double-click the paintbrush tool in the toolbox to display its Options palette. The default opacity setting in the Paintbrush Options palette is 100%.

Simply clicking any tool in the toolbox selects the tool. Double-clicking the tool displays its Options palette. Generally, each painting and editing tool has its own options and brushes that you specify in the Options palette and Brushes palette, respectively.

2 Experiment with changing the opacity level of paint in either of these ways:

• By dragging the Opacity slider in the painting tool's Options palette. (Click the arrowhead next to the Opacity text box to display the Opacity slider.)

• By typing a number on your keypad. If you type a number from 1 to 9, the opacity changes in 10% increments; type 0 for 100%. (If you want to set the opacity to an increment other than 10%, type the 2-digit number quickly.)

Dragging Opacity slider   *Typing new Opacity value*

Note: *For Windows, the NumLock key must be on to use the keypad to set brush opacity.*

3 When you've finished experimenting, return the opacity setting to 100%.

Painting within a selection

As you saw at the beginning of the lesson, you can paint anywhere in an image, simply by not making a selection. Now you'll confine painting to a selection you'll make with the magic wand tool. When you select an area, any painting you do affects only the area within the selection. By selecting the area within the coyote first, you won't get any paint outside the edges of the selection.

1 In the toolbox, click the magic wand tool (✎).

2 Click within the coyote's body. Then hold down Shift, and click within the coyote's head and tail. Continue clicking until you've selected all the area within the coyote's body.

Magic wand selection   *Selection extended*

Before you begin painting, you'll create a new layer on which to paint so that you can edit your painting repeatedly without affecting the black-and-white line drawing.

3 To open the Layers palette, choose Window > Show Layers. Click the New Layer button at the bottom of the Layers palette. To rename the layer, double-click the layer, enter the name **Painting**, and then click OK.

Note: *This new layer is empty. So if you try to select anything on this layer with the magic wand tool, you'll select the entire layer.*

4 In the toolbox, double-click the paintbrush tool to select its Options palette. Check to make sure that the opacity setting is 100%.

5 Using the brown color you selected earlier, paint a few areas within the coyote selection (don't fill in the selection completely).

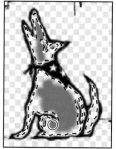

New Layer button   *Painting layer*

By default, Photoshop represents transparency (the absence of color or pixels) with a checkerboard pattern. Notice that where you applied the brown paint at an opacity level of 100%, the checkerboard is no longer visible. (Later you'll learn how to turn this gray pattern off if you want to.)

6 Now click the arrowhead next to the Opacity text box in the Paintbrush Options palette to display the Opacity slider, and drag the Opacity slider to about 60%.

7 Select another shade of brown (or any other color you like), and continue painting within the selection until you've painted the entire selection.

8 Choose View > Hide Edges to hide the selection border.

Notice that where you painted with the brown color at 60% opacity, part of the checkerboard shows through, indicating partial transparency.

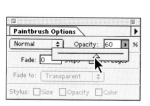

Opacity set to 60%   *Showing edges of selection border*

Now you'll soften and blur the paint you've applied to the coyote using a filter.

9 Choose Filter > Blur > Gaussian Blur.

10 Make sure that the Preview option is turned on, and then experiment by dragging the Radius slider to the right. The higher the value in the Radius text box, the more blurred the colors in the selection. Click OK to apply the blur.

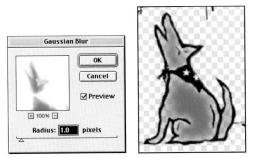

Gaussian Blur filter applied   Result

11 Choose Select > Deselect to deselect everything.

If you deselect first and then apply the filter, the blurring applies to the entire image, not just the selection.

Now you'll change the order of the layers so that the black outline of the coyote appears on top of the brown paint you've applied.

12 In the Layers palette, drag the Painting layer down to position it below the Drawing layer.

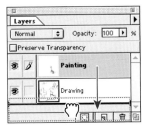

*Positioning Painting layer below
Drawing layer*

At this point, you'll turn off the checkerboard so you can easily see the changes you make.

13 Choose File > Preferences > Transparency & Gamut. For Grid Size, choose None; then click OK.

Gray checkerboard transparent grid   *White transparent grid*

You can also choose a color for the transparent grid display. Don't confuse this color with the background or with actual color added to an image, however.

Creating hard-edged lines with the pencil tool

Next you'll try out the pencil tool, adding lines to the artwork and closing up the cactus to make it easier to select.

1 In the toolbox, click the Default Colors icon to return the foreground and background colors to their defaults—black and white, respectively.

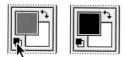

Resetting default colors

2 Click the pencil tool in the toolbox to select it.

3 In the Brushes palette, select a small brush from the top row.

Notice that the brush selection for the pencil tool consists only of hard-edged brushes. The pencil tool draws only with hard edges.

4 Drag with the pencil tool to close the bottom of the cactus.

5 Draw another line for the horizon. Make the horizon line appear behind the cactus, running from the left side of the drawing to the base of the mountains.

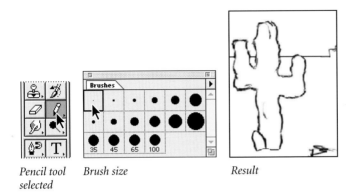

Pencil tool   Brush size   Result
selected

Painting with a watercolor effect

Next you'll paint the mountain using the Wet Edges option of the paintbrush tool. This option creates a watercolor effect by building up (darkening) the edges of brush strokes.

To choose colors for the mountains, you'll use the Adobe Photoshop Color Picker. The color picker lets you select the foreground or background color from a color spectrum or enter values to define a color. It is also used to choose custom color systems, such as Pantone® or Focoltone® colors.

1 To open the color picker, click the foreground color box in the toolbox.

The swatch in the top right of the Color Picker dialog box indicates the current foreground color.

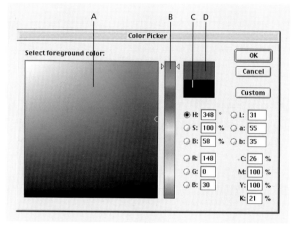

A. *Color field* B. *Color bar* C. *Current foreground color swatch*
D. *New foreground color swatch*

2 Drag the triangles along the color bar to find a color range that appeals to you for painting the mountains.

When the default is set to other than black, dragging updates the swatch at the right side of the dialog box. The top half of the swatch displays the new color, and the bottom half of the swatch displays the previous foreground or background color.

3 To select a different shade of the new color, click the desired shade in the color field at the left side of the color picker. Click OK to close the color picker.

The foreground color box in the toolbox shows the new color.

4 Double-click the paintbrush tool to display its Options palette. Turn on the Wet Edges option.

5 Click the Brushes palette tab to bring the Brushes palette forward. Select a medium-sized, soft-edged brush from the middle row.

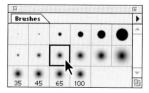

6 Move the paintbrush into the window and begin painting the mountains. Don't worry if you paint a little outside the edges of the mountains. You'll have a chance to clean up any stray paint in the next section.

If you'd like to paint with some straight lines, hold down Shift as you drag the paintbrush.

If paint doesn't appear where you expected, check to make sure that:

• You're painting within the selection, and on the correct layer (Painting).

• You selected the desired tool (here, the paintbrush tool).

• You chose the desired options and brush. (Some options, such as Fade, may cause paint to become transparent.)

Whenever a painting or editing tool doesn't perform as you expect it to, you should check all of these possibilities.

7 Use the sliders or color bar in the Colors palette, or use the Swatches palette to select different foreground colors to add different colors to the mountains as you paint.

Painting mountains   *Painting with different
foreground colors*

You can also reverse the foreground and background color by clicking the Switch Colors icon in the toolbox. (Clicking the Default Colors icon returns the foreground color to black and the background color to white.)

8 In the Paintbrush Options palette, turn off the Wet Edges option.

You won't use this option again in this lesson. Because Photoshop remembers the last used setting for each brush, you must turn off this option so that the paintbrush won't continue to paint with it.

9 Choose File > Save to save your work.

Erasing

Now you'll use the eraser tool to touch up mistakes you may have made. It's better to think of the eraser tool as returning transparency rather than "erasing" colored pixels. (You can also use the eraser to return an area of an image to its previously saved state.)

1 Click the eraser tool (✐) in the toolbox and move the pointer into the image area. By default, the eraser is the same shape and size as the default paintbrush.

2 In the Brushes palette, select a small, hard-edged brush from the top row.

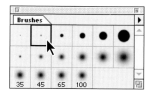

When you switch tools, Photoshop remembers the last brush settings you set for a painting or editing tool.

3 Drag the eraser tool over any area around the mountains where you want to get rid of any stray paint.

Filling with the paint bucket tool

Now you'll select the cactus and fill it with color. A quick way to fill a selection with color is by clicking it with the paint bucket tool.

1 In the Layers palette, make sure that the Painting layer is the active layer.

2 In the toolbox, double-click the lasso tool (♒) to display its Options palette.

3 In the Lasso Options palette, enter a value of **3** in the Feather text box.

4 Create a rough selection around the cactus, using the cactus as a guide.

5 End the selection by crossing the starting point.

6 Click the paintbucket tool in the toolbox. This tool fills a selection or image with flat color.

7 In the Swatches palette, select a light green color.

8 Click inside the cactus selection to fill it with color.

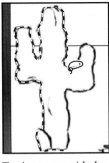 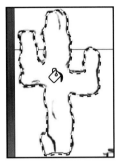 

Tracing cactus with the lasso tool   *Filling with the paint bucket tool*   *Result*

9 Choose Select > Deselect.

Using custom brushes

To finish painting the cactus, you'll use some custom brushes and add texture. To use custom brushes in Photoshop, you load the brushes into the Brushes palette, and then select a brush shape.

1 Select the paintbrush tool in the toolbox.

2 Choose Load Brushes from the Brushes palette menu.

3 In the Lesson04 folder, select Assorted.abr, and then click Open to add the custom brushes to the Brushes palette.

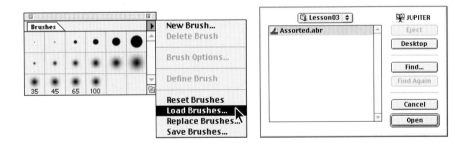

Note: For this lesson, we've placed the custom brushes in the Lesson04 folder. For future reference, the custom brushes are located in the Photoshop subdirectory (Windows) or the Goodies\Brushes\Assorted Brushes folder (Mac OS).

4 In the fifth row of the Brushes palette, click to select the texture brush.

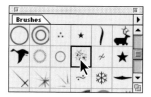

5 In the Swatches palette, select a lighter green or yellow color to add texture.

6 Using the brush tool, click inside the cactus to add texture.

To complete the cactus texture, you'll add some spines.

7 In the toolbox, click the Default Colors icon to return the foreground color to its default of black.

8 In the Brushes palette, click to select the second brush in the sixth row—a spiny-shaped brush.

9 Click at the edges of the cactus to add prickles.

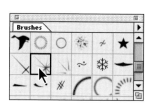   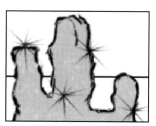

Selecting spiny custom brush   *Result*

10 Choose Select > Deselect.

11 Choose File > Save to save your work.

Airbrushing and smudging

Now you'll paint the clouds using the airbrush tool. The airbrush tool applies paint in the same way as a traditional airbrush. The default pressure for the airbrush tool is 50%, but the rate at which you drag the tool also influences the density of the paint. The more slowly you drag, the more dense the application of the paint.

To choose colors for the clouds, you'll select them from the Swatches palette and from the existing colors in the border of the drawing. Choosing a color within an image is called *sampling* a color. You can save sampled colors for future use by storing them in the Swatches palette.

1 In the Layers palette, make sure that the Painting layer is the active layer (so that you can paint without affecting the black-and-white line drawing).

2 In the Brushes palette, select a small soft-edged brush from the second row of brushes.

3 Double-click the airbrush tool (✎)to display its Options palette. Notice that the default pressure for the airbrush tool is 50%.

4 In the Swatches palette, click a gray swatch and paint a portion of the clouds using the airbrush. Don't worry if you paint a bit outside the outlines of the clouds.

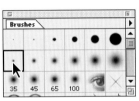   

Brush selected in palette   *Airbrush applied to clouds*

Next, you'll sample a color from the border of the image to add as a color for the clouds.

5 With the airbrush tool still selected, hold down Alt (Windows) or Option (Mac OS). The pointer becomes the eyedropper (✒). (You can also select the eyedropper tool in the toolbox. But you must remember to reselect the airbrush tool when you have finished.)

6 Click the eyedropper in the green border to sample the green color and to make it the new foreground color.

Sampling color from the border   *Color applied to clouds*

7 Release Alt/Option. The pointer becomes the airbrush tool again. Continue painting the clouds with the airbrush tool.

Note: Although you can always select the eyedropper tool from the toolbox to sample a color, you can also select the eyedropper tool using Alt (Windows) or Option (Mac OS) whenever a painting tool is selected.

Before you select another color, you'll save the green color in the Swatches palette.

8 Click the Swatches palette tab.

9 Position the pointer in the blank area at the bottom of the Swatches palette. The pointer becomes a paint bucket.

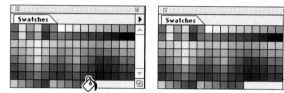

Paint bucket in Swatches palette

Clicking adds color

10 Click the paint bucket in the blank area; the green color is added to the Swatches palette.

Note: You don't have to save a sampled color to work with it—you've done it here just to learn how to save colors in the Swatches palette. To remove a swatch from the Swatches palette, Control-click (Windows) or Command-click (Mac OS) the swatch. Holding down Control/Command turns the paintbucket pointer into the scissors pointer, and clicking removes the swatch.

11 Finish painting the clouds using either sampled colors or colors from the Swatches palette.

As a final touch, you'll use the smudge tool to smudge the colors in the clouds. The smudge tool moves and mixes different colored pixels as you drag.

12 Select the smudge tool (✥), located under the blur tool in the hidden tools palette. To select a hidden tool, you position the pointer on the visible tool and drag to highlight the tool you want.

13 In the Brushes palette, select a smaller soft brush from the second row.

14 Drag the tool in the clouds to create swirls.

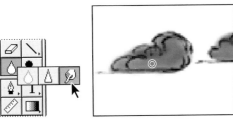

Smudge tool selected *Mixed color*
in palette

The smudge tool uses a default opacity of 50% to softly mix colors. You can increase the opacity to make the effect more pronounced.

Creating gradients

Next you'll use the radial gradient tool to apply a gradient to the sun. The gradient tools let you apply a gradual transition between multiple colors. The gradient pull-out menu in the toolbox includes five different tools. The radial gradient tool shades concentrically from the starting point to the ending point in the image or selection.

1 In the Layers palette, make sure that the Painting layer is the active layer. You'll continue to work on this layer.

2 Using the zoom tool (🔍), drag over the sun to zoom in on that part of the image.

3 Select the ellipse marquee tool (◯) hidden under the rectangular marquee tool, and double-click to display its Options palette. (To select a hidden tool, you position the pointer on the visible tool and drag to highlight the tool you want.)

To fill only part of the image, you must select the desired area first. Otherwise the gradient fill is applied to the entire active layer.

4 In the Marquee Options palette, enter a value of **2** in the Feather text box. Feathering blurs the edges of a selection.

5 Hold down Alt (Windows) or Option (Mac OS), and then drag from the center point of the sun to the outside edge to create a circular selection.

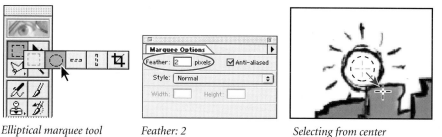

Elliptical marquee tool selected   *Feather: 2*   *Selecting from center*

6 Select and double-click the radial gradient tool. Remember that to select a hidden tool, you position the pointer on the visible tool and drag to highlight the tool you want.

7 In the Radial Gradient Options palette, select Orange, Yellow, Orange from the Gradient pop-up menu. Set the opacity to 50% or 60%.

8 In the image, drag from the center of the sun to the outside edge to apply the gradient.

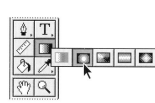

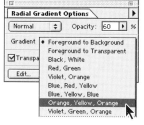

Radial gradient tool selected   *Orange, Yellow, Orange option*   *Applying gradient from center*

9 Choose Select > Deselect to deselect everything.

10 Double-click the zoom tool in the toolbox to zoom out of the image.

About the gradient tools

The gradient tools create a gradual blend between multiple colors. You can choose from existing gradient fills or create your own. You draw a gradient by dragging in the image from a starting point (where the mouse is pressed) to an ending point (where the mouse is released). The starting and ending points affect the gradient appearance according to the gradient tool used.

The gradient pull-out menu in the toolbox includes these tools:

• *Linear gradient shades from the starting point to the ending point in a straight line.*

• *Radial gradient shades from the starting point to the ending point in a circular pattern.*

• *Angular gradient shades in a counter-clockwise sweep around the starting point.*

• *Reflected gradient shades using symmetric linear gradients on either side of the starting point.*

• *Diamond gradient shades from the starting point outward in a diamond pattern. The ending point defines one corner of the diamond.*

–From the Adobe Photoshop User Guide, Chapter 9

Creating soft-edged effects

You can use the Fade option on any of the painting tools (the paintbrush, airbrush, or pencil tools) to cause paint to fade to the background color or to fade to transparent over the length of a brush stroke. You'll use this option with the paintbrush tool again to create rays around the sun.

First, you'll learn another way to select a foreground color using the Color palette. The Color palette contains sliders and a color bar that let you change the foreground and background colors. The current foreground and background colors are displayed in the Color palette; the swatch with the outline determines which swatch is selected.

1 In the Layers palette, make sure that the Painting layer is the active layer. You'll continue to work on this layer.

2 Click the Color palette tab to bring it to the front of the palette group. Make sure that the swatch in the top left corner of the Color palette is selected. When a swatch is selected, it has a border.

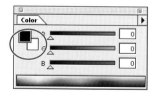

Active swatch (foreground color)

Note: *If the swatch is already selected and you click it, you'll open the Adobe Photoshop Color Picker. If necessary, click Cancel to close the color picker.*

You can select colors in the Color palette either by dragging the sliders or by dragging through the color bar at the bottom of the palette. You'll select a color from the color bar.

3 Position the pointer in the color bar; the pointer becomes an eyedropper.

Just to see what happens, drag the eyedropper through the color bar to see how the foreground box changes color as you drag. Select a reddish-brown color from the color bar to paint the rays around the sun.

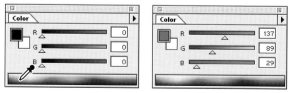

Dragging eyedropper pointer   Result
in the color bar to select a color

Double-click the airbrush tool in the toolbox to display its Options palette. Enter a value of **15** in the Fade text box. In the Fade To menu, make sure that Transparent is selected so the paint will fade to transparency.

The value you enter in the Fade text box determines how long the painting tool will apply paint before it begins to fade. The higher the value you set, the longer the brush paints before beginning to fade. Turning on the Fade option lets you select an option from the Fade To menu.

4 In the Brushes palette, select a small, soft-edged brush.

5 Position the pointer in the window and drag to draw rays around the sun. You'll notice that they begin to fade as you drag.

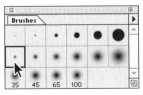 

Fade option: 15 steps *Small, soft-edged brush* *Drawing with airbrush tool*

Painting with gradients and modes

You'll try out different blending modes as you create a background sky for the artwork. You'll continue working on the Painting layer that you created at the start of the lesson.

1 Make sure that the Painting layer is active—selecting it, if necessary, in the Layers palette. Make sure that the Preserve Transparency option is off.

2 Select the rectangle marquee tool ([⃞]) in the toolbox. Drag a selection marquee from the horizon line to the top of the image.

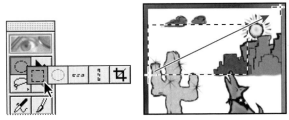

Sky selected with rectangular marquee tool

Now you'll apply a gradient to the sky. As you saw when you applied a radial gradient, a gradient blends from one color to another over the length of a selection. You can choose from several predefined gradients in the Gradient Options palette. You also can create your own gradients.

3 In the toolbox, position the pointer on the radial gradient tool and drag to the right to select the linear gradient tool (▣) from the hidden tools.

Photoshop includes five gradient tools, which differ in the point from which they blend colors. The linear gradient tool blends colors from the starting point to the ending point in a straight line.

4 In the Gradient Tool Options palette, for Gradient select Foreground to Background. A sample of the gradient you select appears at the bottom of the Gradient palette. If desired, change the opacity to 80% or 90%.

5 Select Violet, Green, Orange from the Gradient pop-up menu. Make sure that Transparency, Dither, and Reverse are deselected.

6 Using the gradient tool, drag downward from the top of the image to the horizon line to apply the linear gradient.

The gradient is applied on top of the cactus and mountains, saturating them with color. You'll undo the gradient so that you can see what happens when you reverse the order of the colors.

7 Choose Edit > Undo to undo the gradient.

8 In the Gradient Options palette, select an opacity of 60% and select the Reverse option to reverse the order in which the colors are applied (from orange, green, and then to violet).

9 Drag from the top of the image down to the horizon line to apply the gradient.

You'll undo gradient again so that you can change its mode and see the effect.

10 Choose Edit > Undo.

11 In the Linear Gradient Options palette, choose Behind from the mode menu.

In the Behind mode, paint is applied only to the transparent part of a layer, to give the appearance of painting behind existing objects. This mode works only in layers with Preserve Transparency off and is analogous to painting on the back of transparent areas in a sheet of acetate.

12 Using the gradient tool, drag from the top of the image downward to the horizon line. The gradient now appears behind the mountains and cactus, for a more realistic sky.

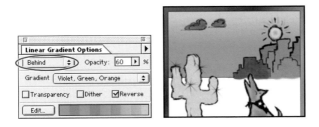

When using a blending mode, it's helpful to think in terms of the following colors when visualizing an effect:

• The *base color* is the original color in the image.

• The *blend color* is the color being applied with the painting or editing tool.

• The *result color* is the color resulting from the blend.

You can set blending modes for layers as well as for painting tools. Painting modes affect only the paint applied by a selected tool; layer modes affect the entire layer.

Try out other painting modes to see their effect.

🗗 For more on the blending modes, see "Selecting a blending mode" in online Help or Chapter 9 of the Adobe Photoshop User Guide. For a gallery illustration of the blending modes, see online Help.

🖊 For an illustration of different blending modes applied to brush strokes, see figure 4-1 in the color signature.

13 When you are satisfied with the results, choose Select > Deselect.

Painting with texture

To complete the image, you'll paint in the desert floor by defining a brush, painting with it, and then applying a filter effect.

In addition to the round brushes that appear by default in the Brushes palette and any custom brushes that you load, you can use part of an image to create a custom brush shape.

1 Make sure that the Painting layer is still active. You'll continue working on this layer.

2 Using the rectangle marquee tool (⬚), drag a selection marquee to select the desert floor.

3 In the Swatches palette, select a light brown or tan color for desert sand.

4 Select the paintbrush tool in the toolbox, and then set the tool options:

• In the Paintbrush Options palette, choose Behind from the mode menu.

• In the Brushes palette, select a large soft brush from the second row.

5 Drag to paint in the desert floor.

6 Choose Select > Deselect.

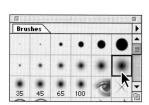
Large, soft brush

Behind mode

As you just saw, in Behind mode any paint is applied behind existing paint. So you can paint freely without affecting existing artwork.

Setting brush options

You can define a number of options for the default brushes and any brushes you create. For custom brushes, only the spacing and anti-aliased options can be changed.

•Diameter controls the size of the brush. Enter a value in pixels or drag the slider.

•Hardness controls the size of the brush's hard center. Type a number, or use the slider to enter a value that is a percentage of the brush diameter.

•Spacing controls the distance between the brush marks in a stroke. To change the spacing, type a number, or use the slider to enter a value that is a percentage of the brush diameter. To paint strokes without defined spacing, deselect this option.

•Angle specifies the angle by which an elliptical brush's long axis is offset from horizontal. Type a value in degrees, or drag the horizontal axis in the left preview box.

•Roundness specifies the ratio between the brush's short and long axes. Enter a percentage value, or drag the points in the left preview box. A value of 100% indicates a circular brush, a value of 0% indicates a linear brush, and intermediate values indicate elliptical brushes.

–From the Adobe Photoshop User Guide Chapter 9

Defining a brush

To complete the artwork, you'll paint the desert floor, defining a brush to add details to it.

1 In the Layers palette, click to select the Drawing layer. Click the eye icon next to the Painting layer to hide that layer.

You'll define a brush using the Drawing layer, which contains only black-and-white values—that is, fully selected or fully deselected pixels. If you select from the Painting layer, your selection (and thus your brush) will color and gray values; the result will be a brush with partially selected pixels.

2 Select the rectangular marquee tool in the toolbox. Only a rectangular selection can be defined as a brush.

3 Drag to select some rays of the sun.

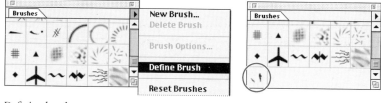

Selecting black-and-white art from Drawing layer

4 In the Brushes palette, choose Define Brush from the Brushes palette menu.

The sun-ray selection is added as a new brush to the Brushes palette. Next, you'll set the brush's options.

Defining brush

Result

5 Double-click the brush in the Brushes palette to select it and set its options.

6 In the Paintbrush Options dialog box, set the spacing to 300%, and click OK.

The amount you set for spacing controls the distance between brush strokes.

Brush spacing options

Result

7 Choose Select > Deselect. Deselecting the rectangular selection also deselects the brush you just defined.

8 In the Layers palette, click the Painting layer to select it and make it visible. You'll finish working on this layer.

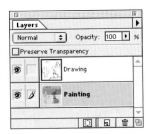

9 Click the paintbrush tool in the toolbox to select it and to reselect the brush you just defined.

10 In the Paintbrush Options palette, set the tool's Opacity to 40%. Choose Normal from the mode menu so that any paint you apply will appear on top of existing paint.

Remember that the painting modes, like painting tool options, affect only the paint applied by the selected tool. Layer modes affect the entire layer.

11 In the Swatches palette, click a dark brown color to contrast with the sand.

12 Using the paintbrush tool, drag to paint in the desert floor.

Another way to add texture to painting is to apply a filter, or to use different tools to apply paint on top of paint.

13 Choose File > Save to save your artwork. You've completed the painting lesson. You're well on your way to learning Adobe Photoshop!

Review questions

1 What is the benefit of making a selection before starting to paint in an area?

2 How are a painting tool, its Options palette, and the Brushes palette related? For example, if you click the paintbrush tool in the toolbox, what effect do the Brushes palette and the Paintbrush Options palette have on the tool?

3 How can you display a painting tool by its size in pixels?

4 How do you create a custom brush?

Review answers

1 Once you've made a selection, you cannot paint outside the boundary of the selection marquee.

2 When you select a painting tool, the Brushes palette displays the size of the painting tool, and the tool's Options palette displays the opacity, the mode, and any other options you may have previously selected. If a tool does not perform the way you expect it to, check the Brushes palette and the tool's Options palette to make sure the options are set the way you want.

3 By choosing File > Preferences > Display & Cursors, and then choosing Brush Size from the Painting Cursors section of the Preferences dialog box.

4 Select the area you want to define as a brush, and then choose Define Brush from the Brushes palette menu.

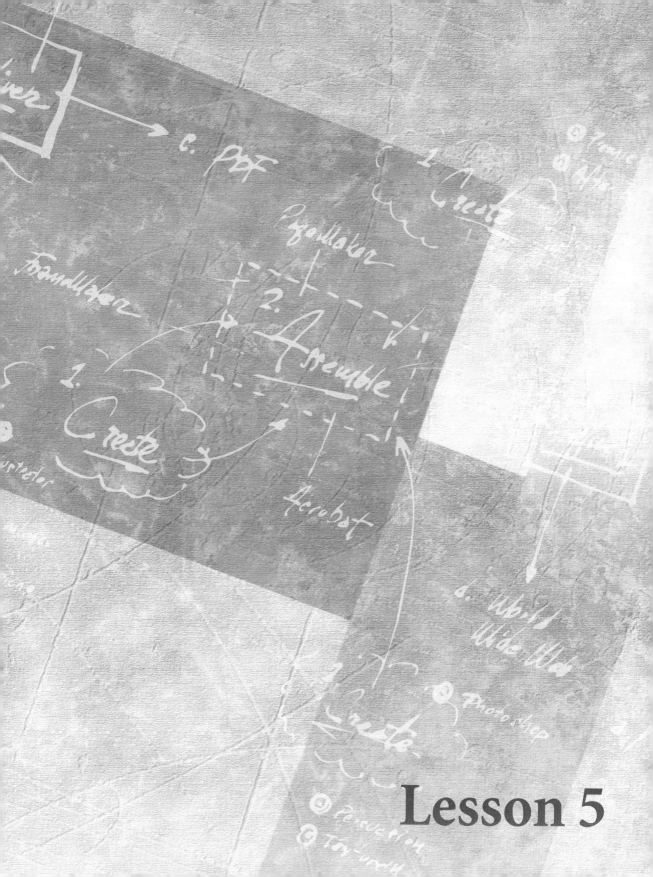

Lesson 5

Masks and Channels

Adobe Photoshop uses masks to isolate and manipulate specific parts of an image. A mask is like a stencil. The cutout portion of the mask can be altered, but the area surrounding the cutout is protected from change. You can create a temporary mask for one-time use, or you can save masks for repeated use.

In this lesson, you'll learn how to do the following:

- Refine a partial selection using a quick mask.

- Save a selection as a channel mask.

- View a mask using the Channels palette.

- Load a saved mask and apply effects.

- Paint in a mask to modify a selection.

- Create and use a gradient mask.

Working with masks and channels

Masks let you isolate and protect parts of an image. When you create a mask from a selection, the area not selected is *masked* or protected from editing. With masks, you can create and save time-consuming selections and then use them again. In addition, you can use masks for other complex editing tasks—for example, to apply color changes or filter effects to an image.

In Adobe Photoshop, you can make temporary masks, called *quick masks*, or you can create permanent masks and store them as special grayscale channels, called *alpha channels*. Photoshop also uses channels to store an image's color information and information about spot color. Unlike layers, channels do not print. You use the Channels palette to view and work with channels.

Getting started

Before beginning this lesson, delete the Adobe Photoshop Preferences file to restore the program's default settings. For step-by-step instructions, see "Restoring default preferences" on page 4.

After you've deleted the Preferences file, restart the Photoshop program. Then open the finished art file for this lesson to see what you'll be creating.

1 Choose File > Open. Locate and open the Lesson05 folder, select End05.psd, and click Open.

An image of an egret appears.

For an illustration of the finished artwork in this lesson, see the color signature.

2 Either make the image smaller and leave it on your screen as you work by choosing View > Zoom Out, or close the image by choosing File > Close.

Now you'll open the start file and work with masks and channels to edit the image.

3 Choose File > Open. Locate and open the Lesson05 folder, select Start05.psd, and click Open.

4 Choose File > Save As, enter the name **Work05.psd**, and click Save.

Creating a quick mask

First you'll use Quick Mask mode to convert a selection border into a temporary mask. Later you will convert this temporary quick mask back into a selection border. Unless you save a quick mask as a more permanent alpha channel mask, the temporary mask will be discarded once it is converted to a selection.

You'll begin by making a partial selection of the egret using the magic wand tool, and then you'll edit the selection using a quick mask.

1 Double-click the magic wand tool ( ) in the toolbox to display its Options palette.

2 Enter a Tolerance value of **16**.

3 Click anywhere in the white area of the egret to begin the selection process.

4 To extend the selection, hold down Shift, and click the magic wand on another white portion of the egret. When you hold down Shift, a plus sign appears next to the magic wand tool. This indicates the tool is adding to the selection.

Magic wand selection   *Selection extended*

The egret is still only partly selected. Now you'll add to this selection using a quick mask.

5 In the toolbox, click the Quick Mask icon. By default you have been working in Standard mode.

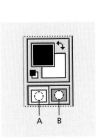 

A. Standard mode Quick mask selection
B. Quick Mask mode showing red overlay

In Quick Mask mode, a red overlay (similar to a piece of *rubylith*, or red acetate, that a print shop uses to mask an image) appears to mask and protect the area outside the selection. You can apply changes only to the unprotected area that is visible and selected. (It's possible to change the color of the red overlay; the color is only a matter of display.)

Note: A partial selection must exist to see the overlay color in Quick Mask mode.

Editing a quick mask

Next you will refine the selection of the egret by adding to or erasing parts of the masked area. You'll use the paintbrush tool to make changes to your quick mask. The advantage of editing your selection as a mask is that you can use almost any Adobe Photoshop tool or filter to modify the mask. (You can even use selection tools.) In Quick Mask mode, you do all of your editing in the image window.

In Quick Mask mode, Photoshop automatically defaults to Grayscale mode. The foreground color defaults to black and the background color defaults to white. When using a painting or editing tool in Quick Mask mode, keep these principles in mind:

- Painting with white erases the mask (the red overlay) and increases the selected area.
- Painting with black adds to the mask (the red overlay) and decreases the selected area.

Adding to a selection by erasing masked areas

You begin by painting with white to increase the selected area within the egret. This erases some of the mask.

1 To make the foreground color white, click the Switch Colors icon above the foreground and background color selection boxes in the toolbox.

Switch Colors icon

2 Choose File > Preferences > Display and Cursors. Click Brush Size under Painting Cursors, and then click OK.

Now the painting tool pointer displays as a brush shape of a certain size. This makes editing with a brush easier.

3 Click the paintbrush tool ( ) in the toolbox. Then click the Brushes palette tab, and select a medium brush from the first row of brushes. As you work, you may want to change the size of your brush. Simply click the Brushes palette tab again, and select a different sized brush. You'll notice that the size of the tool brush pointer changes.

4 As you edit your quick mask, you can magnify or reduce your view of the image. When you zoom in, you can work on details of the image. When you zoom out, you can see an overview of your work.

You can zoom in or magnify your view in these ways:

• Select the zoom tool, and click the area you want to magnify. Each click magnifies the image some more. When the zoom tool is selected, you can also drag over the part of the image you want to magnify.

• Select the zoom tool from the keyboard by holding down Ctrl+Spacebar (Windows) or Command+Spacebar (Mac OS); then release the keys to go back to painting.

You can zoom back out in the following ways:

• Double-click the zoom tool to return the image to 100% view.

• Select the zoom tool. Hold down Alt (Windows) or Option (Mac Os) to activate the zoom-out tool, and click the area of the image you want to reduce.

• Select the zoom-out tool from the keyboard by holding down Alt+Spacebar (Windows) or Option+Spacebar (Mac OS) and click to reduce the view; then release the keys to go back to painting.

5 Move the paintbrush onto the window, and begin painting over the red areas within the egret's body. As you paint with white, the red areas are erased.

Don't worry if you paint outside the outline of the egret's body. You'll have a chance to make adjustments later by masking areas of the image as needed.

Unedited mask   *Painting with white*   *Result*

6 Continue painting with white to erase all of the mask (red) in the egret, including its beak and legs. As you work you can easily switch back and forth between Quick Mask mode and Standard mode to see how painting in the mask alters the selected area.

Standard mode

Notice that the selection border has increased, selecting more of the egret's body.

Edited mask in Standard mode   *Quick mask selection*

For an illustration of the selection in Standard and Quick Mask modes, see figure 5-1 in the color signature.

If any areas within the body of the egret appear still to be selected, it means that you haven't erased all of the mask.

Selection in Standard
mode

Erasing in Quick Mask
mode

7 Once you've erased all of the red areas within the egret, click the Standard mode icon again to view your quick mask as a selection. Don't worry if the selection extends a bit beyond the egret. You can fix that.

8 If you zoomed in on the image for editing, choose any of the techniques in step 4 on page 129 to zoom out.

9 Choose File > Save to save your work.

Subtracting from a selection by adding masked areas

You may well have erased the mask beyond the edges of the egret. This means that part of the background is included in the selection. Now you will return to Quick Mask mode and restore the mask to those edge areas by painting with black.

1 Click the Quick Mask icon to return to Quick Mask mode.

2 To make the foreground color black, click the Switch Colors icon above the foreground and background color selection boxes in the toolbox. Make sure that the black color box now appears on top. Remember that in the image window, painting with black will add to the red overlay.

3 Choose a brush from the Brushes palette. Select a small brush from the first row of brushes, because you'll be refining the edges of the selection.

4 Now paint with black to restore the mask (the red overlay) to any of the background area that is still unprotected. Only the area inside the egret should remain unmasked. Remember that you can zoom in and out as you work. You can also switch back and forth between Standard mode and Quick Mask mode.

*Painting with black to
restore mask*

For an illustration of painting in Quick Mask mode, see figure 5-2 in the color signature.

5 Once you're satisfied with your selection, switch to Standard mode to view your final egret selection. Double-click the hand tool (✋) in the toolbox to make the egret image fit in the window.

Using alpha channels

In addition to the temporary masks of Quick Mask mode, you can create more permanent masks by storing and editing selections in alpha channels. You create a new alpha channel as a mask. For example, you can create a gradient fill in a blank channel and then use it as a mask. Or you can save a selection to either a new or existing channel.

An alpha channel has these properties:

• Each image can contain up to 24 channels, including all color and alpha channels.

• All channels are 8-bit grayscale images, capable of displaying 256 levels of gray.

• You can add and delete alpha channels.

• You can specify a name, color, mask option, and opacity for each channel. (The opacity affects the preview of the channel, not the image.)

• All new channels have the same dimensions and number of pixels as the original image.

• You can edit the mask in an alpha channel using the painting and editing tools.

• Storing selections in alpha channels makes the selections permanent, so that they can be used again in the same image or in a different image.

–From the Adobe Photoshop User Guide, Chapter 10

Saving a selection as a mask

Now you'll save the egret selection as an alpha channel mask. Your time-consuming work won't be lost, and you can use the selection again later.

Quick masks are temporary. They disappear when you deselect. However, any selection can be saved as a mask in an alpha channel. Think of alpha channels as storage areas for information. When you save a selection as a mask, a new alpha channel is created in the Channels palette. (An image can contain up to 24 channels, including all color and alpha channels.) You can use these masks again in the same image or in a different image.

1 To display the Channels palette, choose Windows > Show Channels.

In the Channels palette, you'll see that your image by default already has color information channels—a full-color preview channel for the RGB image and a separate channel for the red, green, and blue channels.

2 Choose Select > Save Selection.

In the Save Selection dialog box, the name of your current document appears in the Destination pop-up menu, and *New* by default appears in the Channel pop-up menu.

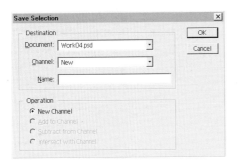

3 Click OK to accept the defaults.

You'll see that a new channel labeled Alpha 1 has been added to the bottom of the Channels palette. All new channels have the same dimensions and number of pixels as the original image. You'll rename this new channel in a moment.

4 Experiment with looking at the various channels individually. Click in the eye icon column next to the channel to show or hide that channel. To show or hide multiple channels, drag through the eye icon column in the palette.

Alpha channel mask visible and selected; other channels hidden

Alpha channels can be added and deleted, and like quick masks, can be edited using the painting and editing tools. For each channel, you can also specify a name, color, mask option, and opacity (which affects just the preview of the channel, not the image).

(To avoid confusing channels and layers, think of channels as containing an image's color and selection information; think of layers as containing painting and effects.)

If you display all of the color channels plus the new alpha mask channel, the image window looks much as it did in Quick Mask mode (with the rubylith appearing where the selection is masked). It is possible to edit this overlay mask much as you did the quick mask. However, in a minute you will edit the mask channel in a different way.

5 When you have finished looking at the channels, click in the eye icon column next to the RGB channel in the Channels palette to redisplay the composite channel view.

6 Choose Select > Deselect to deselect everything.

7 To rename the channel, double-click the Alpha 1 channel in the Channels palette. Type the name **Egret** in the Channel Options dialog box, and click OK.

Editing a mask

Now you'll touch up your selection of the egret by editing the mask channel. It's easy to miss tiny areas when making a selection. You may not even see these imperfections until you view the saved selection as a channel mask.

You can use most painting and editing tools to edit a channel mask, just as you did when editing in Quick Mask mode. This time you'll display and edit the mask as a grayscale image.

1 To display only the channel mask, drag through the eye icon column in the Channels palette, and deselect all of the color information channels. When you have finished, only the Egret channel displays an eye icon. The image window displays a black-and-white mask of the egret selection. (If you left all of the channels selected, then the colored egret image would appear with a red overlay.)

Look for any black or gray flecks within the body of the egret. You'll erase them by painting with white to increase the selected area. Remember these guidelines on editing a channel with a painting or editing tool:

• Painting with white erases the mask and increases the selected area.

• Painting with black adds to the mask and decreases the selected area.

• Painting with gray values adds to or subtracts from the mask in varying opacity, in proportion to the level or gray used to paint. For example, if you paint with a medium gray value, when you use the mask as a selection the pixels will be 50% selected. If you paint with a dark gray and then use the mask as a selection, the pixels will be less than 50% selected (depending on the gray value you choose). And if you paint with a light gray, when you use the mask as a selection, the pixels will be more than 50% selected.

2 Make sure that the Egret channel is the active channel by clicking on the channel in the Channels palette. A selected channel is highlighted in the Channels palette.

3 Now make sure that white is the foreground color. (See step 1 on page 129.) Then select a small brush in the Brushes palette, and paint out any black or gray flecks.

Selection in channel   *Painting out black or gray*

4 If any white specks appear in the black area of the channel, make black the foreground color, and paint those out as well. Remember that when you paint with black you increase the masked area and decrease the selection.

5 Choose File > Save to save your work.

Loading a selection using shortcuts

When you have finished modifying an alpha channel or simply want to use a previously saved selection, you can load the selection into the image. To load a saved selection using shortcuts, do one of the following in the Channels palette:

• Select the alpha channel, click the Load Selection button at the bottom of the palette, and then click the composite color channel near the top of the palette.

• Ctrl-click (Windows) or Command-click (Mac OS) the channel containing the selection you want to load.

• To add the mask to an existing selection, press Ctrl+Shift (Windows) or Command+Shift (Mac OS), and click the channel.

• To subtract the mask from an existing selection, press Ctrl+Alt (Windows) or Command+Option (Mac OS), and click the channel.

• To load the intersection of the saved selection and an existing selection, press Ctrl+Alt+Shift (Windows) or Command+Option+Shift (Mac OS), and select the channel

–From the Adobe Photoshop User Guide, Chapter 10

Loading a mask as a selection and applying effects

Now you'll load the Egret channel mask as a selection. The channel mask remains stored in the Channels palette even after you've loaded it as a selection. This means you can reuse the mask whenever you want.

1 In the Channels palette, click the RGB preview channel to display the entire image.

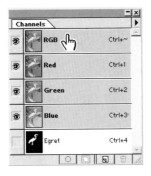

2 Choose Select > Load Selection. For Channel, choose Egret and click OK.

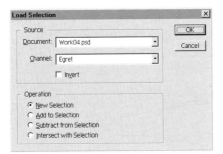

The egret selection appears in the image window.

Now that you've corrected any flaws in the selection by painting in the channel, you'll adjust the tonal balance of the egret and then invert the selection to add a filter to the background.

3 Choose Image > Adjust > Auto Levels. This automatically adjusts the tonal balance of the colors in the selection.

(Auto Levels defines the lightest and darkest pixels in each channel as white and black, and then redistributes the intermediate pixel values proportionately. Lesson 6, "Photo Retouching," takes you through basic image correction, including adjusting an image's tonal range.)

4 Choose Edit > Undo to compare the adjustment you just made. Then choose Edit > Redo to reapply the adjustment.

5 Choose Select > Inverse. Now the previous selection (the egret) is protected, and the background is selected. You can apply changes to the background without worrying about the egret.

6 Choose Filter > Artistic > Colored Pencil. If desired, experiment with the sliders to see the changes before you apply the filter.

Preview different areas of the background by dragging in the preview window of the Colored Pencil filter dialog box. This preview option is available with all filters.

Filter preview   Filter applied

7 Click Apply when you're satisfied with the Colored Pencil settings. The filter is applied to the background selection.

You can experiment with other filter effects for the background. Just choose Edit >Undo to undo your last performed operation.

8 Choose Select > Deselect to deselect everything.

9 Choose File > Save to save your work.

Creating a gradient mask

In addition to using black to indicate what's hidden and white to indicate what's selected, you can paint with shades of gray to indicate partial transparency. For example, if you paint in a channel with a shade of gray that is at least halfway between white and black, the underlying image becomes partially (50% or more) visible.

You'll experiment by adding a gradient (which makes a transition from black to gray to white) to a channel and then filling the selection with a color to see how the transparency levels of the black, gray, and white in the gradient affect the image.

1 In the Channels palette, create a new channel by clicking the New Channel (▣) button at the bottom of the palette.

The new channel labeled Alpha 1 appears at the bottom of the Channels palette.

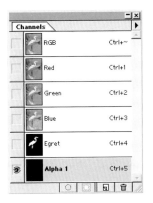

2 Double-click the new channel to open the Channel Options dialog box, and rename the channel **Gradient**. Click OK.

3 Double-click the linear gradient tool (▣) in the toolbox to select the tool and its Options palette.

4 In the Gradient Tool Options palette, choose Black, White from the Gradient menu.

5 Hold down Shift, and drag the gradient tool from the top of the window to the bottom of the window. The gradient is applied to the channel.

Loading the gradient mask as a selection and applying effects

Now you'll load the gradient as a selection and fill the selection with a color.

When you load a gradient as a selection and then fill the selection with a color, the opacity of the fill color varies over the length of the gradient. Where the gradient is black, no fill color is present; where the gradient is gray, the fill color is partially visible; and where the gradient is white, the fill color is completely visible.

1 In the Channels palette, click the RGB channel to display the full-color preview channel. Next, you'll load the Gradient channel as a selection.

2 *Without* deselecting the RGB channel, position the pointer over the Gradient channel. Drag the channel to the Load Selection button (▣) at the bottom of the palette to load the gradient as a selection.

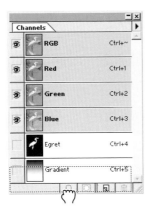

3 In the toolbox, make sure that the foreground and background colors are set to their default (black and white). If necessary, click the Default Colors icon at the bottom left corner of the color selection boxes.

A selection border appears in the window. Although the selection border appears over only about half the image, it is correct. Selection borders are displayed based on the following pixel information: If the pixel value is 0% to 50% opaque, a selection border does not appear, but if the pixel value is 51% to 100% opaque, a selection border appears.

4 Press Delete to fill the gradient selection with the current background color, which is white.

5 Choose Select > Deselect to deselect everything.

6 If desired, choose File > Save to save your work.

You have completed the Masks and Channels lesson. Although it takes some practice to become comfortable using channels, you've learned all the fundamental concepts and skills you need to get started using masks and channels.

Review questions

1 What is the benefit of using a quick mask?

2 What happens to a quick mask when you deselect?

3 When you save a selection as a mask, where is the mask stored?

4 How can you edit a mask in a channel once you've saved it?

5 How do channels differ from layers?

Review answers

1 Quick masks are helpful for creating quick, one-time selections. In addition, using a quick mask is an easy way to edit a selection using the painting tools.

2 Quick masks disappear when you deselect.

3 Masks are saved in channels, which can be thought of as storage areas in an image.

4 You can paint directly on a mask in a channel using black, white, and shades of gray.

5 Channels are used as storage areas for saved selections. Unless you explicitly display a channel, it does not appear in the image or print. Layers can be used to isolate various parts of an image so that they can be edited as discrete objects with the painting or editing tools or other effects.

Lesson 6

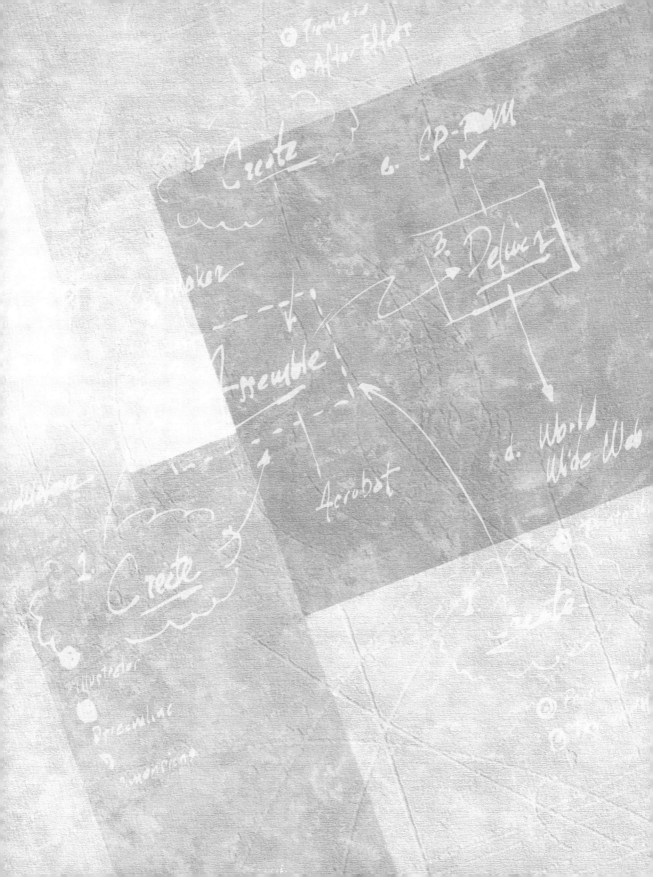

Photo Retouching

Adobe Photoshop provides you with a variety of tools and commands for improving the quality of a photographic image. This lesson explains techniques for basic image correction by stepping you through the process of acquiring, resizing, and retouching a photo intended for a print layout.

In this lesson, you will learn to do the following:

• Choose the correct resolution for a scanned photograph.

• Crop an image to final size.

• Adjust the tonal range of an image.

• Remove a color cast from an image using an adjustment layer.

• Use the Replace Color command to change the hue and saturation of a selected color in a photograph.

• Adjust the saturation and brightness of isolated areas of an image using the sponge and dodge tools.

• Use the rubber stamp tool to eliminate an unwanted object from an image.

• Replace parts of an image with another image.

• Apply the Unsharp Mask filter to finish the photo-retouching process.

• Save an Adobe Photoshop file in a format that can be used by a page-layout program.

Strategy for retouching

In Photoshop, you can retouch photographic images in ways once left only to highly trained professionals. You can correct problems in color quality and tonal range created during the original photography or during the image's scan. You can also correct problems in composition and sharpen the overall focus of the image.

Basic steps

Most retouching in Photoshop follows these general steps:

• Check the scan quality and make sure that the resolution is appropriate for how the image will be used.

• Crop the image to final size.

• Adjust the overall contrast or tonal range of the image.

• Remove any color casts.

• Adjust the color and tone in specific parts of the image to bring out highlights, midtones, shadows, and desaturated colors.

• Sharpen the overall focus of the image.

Intended use

The retouching techniques you apply to an image depend in part on how the image will be used. Whether an image is intended for black-and-white publication on newsprint or for full-color Internet distribution will affect everything from the resolution of the initial scan to the type of tonal range and color correction that the image requires.

To illustrate one application of retouching techniques, this lesson takes you through the steps of correcting a photograph intended for four-color print publication. The image is a scanned photograph of Venice that will be placed in an Adobe PageMaker® layout for an A4-size magazine. The original size of the photo is 5 inches by 7 inches and its final size in the print layout will be 3.75 inches by 6 inches.

Original image *Image cropped and retouched* *Image placed into page layout*

For illustrations of the original and retouched photographs for this lesson, see figures 6-1 and 6-2 in the color signature.

Resolution and image size

The first step in retouching a photograph in Photoshop is to make sure that the image is the correct resolution. The term *resolution* refers to the number of small squares known as *pixels* that describe an image and establish its detail. Resolution is determined by *pixel dimensions* or the number of pixels along the width and height of an image.

Pixels in photographic image

Types of resolution

In computer graphics, there are different types of resolution:

The number of pixels per unit of length in an image is called the *image resolution*, usually measured in pixels per inch (ppi). An image with a high resolution has more pixels, and therefore a larger file size, than an image of the same dimensions with a low resolution.

The number of pixels per unit of length on a monitor is the *monitor resolution*, usually measured in dots per inch (dpi). In Adobe Photoshop, image pixels are translated directly into monitor pixels. Thus, if the image resolution is higher than the monitor resolution, the image appears larger on-screen than its specified print dimensions. For example, when you display a 1-inch-by-1-inch, 144-ppi image on a 72-dpi monitor, the image fills a 2-inch-by-2-inch area of the screen.

3.75 in. x 6 in. @ 72 ppi; 100% view on-screen 3.75 in. x 6 in. @ 200 ppi; 100% view on-screen
file size 342K   file size 2.48 MB

The number of ink dots per inch produced by an imagesetter or laser printer is the *printer* or *output resolution*. Higher resolution printers combined with higher resolution images generally produce the best quality. The appropriate resolution for a printed image is determined both by the printer resolution and by the *screen frequency* or lines per inch (lpi) of the halftone screens used to reproduce images.

Resolution for this lesson

To determine the image resolution for the photograph in this lesson, we followed the computer graphics rule of thumb for color or grayscale images intended for print on large commercial printers: Scan at a resolution 1.5 to 2 times the screen frequency used by the printer. Because the magazine in which the image will be printed uses a screen frequency of 133 lpi, the image was scanned at 200 ppi (133 by 1.5).

For more information on resolution and image size, see "Getting Images into Photoshop" in online Help or Chapter 3 in the Adobe Photoshop User Guide.

Getting started

Before beginning this lesson, delete the Adobe Photoshop Preferences file to restore the program's default settings. For step-by-step instructions, see "Restoring default preferences" on page 4. Then restart the Photoshop program.

Now you'll open the final image to see how the adjustments you'll make will affect the final artwork.

1 Choose File > Open. Locate and open the Lesson06 folder; then select End06.psd and click Open.

2 If you like, choose View > Zoom Out to make the image smaller, and leave it on your screen as you work. If you don't want to leave the image open, choose File > Close.

Now open the start file to view the photograph you will be retouching. (Although the photograph for this lesson was originally scanned at 200 dpi as described above, the file in which you will be working is actually a low-resolution file. The resolution was changed to limit the file size and to make work on the exercises more efficient.)

3 Choose File > Open. Locate and open the Lesson06 folder, select Start06.psd, and click Open.

4 Choose File > Save As, type the name **Work06.psd**, and click Save.

Cropping an image

Once you've scanned an image and opened it in Photoshop, you're ready to retouch it. To start, you'll use the crop tool to scale the photograph for this lesson so that it fits the space designed for it.

1 Hold down the mouse button on the rectangular marquee tool (⬚) in the toolbox, and drag to the crop tool (⛶) to select it. Then double-click the crop tool to display its Options palette, select Fixed Target Size, and enter the dimensions of the finished image—3.75 inches (width) by 6 inches (height).

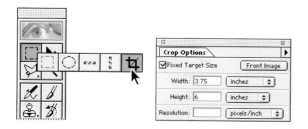

2 Next drag a marquee around the image, making sure that you include the top of the tower and the orange tarp in the bottom right gondola. Notice that as you drag the marquee it retains the same proportion as the dimensions you specified for the target size.

Because the photograph was scanned in slightly crooked, you'll now use the crop tool to straighten the image before applying the new dimensions to it.

3 Move the pointer outside the crop marquee, and drag clockwise until the marquee is parallel with the image.

4 Place the pointer within the crop marquee, and drag until the right edge of the marquee lines up with the right edge of the image.

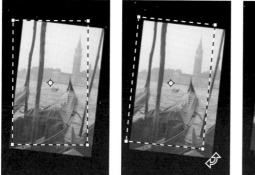

Initial crop marquee   *Marquee rotated*   *Marquee moved*

5 If necessary, fine-tune the size of the marquee by dragging its bottom right corner handle.

6 Press Enter (Windows) or Return (Mac OS). The image is now cropped.

Marquee resized   *Image cropped*

7 Choose File > Save.

Adjusting the tonal range

The tonal range of an image represents the amount of *contrast*, or detail, in the image and is determined by the image's distribution of pixels, ranging from the darkest pixels (black) to the lightest pixels (white). You'll now correct the photograph's contrast using the Levels command.

1 Choose Image > Adjust > Levels, and make sure that the Preview option is checked.

Notice the histogram in the dialog box. The triangles at the bottom of the histogram represent the shadows (black triangle), highlights (white triangle), and midtones or gamma (gray triangle). If your image had colors across the entire brightness range, the graph would extend across the full width of the histogram, from black triangle to white triangle. Instead, the graph is clumped toward the center, indicating there are no very dark or light colors.

You can adjust the black and white points of the image to extend its tonal range.

2 Drag the left and right triangles inward to where the histogram indicates the darkest and lightest colors begin. Click OK to apply the changes.

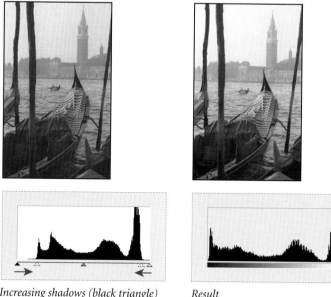

Increasing shadows (black triangle) and adding highlights (white triangle)   *Result*

3 Choose Image > Histogram to view the new histogram. The tonal range now extends throughout the entire range of the histogram. Click OK.

4 Choose File > Save.

Using the color correction tools

All Adobe Photoshop color correction tools work essentially the same way: by mapping existing ranges of pixel values to new ranges of values. The difference between the tools is the amount of control you have.

For example, the Brightness/Contrast command makes the same adjustment to every pixel in the selection or image—if you increase the brightness value by 30, 30 is added to the brightness value of every pixel. On the other hand, two of the color adjustment tools are particularly useful because of the control and flexibility they provide. Levels allows you precise adjustments using three variables (highlights, shadows, and midtones). Curves replicates high-end color correction systems and lets you isolate 16 ranges of pixel values between pure highlight and pure shadow.

You can use most color adjustment tools in three ways: applying them to one or more channels, to a regular layer, or to an adjustment layer. When you make color adjustments to a channel or a regular layer, you permanently alter the pixels on that layer.

With an adjustment layer, your color and tonal changes reside only within the adjustment layer and do not alter any pixels. The effect is as if you were viewing the visible layers through the adjustment layer above them. This lets you experiment with color and tonal adjustments without permanently altering pixels in the image. Adjustment layers are also the only way to affect multiple layers at once.

–From the Adobe Photoshop User Guide, Chapter 6

Removing a color cast

Some images contain color casts (imbalances of color), which may occur during scanning or which may have existed in the original image. The photograph of the gondolas has a color cast—it's too red.

Note: To see a color cast in an image on your monitor, you need a 24-bit monitor (one that can display millions of colors). On monitors that can display only 256 colors (8 bits), a color cast is difficult, if not impossible, to detect.

You will now use a Color Balance adjustment layer to correct the photograph's color cast. An adjustment layer lets you edit an image as many times as you like without permanently changing the original pixel values. Using an adjustment layer to adjust color balance is a particular advantage for images you plan to print. After you see the color proof or printed copy, you can make additional changes to the image, if necessary.

1 Choose Layer > New > Adjustment Layer.

2 For Type, choose Color Balance.

3 Click OK to create the adjustment layer and to display the Color Balance Layer dialog box.

4 Select the Preview option.

5 To adjust the midtones so that they're less red, drag the top slider to the left (we used -15) and the middle slider to the right (we used +8).

6 Click OK to apply the changes to the Color Balance adjustment layer. Notice that a Color Balance layer has appeared in the Layers palette.

7 In the Layers palette, click the eye icon next to the Color Balance layer to hide and show the layer. You'll see the difference between the adjusted colors and the original colors.

8 Choose File > Save.

Note: When you double-click an adjustment layer in the Layers palette, the corresponding dialog box appears, where you can edit the values of the adjustment layer.

Adjusting color balance

Every color adjustment affects the overall color balance in your image. You have numerous ways to achieve similar effects, so determining which adjustment is appropriate depends on the image and on the desired effect.

It helps to keep a diagram of the color wheel on hand if you're new to adjusting color components. You can use the color wheel to predict how a change in one color component affects other colors and also how changes translate between RGB and CMYK color models. For example, you can decrease the amount of any color in an image by increasing the amount of its opposite on the color wheel—and vice versa. Similarly, you can increase and decrease a color by adjusting the two adjacent colors on the wheel, or even by adjusting the two colors adjacent to its opposite.

For example, in a CMYK image you can decrease magenta by decreasing either the amount of magenta or its proportion (by adding cyan and yellow). You can even combine these two corrections, minimizing their effect on overall lightness. In an RGB image, you can decrease magenta by removing red and blue or by adding green. All of these adjustments result in an overall color balance containing less magenta.

–From the Adobe Photoshop User Guide, Chapter 6

Replacing colors in an image

With the Replace Color command, you can create temporary masks based on specific colors and then replace these colors. *Masks* let you isolate an area of an image, so that changes affect just the selected area and not the rest of the image. Options in the Replace Color command's dialog box allow you to adjust the hue, saturation, and lightness components of the selection. *Hue* is color, *saturation* is the purity of the color, and *lightness* is how much white or black is in the image.

You'll use the Replace Color command to change the color of the orange tarp in the gondola at the bottom right corner of the image.

1 In the Layers palette, select the Background.

2 Select the zoom tool ( ), and click once on the tarp to zoom in on it.

3 Hold down the mouse button on the crop tool, drag to select the rectangle marquee tool, and then drag a selection around the tarp. Don't worry about making a perfect selection, but be sure to include all the tarp.

4 Choose Image > Adjust > Replace Color to open the Replace Color dialog box. By default, the Selection area of the Replace Color dialog box displays a black rectangle, representing the current selection.

You will now use the eyedropper tool to select the area of color that will be masked and replaced with a new color. Three eyedropper tools are displayed in the Replace Color dialog box.

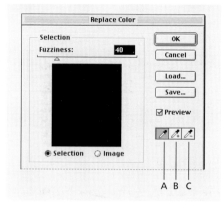

A. *Select single color* B. *Add to selection*
C. *Subtract from selection*

The first eyedropper tool ( ) selects a single color, the eyedropper-plus tool ( ) is used to add colors to a selection, and the eyedropper-minus tool ( ) is used to subtract colors from a selection.

5 Click the eyedropper tool in the dialog box, and click once on the orange tarp to select it.

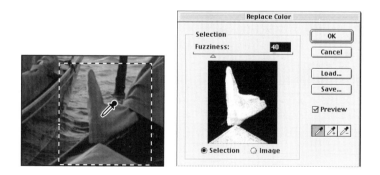

6 Then select the eyedropper-plus tool, and drag over the other areas of the tarp until the entire tarp is highlighted in white in the dialog box.

7 Adjust the tolerance level of the mask by moving the Fuzziness slider to 61. Fuzziness controls the degree to which related colors are included in the mask.

8 In the Transform area of the Replace Color dialog box, drag the Hue slider to 149, the Saturation slider to –17, and the Lightness slider to -39. The color of the tarp is replaced with the new hue, saturation, and lightness.

9 Click OK to apply the changes.

10 Double-click the hand tool (✌) to fit the image on-screen.

11 Choose Select > Deselect.

12 Choose File > Save.

Adjusting saturation with the sponge tool

Now you'll saturate the color of the gondolas in the foreground using the sponge tool. When you change the saturation of a color, you adjust its strength or purity. The sponge tool is useful in letting you make subtle saturation changes to specific areas of an image.

1 Hold down the mouse button on the dodge tool (✦) in the toolbox, and drag to the sponge tool (◉).

2 Click the Options tab, and choose Saturate from the pop-up menu. To set the intensity of the saturation effect, click the arrow next to the Pressure text box, and drag the Pressure pop-up slider to 90%.

3 Select a large, feathered brush from the second row of the Brushes palette.

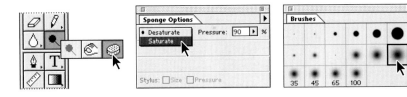

4 Drag the sponge back and forth over the gondolas to saturate their color.

Original   Result

Adjusting lightness with the dodge tool

Next you'll use the dodge tool to lighten the highlights along the gondola's hull and exaggerate the reflection of the water there. The dodge tool is based on the traditional photographer's method of holding back light during an exposure to lighten an area of the image.

1 Hold down the mouse button on the sponge tool, and drag to the dodge tool (✹). Then choose Highlights from the menu in the Tool Options palette, and set Exposure to 50%.

2 Select a medium, feathered brush from the second row of the Brushes palette.

3 Drag the dodge tool back and forth over the gondola's hull to bring out its highlights.

Original   Result

Removing unwanted objects

With Adobe Photoshop, you can remove unwanted objects from a photograph. Using the rubber stamp tool, you can remove an object or area by "cloning" an area of the image over the area you want to eliminate.

You'll eliminate the small boat near the center of the image by painting over it with a copy of the water.

1 Select the zoom tool; then click the small boat to magnify that part of the image.

2 Double-click the rubber stamp tool (⊕) in the toolbox, and make sure that the Aligned option in the Rubber Stamp Options palette is deselected.

3 Center the rubber stamp tool over the water between the large gondola and the post to its right. Then hold down Alt (Windows) or Option (Mac OS), and click to sample or copy that part of the image. Make sure that the area you sample blends well with the area around the object you are removing.

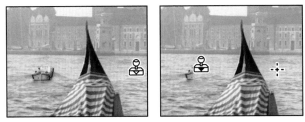

Clicking to sample image   *Dragging to paint over image*

4 Drag the rubber stamp tool over the boat to paint over it with a copy of the water you just sampled. Notice the cross hair that follows your cursor as you paint; it represents the point from which the rubber stamp tool is cloning.

5 Double-click the hand tool in the toolbox to fit the image on-screen.

6 Choose File > Save.

Replacing part of an image

Because the sky is fairly drab and overcast in this photograph, you'll replace it with a more interesting sky from another file. You'll begin by selecting the current sky.

1 Select the magic wand tool (✱). Click to select part of the sky. Hold down Shift, and click the rest of the sky to select it.

2 Open the Clouds.psd file located in the Lesson06 folder.

3 Choose Select > All; then choose Edit > Copy. Close the Clouds.psd file.

4 Choose Edit > Paste Into to paste the clouds into the current selection. Notice that a new layer has been added to the Layers palette.

5 Select the move tool (▶), and drag the clouds into the position you want.

Sky selected *Clouds pasted into sky* *Clouds moved into position*

Now you'll change the clouds' opacity to make them blend better with the rest of the image.

6 Use the keyboard shortcut of typing any number from 01 (1%) to 100 (100%) to set the new cloud layer's opacity (we used 55%).

7 Choose File > Save.

Opacity set to 55% *Result*

You will now flatten the image into a single layer so that you can apply the Unsharp Mask filter, the final step in retouching the photo. Because you may want to return to a version of the file with all its layers intact, you will use the Save As command to save the flattened file with a new name.

8 Choose Layer > Flatten Image.

9 Choose File > Save As. In the dialog box, type a new filename, and click Save.

Sharpening the image

Unsharp masking, or USM, is a traditional film compositing technique used to sharpen edges in an image. The Unsharp Mask filter corrects blurring introduced during photographing, scanning, resampling, or printing. It is useful for images intended both for print and online.

The Unsharp Mask filter locates pixels that differ from surrounding pixels by the threshold you specify and increases the pixels' contrast by the amount you specify. In addition, you specify the radius of the region to which each pixel is compared.

The effects of the Unsharp Mask filter are far more pronounced on-screen than in high-resolution output. If your final destination is print, experiment to determine what dialog box settings work best for your image.

–From the Adobe Photoshop User Guide, Chapter 6

Applying the Unsharp Mask filter

The last step you take when retouching a photo is to apply the Unsharp Mask filter, which adjusts the contrast of the edge detail and creates the illusion of a more focused image.

1 Choose Filter > Sharpen > Unsharp Mask. Make sure that the Preview option is selected so that you can view the effect before you apply it. To get a better view, you can place the pointer within the preview window and drag to see different parts of the image. You can also change the magnification of the preview image with the plus and minus buttons located below the window.

2 Drag the Amount slider until the image is as sharp as you want (we used 120%); then click OK to apply the Unsharp Mask filter.

For more information about the Unsharp Mask filter, see "Making Color and Tonal Adjustments" in online Help or Chapter 6 in the Adobe Photoshop User Guide.

Saving the image

Before you save a Photoshop file for use in a four-color publication, you must change the image to CMYK color mode so that it will be printed correctly in four-color process inks. You can use the Mode command to change the image's color mode.

For more information on color modes, see "Choosing a Color Mode" in online Help or Chapter 4 in the Adobe Photoshop User Guide.

1 Choose Image > Mode > CMYK.

You can now save the file in the correct format required for Adobe PageMaker and your publication. Because PageMaker uses the Tagged-Image File Format (TIFF) for images that will be printed in process or CMYK colors, you will save the photo as a TIFF file.

2 Choose File > Save As.

3 In the dialog box, select TIFF from the Save As menu (Windows) or Format menu (Mac OS).

4 Click Save.

5 In the TIFF Options dialog box, click the correct Byte Order for your system.

The image is now fully retouched, saved, and ready for placement in the PageMaker layout.

For an illustration of the finished artwork in this lesson, see the color signature.

Review questions

1 What is resolution?

2 How can you use the crop tool in photo retouching?

3 How can you adjust the tonal range of an image?

4 How can you correct a color cast in a photograph?

5 What is saturation and how can you adjust it?

6 Why would you use the Unsharp Mask filter on a photo?

Review answers

1 The term *resolution* refers to the number of pixels that describe an image and establish its detail. The three different types of resolution include image resolution, measured in pixels per inch (ppi); monitor resolution, measured in dots per inch (dpi); and printer or output resolution, measured in ink dots per inch.

2 You can use the crop tool to scale and straighten an image.

3 You can use the black and white triangles below the Levels command histogram to control where the darkest and lightest points in the image begin and thus extend its tonal range.

4 You can correct a color cast with a Color Balance adjustment layer. The adjustment layer lets you change the color of the image as many times as you like without permanently affecting the original pixel values.

5 Saturation is the strength or purity of color in an image. You can increase the saturation in a specific area of an image with the sponge tool.

6 The Unsharp Mask filter adjusts the contrast of the edge detail and creates the illusion of a more focused image.

Lesson 7

Basic Pen Tool Techniques

The pen tool draws precise straight or curved lines called paths. You can use the pen tool as a drawing tool or as a selection tool. When used as a selection tool, the pen tool always draws smooth, anti-aliased outlines. These paths are an excellent alternative to using the standard selection tools for creating intricate selections.

In this lesson, you'll learn how to do the following:

- Practice drawing straight and curved paths using the pen tool.
- Save paths.
- Fill and stroke paths.
- Edit paths using the path editing tools.
- Convert a path to a selection.
- Convert a selection to a path.

Getting started

Before beginning this lesson, delete the Adobe Photoshop Preferences file to restore the program's default settings. For step-by-step instructions, see "Restoring default preferences" on page 4. Then restart the Photoshop program.

Now you'll begin by working with templates that guide you through the process of creating straight paths, curved paths, and paths that are a combination of both. In addition, you'll learn how to add points to a path, how to subtract points from a path, and how to convert a straight line to a curve and vice versa. After you've practiced drawing and editing paths using the templates, you'll open an image and practice drawing a path.

1 Choose File > Open. Locate and open the Lesson07 folder; then select Straight.psd, and click Open.

An image containing a template of straight lines appears. You'll practice drawing straight paths using a template, so that you can practice drawing the paths as many times as you like.

For an illustration of the finished artwork in this lesson, see the color signature.

2 Choose File > Save As, enter the name **Lesson7.psd**, and click Save.

3 If desired, select the zoom tool (🔍), and drag over the image to magnify the view.

Drawing paths with the pen tool

The pen tool draws straight and curved lines called *paths*. A path is any line or shape you draw using the pen, magnetic pen, or freeform pen tool. Of these tools, the pen tool draws paths with the greatest precision; the magnetic pen and freeform pen tool let you draw paths as if you were drawing with a pencil on paper.

Paths can be open or closed. Open paths have two distinct endpoints. Closed paths are continuous; for example, a circle is a closed path. The type of path you draw affects how it can be selected and adjusted. Paths do not print when you print your artwork. (That is because paths are vector objects that contain no pixels, unlike the bitmap shapes drawn by the pencil and other painting tools.)

1 Click the pen tool ( ) in the toolbox.

Press Shift+P on the keyboard to select the pen tool. Continue to press Shift+P to scroll through the pen tools.

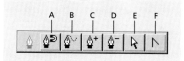

A. *Magnetic pen*
B. *Freeform pen*
C. *Add-anchor-point (+)*
D. *Delete-anchor-point (−)*
E. *Direct-selection (A)*
F. *Convert-anchor-point*

2 Click the Paths palette tab to bring the palette to the front of its group. The Paths palette displays thumbnail previews of the paths you draw.

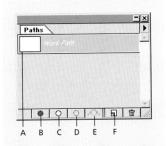

A. *Thumbnail preview* B. *Fill Path*
C. *Stroke Path* D. *Make Selection*
E. *Make Path* F. *New Path*

Drawing straight paths

Straight paths are created by clicking the mouse button. The first time you click the mouse button, you set a starting point for a path. Each time thereafter that you click the mouse, a straight line is drawn between the previous point and the current point.

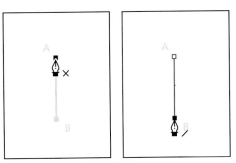

Click to set a starting point…   *click again to draw a straight line.*

1 Position the pen tool on point A and click the pen tool; then click point B to create a straight line path.

As you draw paths, a temporary storage area named Work Path appears in the Paths palette to keep track of the paths you draw.

2 End the path by clicking the pen tool in the toolbox.

The points that connect paths are called *anchor points*. You can drag individual anchor points to edit segments of a path, or you can select all the anchor points to select the entire path.

You'll learn more about anchor points later in this lesson.

3 Double-click the Work Path in the Paths palette to open the Save Path dialog box. Type the name **Straight lines** and click OK to rename the path. The path is renamed, and remains selected in the Paths palette.

You must save a work path to avoid losing its contents. If you deselect the work path without saving and then start drawing again, a new work path will replace the first one.

About anchor points, direction lines, and direction points

A path consists of one or more straight or curved segments. Anchor points mark the endpoints of the path segments. On curved segments, each selected anchor point displays one or two direction lines, ending in direction points. The positions of direction lines and points determine the size and shape of a curved segment. Moving these elements reshapes the curves in a path.

A path can be closed, with no beginning or end (for example, a circle), or open, with distinct endpoints (for example, a wavy line).

Smooth curves are connected by anchor points called smooth points. Sharply curved paths are connected by corner points.

When you move a direction line on a smooth point, the curved segments on both sides of the point adjust simultaneously. In comparison, when you move a direction line on a corner point, only the curve on the same side of the point as the direction line is adjusted.

–From the Adobe Photoshop User Guide, Chapter 7

Moving and adjusting paths

You use the direct-selection tool to select and adjust an anchor point, a path segment, or an entire path.

1 Select the direct-selection tool ( ) from the hidden tools palette under the pen tool. A small triangle to the right of the pen tool icon indicates a pull-out menu of hidden tools.

 To get the direct-selection tool, press A. You can also get the direct-selection tool when the pen tool is active by holding down Ctrl (Windows) or Command (Mac OS).

2 Click the path in the window to select it, and then move the path by dragging anywhere on the path using the direct-selection tool.

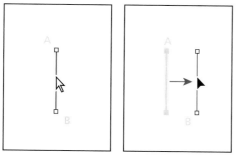

Selecting a path   Moving a path

3 To adjust the angle or length of the path, drag one of the anchor points with the direct-selection tool.

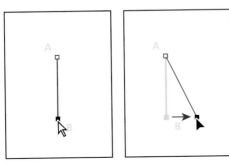   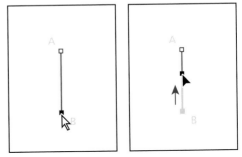

Adjusting the path angle   *Adjusting the path length*

4 Select the pen tool in the hidden tools palette in the toolbox (right now it's under the direct-selection tool).

5 To begin the next path, click point C with the pen tool. Notice that an *x* appears in the Paths palette to indicate that you are starting a new path.

6 Click point D to draw a path between the two points.

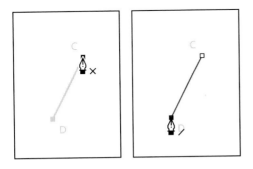

7 End the path using either of the following methods:

• Click the pen tool in the toolbox.

• Hold down Ctrl (Windows) or Command (Mac OS), and click away from the path. Holding down Ctrl/Command while the pen tool is active selects the direct-selection tool.

8 Click point E to begin the next path. Then hold down Shift and click points F, G, H, and I. Holding down Shift as you click the subsequent points constrains the path to a 45° angle.

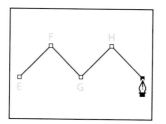

If you make a mistake while you're drawing, choose Edit > Undo to undo the last anchor point. Then click the pen tool to continue.

9 End the path using one of the methods you've learned.

When a path contains more than one segment, you can drag individual anchor points to adjust individual segments of the path. You can also select all of the anchor points in a path to edit the entire path.

10 Select the direct-selection tool in the hidden tools palette under the pen tool.

11 Try dragging individual anchor points to move segments of the zigzag path you just drew.

12 To select an entire path, Alt-click (Windows) or Option-click (Mac OS) with the direct-selection tool. When an entire path is selected, all the anchor points are solid.

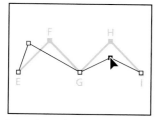 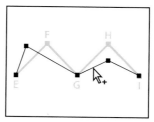

Dragging individual points   *Alt/Option-clicking to select entire path*

13 Drag the path to move the entire path; then choose Edit > Undo to undo the move.

Creating closed paths

Next, you'll draw a closed path. Creating a closed path differs from creating an open path in the way that you end the path.

1 Select the pen tool in the toolbox.

2 Click point J to begin the path; then click point K and point L.

When you position the pen tool over the starting point to end the path, a small circle appears with the pen tool to indicate that the path will be closed when you click.

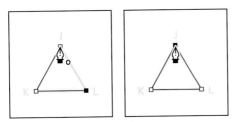

Circle indicating path will be closed, and result

3 To close the path, position the pointer over the starting point (point J), and click.

Closing the path ends the path. In contrast, to end an open path you have to click the pen tool in the toolbox or Ctrl/Command-click away from the path.

If desired, practice drawing another closed path using the star shape on the template as a guide.

At this point, all of the paths you've drawn appear in the Straight Lines path in the Paths palette. Each individual path on the Straight Lines path is called a *subpath*.

You can convert any path you have drawn into a selection and combine this selection with others. (You'll try this later.) You can also convert selection borders into paths and fine-tune them.

Painting paths

Painting paths adds pixels to them that appear when you print an image. Filling paints a closed path with color, an image, or a pattern. Stroking paints color along the path. To fill or stroke a path, you must first select it.

1 Click the Swatches palette tab to bring the palette forward. Click a swatch to select a foreground color to use to paint the path.

2 Select the direct-selection tool (↖) in the hidden tools palette under the pen tool.

3 In the image window, click the zigzag line with the direct-selection tool to select it. Then choose Stroke Subpath from the Paths palette menu.

4 For Tool, choose Airbrush, and click OK. The path is stroked with the current airbrush settings.

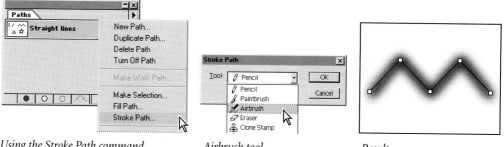

Using the Stroke Path command   *Airbrush tool*   *Result*

Note: *You can select a painting tool and set attributes before you select the tool in the Stroke Subpath dialog box.*

Now try filling one of the paths.

5 In the Swatches palette, click a swatch to select a different foreground color for the fill.

6 Click the triangular closed path with the direct-selection tool. Then choose Fill Subpath from the Paths palette menu. The Fill dialog box appears.

7 Click OK to accept the defaults. The triangular path is filled with the foreground color.

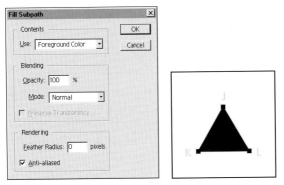

Using the Fill command to fill a   *Result*
closed path

8 To hide the paths, click below the path names in the blank area of the Paths palette.

9 Choose File > Close, and do not save changes.

Drawing curved paths

Curved paths are created by clicking and dragging the mouse button. The first time you click and drag the mouse, you set a starting point for the curved path and also determine the direction of the curve. Then when you drag the mouse, a curved path is drawn between the previous point and the current point.

As you drag the pen tool, Photoshop draws *direction lines* and *direction points* from the anchor point. Direction lines and points are used to edit the shape of curves and to change the direction of curves. You'll edit paths using the direction lines and direction points in a few minutes.

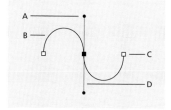

Direction lines and points setting the
curve direction
A. Direction point B. Curved segment
C. Anchor point D. Direction line

Like paths, direction lines and points do not print when you print your artwork because they are vector objects that contain no pixels.

1 Choose File > Open. Locate and open the Lesson07 folder, then select Curves.psd, and click Open.

2 Select the pen tool from the hidden tools palette in the toolbox.

3 Position the mouse button on point A of the first curve. Hold down the mouse button, and drag toward the red dot.

4 To complete the first curve of the path, drag from point B to the red dot. If you make a mistake while you're drawing, choose Edit > Undo to undo the last point you drew. Then continue drawing the path.

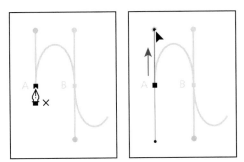 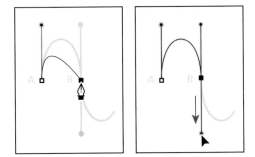

Position pointer on point A and drag to draw a curve. *Drag again to complete the curve.*

5 Complete the curved path by dragging from point C to the red dot and from point D to the red dot. End the path using one of the methods you learned.

6 Now you'll save the temporary work path so that you don't lose its contents.

7 Double-click the Work Path in the Paths palette to open the Save Path dialog box. Type the name **Curve1**, and click OK to rename the path. The named path is selected in the Paths palette.

You must save the work path before you deselect it to prevent a new work path from replacing the first one as you start drawing again.

Creating separate paths

Now that you've created a new path in the Paths palette, as you continue to draw the path, you create a connected series of segments, or subpaths. Subpaths are saved automatically.

But sometimes, you'll want to create separate named paths for each path you draw. To start a new Work Path, you click away from the current path in the Paths palette.

1 In the Paths palette, click in the blank area below the Curve1 path to deselect the path.

When you deselect a path in the Paths palette, any paths on the named path are deselected (hidden). To make them reappear, you click the desired path in the Paths palette (don't click the path now, because you're going to create a new one in a moment).

2 Drag up from point E to the red dot; then drag up from point F to the red dot. You'll notice that as soon as you begin drawing, a new Work Path appears in the Paths palette.

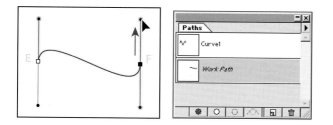

3 End the path using one of the methods you learned.

4 Double-click the Work Path in the Paths palette, name the path **Curve2**, and then click OK.

5 Click away from the path in the Paths palette to deselect it.

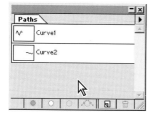

Now you'll create a closed curved path.

6 Drag up from point G to the red dot; then drag down from point H to the red dot. To close the path, position the pointer over point G, and click.

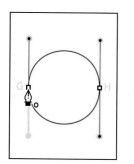

7 In the Paths palette, double-click the Work Path, save the path as **Closed Path**, and then click away from the path to deselect it.

Now you'll have a chance to edit the curved paths you've drawn.

8 Select the direct-selection tool (⬚) from the hidden tools under the pen tool.

💡 *Hold down Ctrl (Windows) or Command (Mac OS) when the pen tool is active to select the direct-selection tool from the keyboard.*

9 In the Paths palette, click the Curve2 path to select it; then click the path in the window to select it.

10 Click one of the anchor points in the curve; then drag a direction point at the end the direction line emanating from the anchor point.

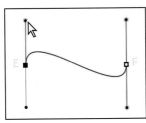 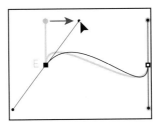

Dragging a direction point...   *to change the direction of a curve*

11 Now, drag an anchor point to change the location of the curve.

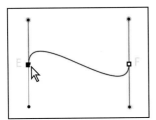 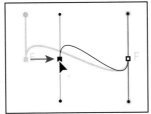

Dragging an anchor point...   *to change the location of the curve*

Stroking and filling paths

In addition to using the Stroke Subpath command, you can stroke paths by dragging a named path onto the Stroke Path button at the bottom of the Paths palette. To determine which painting option you want to stroke the path with, select the desired painting tool in the toolbox before you drag the path onto the Stroke Path button.

1 Click the paintbrush tool (✐) in the toolbox.

2 Drag the Curve1 path onto the Stroke Path button at the bottom of the Paths palette to stroke it with the current paintbrush settings.

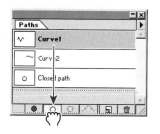

Note: You can also fill or stroke a path by clicking the Fill Path or Stroke Path button at the bottom of the Paths palette. Make sure that the path is selected in the palette before you click the button.

3 Drag the Closed path onto the Fill Path button at the bottom of the Paths palette to fill it with the current foreground color.

(When you fill an open path, Photoshop automatically draws an invisible line between the starting point and the ending point, and fills the segments between them.)

4 Choose File > Close, and do not save changes.

Combining straight and curved lines

Now that you've learned how to draw straight and curved paths individually, you'll put them together to create paths that combine straight and curved lines.

To create a path that combines straight and curved lines, you create a corner point to indicate the transition from a straight line to a curved line (or vice versa).

1 Choose File > Open. Locate and open the Lesson07folder; then select Combo.psd and click Open.

2 Select the pen tool in the toolbox.

3 Drag up from point A to the red dot; then drag from point B downward to the red dot.

4 At point B, you must create a corner point to change the direction of the next curve. Alt-click (Windows) or Option-click (Mac OS) point B to set a corner point.

5 Now, drag from the same point (point B) up to the red dot to change the direction of the next curve.

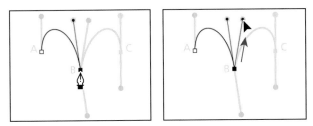

Alt-clicking (Windows) or Option-clicking (Mac OS) to set a corner point; then dragging in the opposite direction

6 Drag from point C to the red dot to complete the path. Then end the path using one of the methods you learned.

7 To start the second path, which begins with a straight line, click point D with the pen tool; then hold down Shift and click point E (don't drag).

8 Position the pen tool on point E and drag to the red dot. Dragging from point E sets the direction of the next curve (which is an upward curve).

9 Drag from point F to the red dot; then Alt-click (Windows) or Option-click (Mac OS) point F to set a corner point.

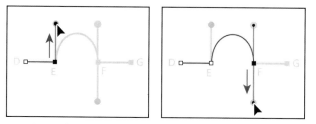

Dragging in the direction of the curve from point E; then dragging in the opposite direction to complete the curve before setting a corner point

10 Hold down Shift, and click point G to create a straight line. Then end the path using one of the methods you learned.

11 To create the next path, click the pen tool on point H, hold down Shift, and then click point I.

12 To set a curve at point I, Alt-drag (Windows) or Option-drag (Mac OS) the red dot.

13 Drag from point J to the red dot.

14 Alt-click (Windows) or Option-click (Mac OS) point J to set a corner point.

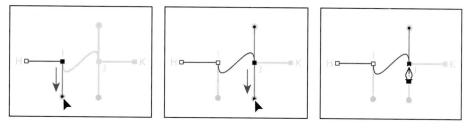

Creating an S-curve by dragging in the opposite direction of a curve; then setting a corner point

15 To complete the path, hold down Shift and click point K. End the path using one of the methods you learned.

16 Choose File > Close, and do not save changes.

Adding and subtracting anchor points

You can add points to a path to increase the number of segments in the path, and you can subtract unneeded or unwanted points from a path.

1 Choose File > Open. Locate and open the Lesson07 folder, then select Edit.psd, and click Open.

Three paths have been created and saved in the Paths palette. You'll edit the paths using the pen tool and the convert-direction point tool.

2 Click the Paths palette tab to bring it to the front; then click the Add and Delete Points path to make it the active path. Two subpaths appear in the window.

3 Select the add-anchor-point tool (✒⁺) from the hidden tools palette in the toolbox. Then position the tool over the red dot at the center of the straight path, and click. An anchor point with direction lines is added to the segment.

4 Release the mouse button. The pointer becomes a hollow arrow, which lets you select and manipulate the path.

5 Now select and drag the path upward.

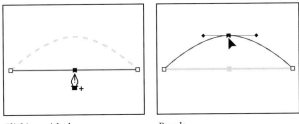

Clicking with the   *Result*
add-anchor-point tool

Next, you'll subtract an anchor point from a path.

💡 *You can always select the direct-selection tool from the keyboard when the pen tool is active by holding down Ctrl (Windows) or Command (Mac OS).*

6 Select the second path with the direct-selection tool.

You must select the path before you can delete points from the path. But you can select the path and the anchor points without first selecting a tool. If a path is active, just move the pen tool over a segment to change it to the add-anchor-point tool. Move the pen tool over an end point to change the tool to the delete-anchor-point tool.

7 Select the delete-anchor-point tool ( ) from the hidden tools palette, position it on the red dot over the center anchor point, and then click to remove the anchor point.

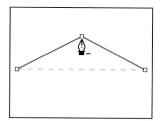
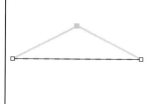

Clicking with the   *Result*
delete-anchor-point tool

Converting points

Sometimes, you may want to change a curve to a corner point or vice versa. Using the convert-direction-point tool, you can easily make the adjustment.

Using the convert-direction-point tool is very much like drawing with the pen tool. To convert a curve to a corner point, you click the anchor point, and to convert a corner to a curve, you drag on the anchor point.

1 In the Paths palette, click the path name Convert Directions to select it.

The shaped path has both corner points and curves. You'll start by converting the corner points to curves, and then you'll convert the curves to corner points.

2 Select the convert-direction-point tool ( ) from the hidden tools palette.

3 Position the convert-direction-point tool on a point of the outer path; then click and drag to convert the point from a corner point to a curve.

4 Convert the rest of the corner points to smooth points to complete the outer path.

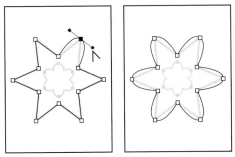

Changing a corner point to a curve with the
convert-direction point tool

5 Now, to convert the curves at the center of the shape to corner points, simply click the anchor point on each curve.

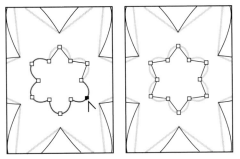

Converting curves to corner points with the
convert-direction-point tool

You can also use the convert-direction-point tool to adjust only one side of a curved segment. You'll try this on the outer path.

6 Click the outer path with the direct-selection tool; then click a curved segment so that direction lines and direction points emanate from one of the anchor points.

7 Select the convert-direction-point tool again.

8 With the path still selected, position the convert-direction-point tool directly on one of the direction points (at the end of a direction line), and drag. Only one side of the curve is adjusted.

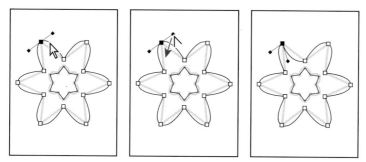

Selecting path with direct-selection tool; then adjusting part of curved segment with the convert-direction-point tool

Remember that you can use the convert-direction-point tool to convert a corner point to a curve, to convert curve to a corner point, and to adjust one side of a curved segment.

9 Choose File > Close, and do not save changes.

Drawing a path around artwork

Now that you've had some practice using the templates, you'll draw a path around artwork in an image. After you've drawn the path, you'll convert it to a selection and then apply a filter to the selection to complete the image.

When drawing a freehand path using the pen tool, use as few points as possible to create the shape you want. The fewer points you use, the smoother the curves.

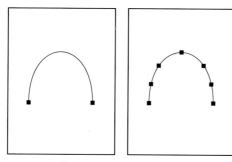

Correct number of points   *Too many points*

1 Choose File > Open. Locate and open the Lesson07 folder; then select Catmask.psd and click Open.

2 Choose File > Save As, enter the name **Catwork.psd**, and then click Save.

First you'll use the pen tool to draw a path around the outside of the mask. Then you'll create a path by creating a selection and then converting it to a path.

3 Select the pen tool from the hidden tools palette in the toolbox.

💡 *Press Shift+P on the keyboard to select the pen tool. Pressing Shift+P repeatedly scrolls through the pen, magnetic pen, and freeform pen tools.*

4 Position the pen tool on point A, and drag to the red dot to set the first anchor point and the direction of the first curve.

5 Position the pen tool on point B, and drag to the red dot.

6 At the tip of the ear, you'll need to set a corner point. Alt-click (Windows) or Option-click (Mac OS) point B to set a corner point. Remember, you set a corner point when the direction of the curve changes and no longer is smooth.

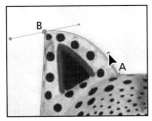
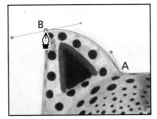

Setting anchor point and   Setting a corner point at B
direction of curve at A

7 Now that you've set a corner point, position the pen tool on point C, and drag to the red dot.

If you make a mistake while you're drawing, choose Edit > Undo to undo the step. Then resume drawing.

The next few points are simple curves.

8 Position the pen tool on point D, and drag to the red dot; then do the same for points E and F.

At point G, you'll complete the curve from point F and then set another corner point at the tip of the ear.

9 Position the pen tool on point G, and drag to the red dot. Then Alt-click (Windows) or Option-click (Mac OS) point G again to set a corner point.

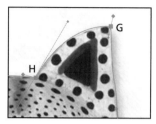

Dragging from point G; then setting a corner point at H

10 Drag point H to the red dot (below the anchor point) to complete the curve of the ear.

11 Still on point H, Alt-drag (Windows) or Option-drag (Mac OS) to the yellow dot to set the direction of the final curve.

12 To end the path, Alt-drag (Windows) or Option-drag (Mac OS) point A to the yellow dot. (This adds a slight curve to the line between the ears.)

13 In the Paths palette, double-click the Work Path, name the path **Face**, and click OK to save it.

14 Choose File > Save to save your work.

Converting selections to paths

Now you'll create a second path using a different method. First, you'll use a selection tool to select a similarly colored area, and then you'll convert the selection to a path.

1 Click the Layers palette tab to display the palette, and then drag the Template layer to the Trash button at the bottom of the palette. You won't need this layer any longer. Only the background should remain.

2 Double-click the magic wand tool ( ) in the toolbox. In the Magic Wand Options palette, enter **60** in the Tolerance text box.

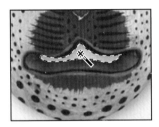

3 Click the gray background where it shows through the cat's mouth.

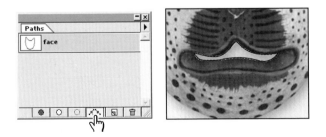

4 If you don't select the entire area the first time, Shift-click again on the mouth with the magic wand to add to the selection.

5 Click the Paths palette tab to bring the Path palette to the front. Then click the Make Path button at the bottom of the palette. The selection is converted to a path, and a new Work Path is created. You can convert any selection made with a selection tool into a path.

Note: If desired, use the tools you've learned to adjust the points on the path.

6 Double-click the Work Path, and name it **Mouth**; then click OK to save the path.

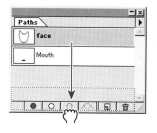

7 Choose File > Save to save your work.

Converting paths to selections

Just as you can convert selection borders to paths, you can convert paths to selections. With their smooth outlines, paths let you make precise selections. Now that you've drawn paths for the cat's face and mouth, you'll convert them to selections and apply a filter to the selection.

1 In the Paths palette, click the Face path to make it active.

2 Convert the Face path to a selection using either of the following methods:

• Choose Make Selection from the Paths palette menu, and click OK.

• Drag the Face path to the Make Selection button at the bottom of the Paths palette.

Next, you'll subtract the mouth selection from the face selection so that you can apply a filter without affecting the gray area of the background, which shows through the cat's mouth.

3 In the Paths palette, click the Mouth path; then choose Make Selection from the Paths palette menu.

4 In the Make Selection dialog box, select Subtract from Selection in the Operation section; then click OK.

The Mouth path is simultaneously converted to a selection and subtracted from the Face selection.

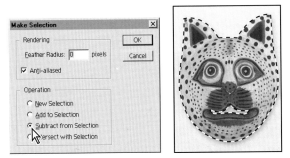

Subtracting the mouth selection   *Result*
from the face selection

5 Before adding a filter to the mask, make sure that the foreground is set to white and the background is set to black (if necessary, click the Default Colors icon in the toolbox, and then click the Switch Colors icon).

6 Choose Filter > Artistic > Neon Glow. Accept the defaults, and click OK to apply the filter.

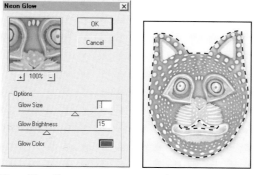

Neon Glow filter   *Result*

The filter has been applied to only the mask area. As a final step, you'll apply a textured filter to the entire image.

7 Choose Select > Deselect to deselect everything.

8 Choose Filter > Texture > Texturizer. Select the Sandstone option from the Texture menu; then click OK to apply the settings.

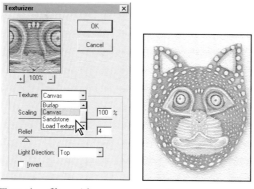

Texturizer filter with   *Result*
Sandstone option

9 Choose File > Save to save your work; then close the file.

You've completed the Basic Pen Tool lesson. Try drawing paths around different objects in your artwork to practice using the pen tool. With practice, you'll find that the pen tool can be invaluable for creating intricate outlines.

Review questions

1 How do you modify individual segments of a path?

2 How do you select an entire path?

3 How do you add points to a path?

4 How do you delete points from a path?

5 When you drag the pen tool to create a curved path, how does the direction in which you drag affect the curve?

6 How can the pen tool be useful as a selection tool?

Review answers

1 You drag the anchor points on the path using the direct-selection tool. You can also edit the shape of curved segments by dragging the direction points at the ends of the direction lines that extend from the anchor point of the curve.

2 To select an entire path, hold down Alt (Windows) or Option (Mac OS), and click the path using the direct-selection tool. When an entire path is selected, all the anchor points are solid.

3 To add points to a path, you select the add-anchor-point tool from the hidden tools under the pen tool and then click the path where you want to add an anchor point.

4 To delete points from a path, you select the delete-anchor-point tool from the hidden tools under the pen tool and then click the anchor point you want to remove from the path.

5 The direction you drag defines the direction of the curve that follows.

6 If you need to create an intricate selection, it can be easier to draw the path with the pen tool and then convert the path to a selection.

Lesson 8

Advanced Layer Techniques

Once you've learned basic layer techniques, you can begin to create more complex effects in your artwork using layer masks, clipping groups, and adjustment layers. Layer masks let you hide or reveal parts of the artwork on a layer. Clipping groups let you define an object on one layer as a mask for artwork on other layers. Adjustment layers let you apply effects that can be edited repeatedly without making a permanent change to the pixels in the image.

In this lesson, you'll learn how to do the following:

• Add guides to an image to help you make selections and align artwork.

• Create and edit layer masks to selectively hide and reveal portions of artwork on a layer.

• Align images and layers.

• Create clipping groups, which let you use an image on one layer as a mask for artwork on other layers.

• Add adjustment layers to an image and use them to apply color and tonal adjustments without permanently changing pixel data.

• Add layer effects to a type layer and apply the effects to multiple layers.

• Delete a layer mask.

• Save layered files.

Getting started

Before beginning this lesson, delete the Adobe Photoshop Preferences file to restore the program's default settings. For step-by-step instructions, see "Restoring default preferences" on page 4. Then restart the Photoshop program.

Now you'll open the final Photoshop image for this project to see what you'll create.

1 Choose File > Open. Locate and open the Lesson08 folder; then select End08.psd, and click Open. A photo collage of four seasons appears.

2 If you like, choose View > Zoom Out to make the image smaller, and leave it on your screen as you work. If you don't want to leave the image open, choose File > Close.

You'll start this lesson by opening an image that contains two layers, and then you'll work with various layering and masking techniques to complete the image.

3 Choose File > Open, locate and select Start08.psd in the Lesson08 folder, and then click Open.

4 Choose File > Save As, enter the name **Work08.psd**, and click Save.

The Layers palette shows that there are two layers in the file—the Tulips layer and the background. At this point, you can see only the Tulips layer, because the background is positioned under the tulips.

5 In the Layers palette, click the eye icon next to the Tulips layer to hide it. The winter scene on the background beneath the Tulips layer is revealed. Make the Tulips layer visible before continuing to the next step.

Adding guides to align artwork

Guides help you align artwork in an image. To create a guide, you turn on the rulers and then drag from the horizontal or vertical ruler. Here you'll add guides to divide the image into four equal quadrants; later you'll make a selection based on one of these quadrants.

1 Choose View > Show Rulers. The default unit of measurement for the rulers is inches. This image is 8 inches by 5 inches.

Note: To change the unit of measurement for the rulers, choose File > Preferences > Units and Rulers, and select the desired unit of measurement from the Units menu.

2 Position the pointer anywhere within the horizontal ruler at the top of the image, and drag downward to align a guide at the 2.5-inch mark on the vertical ruler. Release the mouse button to place the guide.

3 Position the pointer anywhere within the vertical ruler at the left side of the image, and drag to the right to align a guide at the 4-inch mark on the horizontal ruler. Release the mouse button to place the guide.

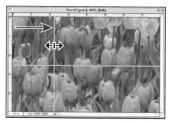

Dragging guide   *Setting guide at 4" horizontally, 2.5" vertically*

Note: If you need to reposition a guide, click the move tool in the toolbox, position the move tool on the guide, and drag to reposition the guide.

4 Choose File > Save.

Using guides and the grid

Guides appear as lines that float over the entire image and do not print. You can move, remove, or lock a guide to avoid accidentally moving it. The grid appears by default as nonprinting lines but can also be displayed as dots. The grid is useful for laying out elements symmetrically.

Guides and grids behave in similar ways:

•Selections, selection borders, and tools snap to a guide or the grid when dragged within 8 screen (not image) pixels. Guides also snap to the grid when moved. You can turn this feature on and off.

•Guide spacing, along with guide and grid visibility and snapping, is specific to an image.

•Grid spacing, along with guide and grid color and style, is the same for all images.

–From the Adobe Photoshop User Guide, Chapter 8

Working with layer masks

Layer masks let you hide or reveal portions of the artwork on an individual layer. When you hide artwork, that part of the layer becomes transparent, and underlying layers show through. You can control how much artwork on a layer is hidden or revealed by making selections for the mask and by painting on the mask using black, white, or shades of gray.

Using a selection with a layer mask

You'll start by selecting one of the quadrants on the Tulips layer and then using a layer mask to hide all but the selected quadrant.

1 In the Layers palette, make sure that the Tulips layer is active.

2 Select the rectangular marquee tool ([⬚]) in the toolbox. Then drag a selection around the bottom left quadrant of the image.

3 Choose Layer > Add Layer Mask > Reveal Selection. The Reveal Selection command displays the selected quadrant of the tulips and hides the rest of the Tulips layer. The winter scene now shows through in the other three quadrants of the image.

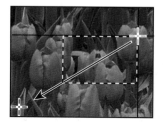
Selecting bottom left quadrant

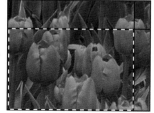
Selection made

Selection revealed through layer mask

In the Layers palette, several changes take place when you add a layer mask. A layer mask thumbnail appears to the right of the Tulips layer thumbnail, indicating that a layer mask has been added. A link icon (⧉) appears between the layer thumbnail and the layer mask thumbnail, indicating that the layer and the mask are linked, and a layer mask icon (▣) appears in the column next to the eye icon, indicating that the layer mask is active.

You can make either the layer or the layer mask active by clicking the corresponding thumbnail.

4 Click the Tulips layer thumbnail. The mask icon changes to a paintbrush icon, indicating that the Tulips layer is active. Then click the layer mask thumbnail to make the layer mask active.

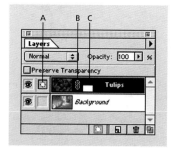

A. Layer mask icon (indicating layer mask is selected) B. Link icon C. Layer mask thumbnail

5 Choose File > Save.

Painting on a layer mask

Painting with white on a layer mask erases some of the mask, revealing artwork on that layer. Painting with black adds to the layer mask, hiding artwork so that the image beneath shows through. Painting with shades of gray on a layer mask partially hides artwork, making it semitransparent.

Now you'll paint on the layer mask with white to reveal the tulip heads that were cut off by the rectangular selection. Don't worry if you bring in some tulip leaves along with the heads. You can paint with black later to remove the leaves.

1 Make sure that white is the foreground color and black is the background color in the toolbox color selection box.

A. Switch Colors icon
B. Foreground color
C. Background color

Note: When you paint a layer mask, the default foreground color is white and the default background color is black.

2 Choose File > Preferences > Display & Cursors. In the Painting Cursors section of the dialog box, select the Brush Size option, and click OK.

3 Select the paintbrush tool ( ) in the toolbox. Then click the Brushes palette tab, and select a large, soft-edged brush.

4 Begin painting above the horizontal guide where the layer mask has cropped the tops of the tulips. (Don't be too careful here.)

As you paint with white, you erase some of the layer mask and the tulip heads appear. In the Layers palette, notice how the layer mask changes as you paint.

Now you can paint with black to hide the green leaf areas that came in accidentally when you painted in the tulip heads.

5 Click the Switch Colors icon to make black the foreground color.

💡 *Pressing x on the keyboard switches the foreground and background colors.*

6 Select a small, soft-edged brush from the Brushes palette.

7 Paint with black to extend the mask and hide the extra leaf areas. Again notice how the layer mask thumbnail changes as you paint.

Painting in white to show tulips and leaves

Painting in black to remove leaves

Result

Viewing layer masks

Photoshop offers different ways to view and hide layer masks in an image. For instance, you can use the Layers palette to view just the layer mask without the layer's artwork.

1 To display the layer mask, hold down Alt (Windows) or Option (Mac OS), and click the layer mask thumbnail. The artwork in the Work08 window disappears and the black-and-white layer mask takes its place.

2 To hide the layer mask and redisplay the artwork, hold down Alt (Windows) or Option (Mac OS), and again click the layer mask thumbnail.

You can also view the tulips artwork without its layer mask simply by turning off the mask.

3 To turn off the layer mask, hold down Shift, and click the layer mask thumbnail on the Tulips layer. A large red *x* appears on the layer mask thumbnail.

4 To turn the layer mask back on, click the layer mask thumbnail in the Layers palette. The *x* disappears, and the tulips are again masked.

5 Choose File > Save.

Unlinking layer masks

By default, layer masks are linked to the artwork on the layer. When you move a mask or the artwork, both the mask and the artwork are repositioned. You can unlink the layer mask and the artwork on the layer if you want to move them independently.

1 In the Layers palette, click the link icon between the layer thumbnail and the layer mask thumbnail to turn off linking.

2 Click the layer thumbnail for the Tulips layer to make the layer active.

3 Select the move tool (✛) in the toolbox, and drag in the image window to move the artwork. Notice that the layer mask does not move with the artwork.

Turning linking off   *Making thumbnail layer active*   *Moving artwork without mask linked*

4 Choose Edit > Undo to undo the move.

5 Click the area between the layer thumbnail and the layer mask thumbnail to relink the layer mask and the artwork.

6 Now move the artwork again. This time the mask moves with the artwork.

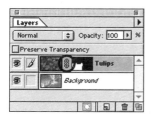
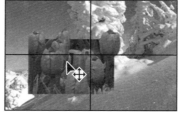

Turning linking on   *Moving artwork with mask linked*

7 Choose Edit > Undo.

Aligning images

Next you'll use guides to help you draw and align a circle on a new layer. Later you'll learn how to mask or clip images inside the circle.

You'll begin by adding two new guides to mark the diameter of the circle.

1 Position the pointer anywhere within the vertical ruler at the left side of the image, and drag to the right to align a guide at the 6-inch mark on the horizontal ruler. Release the mouse button, and drag another vertical guide to the 2-inch mark on the horizontal ruler.

Now you're ready to draw the circle.

2 In the Layers palette, make sure that the Tulips layer is selected, and then click the New Layer button (□) at the bottom of the palette.

3 Double-click the new layer, enter the name **Circle** in the Layer Options dialog box, and click OK. The Circle layer should be at the top of the Layers palette.

4 Select the ellipse marquee tool (○) from the hidden tools palette under the rectangle marquee.

5 Position the cross hair at the intersection of the two center guides you created at the beginning of the lesson, click, and begin dragging. Then without releasing the mouse button, hold down Alt+Shift (Windows) or Option+Shift (Mac OS), and continue dragging from the center point to the two new vertical guides. Release the mouse button; then release the Alt/Option key. (Holding down the Alt/Option key draws the circle from the center point, and Shift constrains the selection marquee to a circle.)

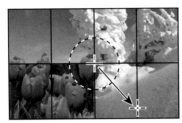
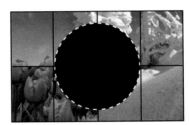

Drawing circle from center point   *Circle filled with black*

Next you'll fill the circle with black.

6 Make sure that the foreground and background colors are set to black and white.

7 Choose Edit > Fill. Accept the default settings of Foreground and 100% opacity. Then click OK to fill the circle with black.

8 Choose Select > Deselect.

9 Choose File > Save.

Aligning layers

Now you'll add two new layers to the image by bringing in images from other files. Then you'll align the layers with the Circle layer so that later you can clip the images to the circle.

1 In the Lesson08 folder, locate and open the Sunflowr.psd and Leaves.psd files.

2 If necessary, reposition the Sunflower, Leaves, and Work08 windows so that you can see a part of each of them. Then click the Sunflower window to make it active.

3 Drag the Sunflower layer from the Layers palette onto the Work08 image. Do not try to center the sunflower on the image. Just place it anywhere.

4 Click the Leaves window to make it active. Then drag the Leaves layer from the Layers palette onto the Work08 image. Again, do not try to center the image.

5 Close the Sunflowr.psd and Leaves.psd files.

You can center the two new images over the circle image by using the Align Linked command. The command allows you to align the contents of linked layers to the contents of the active layer.

6 Click the Circle layer to make it active.

7 Click the link column to the right of the eye icon for Layer 1 and Layer 2 to link them to the Circle layer.

8 Choose Layer > Align Linked > Vertical Center. The sunflower and leaves images shift into vertical alignment with the circle image.

9 Choose Layer > Align Linked > Horizontal Center. The sunflower and leaves images shift again into horizontal alignment with the circle.

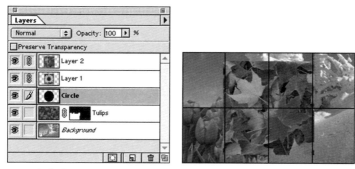

Layers linked   *Layers aligned*

All three images are now centered on top of each other. To see how they are aligned, you can turn off some layers by clicking their eye icons in the Layers palette.

10 Click the eye icon for Layer 2 to hide the layer. Then click the eye icon for Layer 1 to hide that layer. Notice how the layers align with the circle image.

11 Click the link icon for Layer 1 and Layer 2 to delink them from the Circle layer.

12 Choose File > Save.

Creating a clipping group

You can mask artwork on one layer using an image from another layer by creating a *clipping group.* In a clipping group, artwork on the *base layer* of the group masks or controls the shape of any successive layers.

You'll now use the circle you drew as the base layer of a clipping group for the Sunflower and Leaves layers.

1 Click Layer 1 to display it and make it active.

2 Choose Layer > Group with Previous. The sunflower is now clipped to the Circle layer and is masked by the shape of the circle.

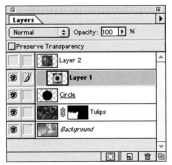 

When you add layers to a clipping group, some changes take place in the Layers palette. The base layer of the clipping group (in this lesson, the circle) is underlined, and any layers above the base layer that are part of the clipping group (in this case, the Sunflower layer) are indented. In addition, the solid lines separating the grouped layers change to dotted lines.

Now you'll redisplay the Leaves layer and use a keyboard shortcut to add the layer to the clipping group.

3 Click Layer 2 to display it and make it active.

4 In the Layers palette, position the pointer on the line between Layer 2 and Layer 1, hold down Alt (Windows) or Option (Mac OS), and click to add the leaves to the clipping group.

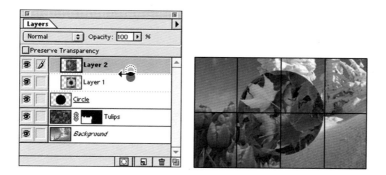

Layer 2 now completely covers Layer 1. You'll adjust the position of the leaves so that the sunflower is partially displayed.

5 Select the move tool in the toolbox and drag Layer 2 toward the bottom of the circle. Continue dragging until the top of the leaves image aligns with the horizontal guide. The sunflower now appears in the top half of the circle and the leaves in the bottom half.

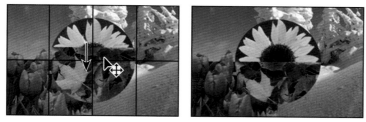

Moving leaves   *Result*

6 Choose View > Hide Guides to turn off the guides while you continue to work.

7 Choose File > Save.

About adjustment layers

An adjustment layer lets you experiment with color and tonal adjustments to an image without permanently modifying the pixels in the image. The color and tonal changes reside within the adjustment layer, which acts as a veil through which the underlying image layers appear.

When you create an adjustment layer, its effect appears on all the layers below it. This lets you correct multiple layers by making a single adjustment, rather than making the adjustment to each layer separately. To confine the effects of an adjustment layer to the layers immediately below it, create a clipping group consisting of these layers.

Adjustment layers have the same opacity and blending mode options as image layers and can be rearranged in order, deleted, hidden, and duplicated in the same manner as well. However, you also specify a color adjustment type for an adjustment layer. Depending on your choice, the dialog box for the selected adjustment command may appear. The adjustment layer takes the name of the adjustment type and is indicated in the Layers palette by a partially filled circle to the right of the name.

Adjustment layers are also layer masks, as indicated by the mask icon to the left of the layer thumbnail. When an adjustment layer is active, the foreground and background colors default to grayscale values. By painting the adjustment layer, you can apply the adjustment to just portions of the underlying layers.

–From the Adobe Photoshop User Guide, Chapter 11

Adding adjustment layers

Adjustment layers can be added to an image to apply color and tonal adjustments without permanently changing the pixel values in the image. For example, if you add a Color Balance adjustment layer to an image, you can experiment with different colors repeatedly, because the change occurs only on the adjustment layer. If you decide to return to the original pixel values, you can hide or delete the adjustment layer.

Here you'll add a Levels adjustment layer to correct the contrast in part of the image. An adjustment layer affects all layers below it in the image's stacking order. Because you'll place the Levels adjustment layer just above the Tulips layer, the adjustment will affect both the Tulips layer and the background winter scene.

1 In the Layers palette, click the Tulips layer to make it active. Then choose Layer > New > Adjustment Layer.

Holding down Ctrl (Windows) or Command (Mac OS) and clicking the New Layer button in the Layers palette creates a new adjustment layer.

2 In the New Adjustment Layer dialog box, choose Levels for Type, and click OK.

3 In the Levels dialog box, drag the histogram's left triangle to the right and position it where the darkest colors begin. Notice how the tonal range improves in both the tulips and the winter scene.

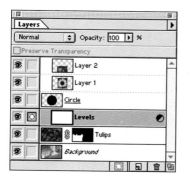

4 Click OK to apply the changes. An adjustment layer named Levels appears in the Layers palette. The new layer does not include a layer thumbnail; only layer mask thumbnails are displayed for adjustment layers.

Next you'll apply a Color Balance adjustment layer to the Work08 image and add the adjustment layer to the circle clipping group.

For an illustration of the image with and without the Color Balance adjustment layer, see figure 8-1 in the color signature.

5 In the Layers palette, click Layer 2 to make it active. Then choose Layer > New > Adjustment Layer.

6 In the New Adjustment Layer dialog box, choose Color Balance for Type, and click OK.

7 In the Color Balance dialog box, make sure the Preview option is selected. Then, by using the sliders or by typing in the text boxes, set the color levels to 47, 22, -41. Click OK.

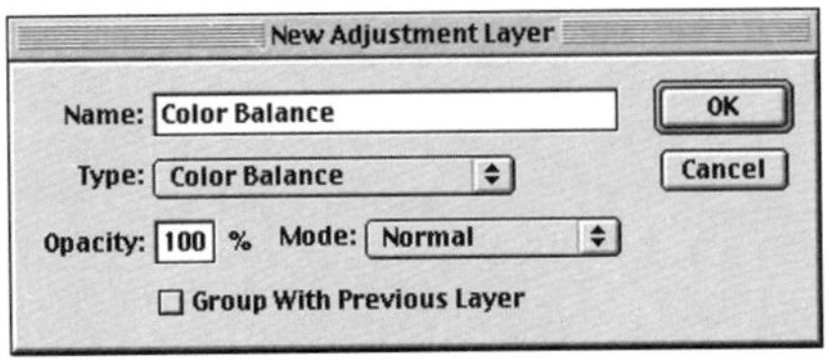

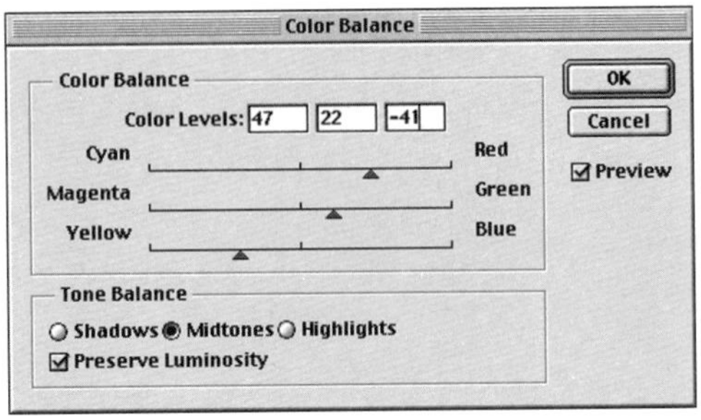

A Color Balance adjustment layer now appears above the Leaves layer in the Layers palette. Notice how the adjustment layer improves the color of the Sunflower and Leaves layers directly below it. But because it is at the top of the image's stacking order, the adjustment layer also affects the tulips and background and distorts their colors.

To contain the color balance to just the Sunflower and Leaves layers, you will add the adjustment layer to the circle clipping group. An adjustment layer that is part of a clipping group affects just the layers in the group.

8 In the Layers palette, position the pointer on the line that separates the Color Balance layer and Layer 2. Hold down Alt (Windows) or Option (Mac OS), and click the line. The adjustment layer is now part of the clipping group and no longer affects colors in the Tulips layer or background winter scene.

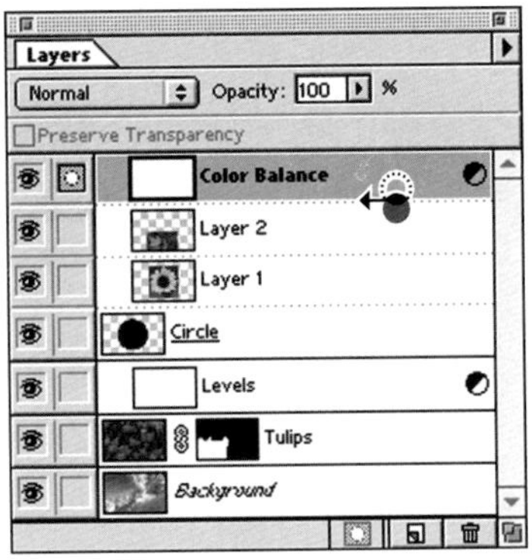

9 Choose File > Save.

About type

Graphics applications create two different kinds of type:

Outline type
Drawing or page-layout programs such as Adobe Illustrator or Adobe PageMaker create outline type. Outline type consists of mathematically defined shapes and can be scaled to any size without losing its crisp, smooth edges. When opening an image that contains outline type, Photoshop rasterizes the type into pixel or bitmap type.

Bitmap type
Paint and image-editing programs such as Adobe Photoshop create bitmap type composed of pixels. The sharpness of bitmap type depends on the type size and the resolution of the image. For example, type that has been scaled up in size may show jagged edges. High-resolution images can display higher-resolution (and therefore smoother) type than low-resolution images.

If you want to create scaleable type or text containing many type characters, import your Photoshop image into an application that supports outline type and create the type using that application.

In Photoshop, you can use these tools to create type in an image:

• The type and vertical type tools let you create colored type that is stored in a new type layer. You can edit the text at any time using the type layer.

• The type mask and vertical type mask tools let you create selection borders in the shape of type. Type selections appear on the active layer, and can be moved, copied, filled, or stroked just like any other selection.

–From the Adobe Photoshop User Guide, Chapter 12

Adding text

Now you'll add the names of the seasons to the image. Because each name is on a different type layer, you'll have the flexibility to position the text exactly where you want it.

1 Make sure that the Color Balance adjustment layer is active in the Layers palette.

2 Select the type tool (**T**), and click somewhere in the upper left quadrant of the image.

3 In the Type Tool dialog box, select a font from the Font menu, and enter a point size in the Size text box. (We chose 50-point Helvetica Inserat Regular.)

4 To select a color for the type, click the color box at the left of the Type Tool dialog box, and move the pointer into the image area. The pointer temporarily changes to the eyedropper tool (✐), which you can use to sample a color from the image.

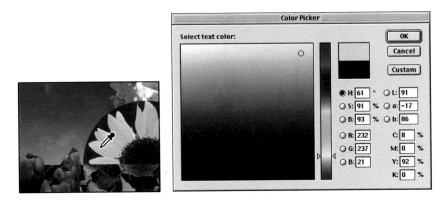

5 Click on a part of the image that is appropriate to the type's season. (We sampled a yellow from the sunflower.) Then click OK to close the Color Picker dialog box.

6 Type **summer** in the large text box at the bottom of the dialog box, and click OK. The text is automatically placed on a new layer in the upper left quadrant of the image where you clicked.

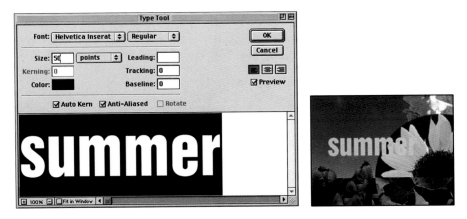

7 Create a new type layer in the same way for the word "fall," but sample a color from the leaves. Then create two similar type layers for the words "spring" and "winter," but this time position the type in the lower right quadrant of the image and sample colors from the tulips and the winter scene.

You can now use the move tool to reposition the layers.

8 Select the move tool, make different type layers active, and experiment moving the layers around until you are satisfied with the placement of the text.

Adding multiple layer effects

Once you have the text arranged on the image, you can add some layer effects to enhance the look of the type. As you learned in Chapter 3, "Layer Basics," layer effects are automated special effects you can apply to a layer with the Effects command.

1 In the Layers palette, click the winter type layer to make it active. Then choose Layer > Effects > Bevel and Emboss.

2 In the Effects dialog box, change Style to Inner Bevel, Depth to 3 pixels, and Blur to 3 pixels.

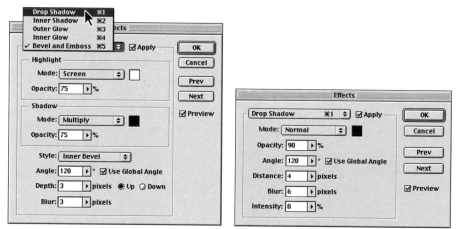

Bevel and Emboss settings   *Drop Shadow settings*

3 Now choose Drop Shadow from the menu at the top of the dialog box.

4 In the new dialog box, click Apply. Then change Mode to Normal, Opacity to 90%, Distance to 4 pixels, and Blur to 6 pixels.

5 Click OK to apply the layer effects. The type for "winter" appears with a combination drop shadow and inner bevel.

You can copy the modified layer effects you just created for the winter type layer and paste them into the other three type layers, so that all the type appears with exactly the same look. By linking the type layers, you can paste the effects in just one step.

6 With the winter type layer still active, choose Layer > Effects > Copy Effects.

7 Click the link column for the spring, fall, and summer type layers to link them to the winter type layer.

8 Choose Layer > Effects > Paste Effects to Linked. All four type layers now have the same layer effects applied.

Layers linked for Paste Effects   *Result*
to Linked command

9 Choose File > Save.

Removing layer masks

Each layer mask in a file increases the file's size. To minimize the size of your files, it's important to remove or merge layer masks after you've made final design decisions.

You'll use the Remove Layer Mask command to merge the layer mask on the Tulips layer with the artwork on the layer.

1 In the Layers palette, select the Tulips layer.

2 Choose Layer > Remove Layer Mask.

3 When the prompt appears, click Apply to merge the layer mask with the artwork on the layer.

4 Choose File > Save.

Flattening a layered image

If you plan to send a file out for proofs, it's also a good idea to save two versions of the file—one containing all the layers so that you can edit the file if necessary and one flattened version to send to the print shop.

1 First, note the file size in the lower left corner of the Work08.psd image.

2 Choose Image > Duplicate, name the duplicate file **Final08.psd**, and click OK.

3 Choose Flatten Image from the Layers palette menu. The Final08.psd file is combined onto a single background.

4 Now check the file size of the Final08.psd image. You'll notice that it is significantly smaller than the Work08.psd image, because it has been flattened onto the background.

5 Choose File > Save.

You've completed the Advanced Layers lesson. If you like, you can also experiment using layer masks, clipping groups, and adjustment layers with your own work.

For an illustration of the finished artwork, see the color signature.

Review questions

1 Why would you paint with black on a layer mask? With white? With gray?

2 How do you turn off a layer mask to view only the artwork on the layer?

3 What is a clipping group? How could you use it in your work?

4 How do adjustment layers work, and what is the benefit of using an adjustment layer?

5 What does an adjustment layer affect when it is added to a clipping group?

Review answers

1 To hide part of the artwork on a layer, you paint with black on the layer mask. To reveal more of the artwork on a layer, you paint with white on the layer mask. To partially reveal artwork on a layer, you paint with shades of gray on the layer mask.

2 Hold down Shift, and click the layer mask thumbnail in the Layers palette.

3 A clipping group consists of at least two layers, where the artwork on the base layer is used as a mask for artwork on the layer or layers above.

4 Adjustment layers are a special type of layer that work specifically with color and tonal adjustments. When you apply an adjustment layer, you can edit an image repeatedly without making a permanent change to the colors or tonal range in the image.

5 When an adjustment layer is added to a clipping group, only the layers in the clipping group are affected.

1-1: Toolbox Overview

The rectangular marquee tool makes rectangular selections.

The elliptical marquee tool makes elliptical selections.

The single row and single column marquee tools make 1-pixel wide selections.

The crop tool trims images.

The move tool moves selections, layers, and guides.

The lasso tool makes freehand selections.

The polygon lasso tool makes freehand and straight-edged selections.

The magnetic lasso tool draws selection borders that cling to the edges of objects.

The magic wand tool selects similarly colored areas.

The airbrush tool paints soft-edged strokes.

The paintbrush tool paints brush strokes.

The eraser tool erases pixels and restores parts of an image to a previously saved state.

The pencil tool draws hard-edged strokes.

The line tool draws straight lines.

The clone stamp tool paints with a copy of an image.

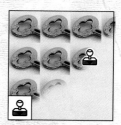

The pattern stamp tool paints with the selection as a pattern.

1-1: Toolbox Overview (cont.)

The history brush tool paints with the selected state or snapshot.

The blur tool blurs hard edges in an image.

The sharpen tool sharpens soft edges.

The smudge tool smudges data in an image.

The dodge tool lightens areas in an image.

The burn tool darkens areas in an image.

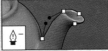

The sponge tool changes the color saturation of an area.

The pen tool lets you draw smooth-edged paths.

The direct-selection tool selects and moves paths and parts of paths.

The add-anchor-point tool adds anchor points to a path.

The delete-anchor- point tool deletes anchor points from a path.

The convert-anchor- point tool converts straight line segments to curved segments, and vice versa.

The freeform pen tool draws paths directly as you drag.

The magnetic pen tool draws paths that cling to the edges of objects.

The type tool creates type on an image.

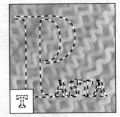

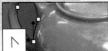

The type mask tool creates selection borders in the shape of type.

1-1: Toolbox Overview (cont.)

The vertical type tool *creates vertical type on an image.*

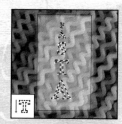

The vertical type mask tool *creates selection borders in the shape of the vertical type.*

The linear gradient tool *creates a straight-line blend between colors.*

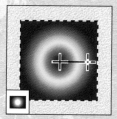

The radial gradient tool *creates a circular blend between colors.*

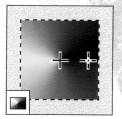

The angle gradient tool *creates an angular blend between colors.*

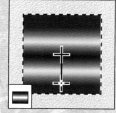

The reflected gradient tool *creates symmetric straight-line blends between colors.*

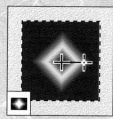

The diamond gradient tool *creates diamond-shaped blends between colors.*

The paint bucket tool *fills similarly colored areas with the foreground color.*

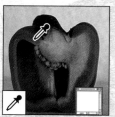

The eyedropper tool *samples colors in an image.*

The color sampler tool *samples up to four locations simultaneously.*

The hand tool *moves an image within its window.*

The zoom tool *magnifies and reduces the view of an image.*

The measure tool *measures distances, locations, and angles.*

Photoshop Tour: Finished artwork

Lesson 2: Finished artwork

Lesson 1: Finished artwork

Lesson 4: Finished artwork

Lesson 3: Finished artwork

3-1: Layer mode samples

Layer 1

Background

Dissolve, 50% opacity

Multiply

Screen

Overlay

Soft Light

Hard Light

Color Dodge

Color Burn

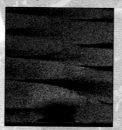

Darken

Lighten

Difference

Exclusion

Hue

Luminosity

Saturation

Color

4-1: Application of brush stroke to background using blending modes

Normal, 100% opacity

Normal, 50% opacity

Dissolve, 50% opacity

Multiply

Screen

Soft Light

Hard Light

Color Dodge

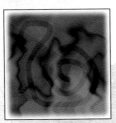
Color Burn

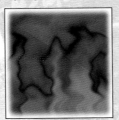
Darken

Lighten

Difference

Exclusion

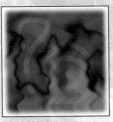
Hue

Luminosity

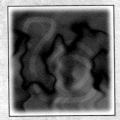
Saturation

Color

Lesson 5: Finished artwork

5-1: Original selection in Standard Mode and Quick Mask mode

A. Selected Areas
B. Hidden Areas

5-2: Painting in Quick Mask mode

Quick Mask mode
Painting with white
Resulting selection

Painting with black
Resulting selection

Lesson 6: Finished artwork

Preserving an extensive body of work assembled by a team of photographers from 1991 to 1995, The Architecture of Italy CD-ROM disc is a compilation of more than three hundred sumptuous photographs. With cross-referenced text provided for each photograph, this collection can be used as a resource for many endeavors. Much more than a "digital coffee-table book, "you are free to modify, rent, lease, distribute, or create derivative works based upon the original images found in this collection.

Included in this collection are St. Mark's Cathedral in Venice; the Tower and Baptistry at Pisa; the Colliseum, the Forum, the Vatican, and highlights from the Vatican Museum in Rome; the Duomo, the Medici Palace, the Ponte Vecchio, and the Gates of Heaven in Florence. More than 75 superb

architectural examples, which have received little recognition, have also been included. Gina Antonelli is known for her works on Italian fine art, as well as several previous photographic publications: "Italy's Best Loved Gardens," the series "Italian Tradition in Color and Form" (Dress; Cuisine; Architecture; Pastimes), and two editions of the book "Italian Traditional Patterns." In addition to completing the Rome and Naples photography assignment, photographer and art historian Tomas Panini assembled and edited the explanatory notes for the 300 photographs. Photographer Anton Harris, having apprenticed at Maria Guerra Atelier in Paris for seven years, contributed his own unique insights to the Venice and Rome assignments. In 1984 Mr. Anton Harris won the Paris Exhibition Prize for his Design Study photographic series, consisting of three books.

6-1: Retouching before

6-2: Retouching after

Lesson 8: Finished artwork

8-1: Adjustment layers

Without adjustment layer

With adjustment layer

Lesson 9: Finished artwork

Lesson 10: Finished artwork

12-1: Color photo

12-2: Black and white with adjustment

13-1: RGB image with red, green, and blue channels

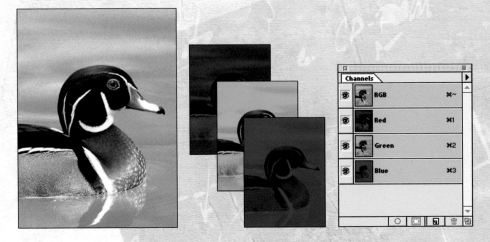

13-2: CMYK image with cyan, magenta, yellow, and black channels

13-3: Color gamuts

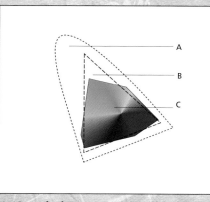

A. Natural color gamut B. RGB color gamut
C. CMYK color gamut

13-4: RGB color model

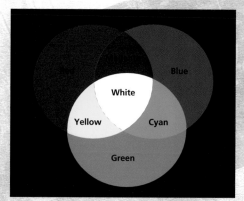

13-5: CMYK color model

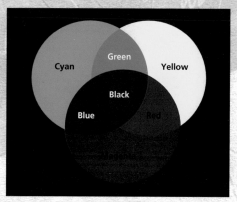

IR1-1: Image with different palette values

256 colors   *8 colors*

IR1-2: Image with different dither values

Dither=100%   *Dither=0%*

Lesson 9

Creating Special Effects

The huge assortment of filters in Adobe Photoshop lets you transform ordinary images into extraordinary digital artwork. You can select filters that simulate a traditional artistic medium—for example, a watercolor, pastel, or sketched effect—or you can choose from filters that blur, bend, wrap, sharpen, or fragment images. In addition to using filters to alter images, you can use adjustment layers and painting modes to vary the look of your artwork.

This project shows you how to do the following:

• Add a grid to an image to help you make precise selections.

• Desaturate a selection without affecting the color in other parts of the image.

• Paint on a layer above the artwork to color the underlying artwork without changing it permanently.

• Add an adjustment layer to make a color correction to a selection.

• Apply filters to selections to create various effects.

Getting started

Before beginning this lesson, delete the Adobe Photoshop Preferences file to restore the program's default settings. For step-by-step instructions, see "Restoring default preferences" on page 4. Then restart the Photoshop program.

Before you begin working, you'll open the finished art to get an idea of what you'll create.

1 Choose File > Open. Locate and open the Lesson09 folder, select End09.psd, and click Open.

An image containing six sets of pears appears. Some of the pears have been painted, and some have had filters applied to them.

For an illustration of the finished artwork in this lesson, see the color signature.

2 To make the image smaller, choose View > Zoom Out. Either you can leave the image on-screen as you work, or you can close the image by choosing File > Close.

Now you'll open the start file and begin working.

3 Choose File > Open. Locate and open the Lesson09 folder, select Start09.psd, and click Open.

4 Choose File > Save As, enter the name **Work09.psd**, and click Save.

Saving and loading a selection

You'll start by making a selection of a set of pears and then saving it. That way you can reuse the selection by reloading it as needed.

1 Use the zoom tool (⊕), and drag over the set of pears in the upper left corner to magnify your view.

2 Position the pointer on the lasso tool ( ) in the toolbox and drag to the right to select the magnetic lasso tool ( ).

3 To draw a freehand segment, drag the pointer along the edge you want to trace. Notice that the pointer doesn't have to be exactly on the edge for the segment to snap to it.

As you move the pointer, the active segment snaps to the strongest edge in the image. Periodically, the magnetic lasso tool adds fastening points to the selection border to anchor previous sections. As you move the pointer over the starting point, a hollow circle appears next to the pointer, indicating that you are about to close the segment.

Dragging with magnetic lasso   *Result*
pointer

4 When a circle appears next to the magnetic lasso pointer, release the mouse button to close the segment.

Note: For best results when tracing the pear stem with the magnetic lasso tool, zoom in on your work and decrease the tool's lasso width and edge frequency values. For example, try tracing the pear using a lasso width of 1 or 2 pixels and an edge frequency of 40.

5 Save the selection of the right pear by choosing Select > Save Selection, and click OK to save the selection in a new channel (Alpha 1 by default). You'll use the selection again for another sets of pears. (To learn more about channels, see Lesson 5, "Masks and Channels.")

6 Choose Select > Deselect to deselect the right pear.

7 Now select the left pear using the magnetic lasso tool.

8 Choose Select > Save Selection, and click OK to save the selection of the right pear in a new channel (Alpha 2 by default).

9 Choose Select > Deselect to deselect the pear. You'll use this selection again for other sets of pears.

You'll begin this lesson by hand-coloring a set of the pairs. You'll begin with the right pear, so you'll need to load the selection you created.

10 Choose Select > Load Selection, and select Alpha 1. Click OK. A selection border appears around the right pear in your image

Hand-coloring selections on a layer

First you'll remove the color from the selection so that you can color it by hand. Then you'll add a layer above the pears and apply any new color on the layer. This way, if you don't like the results, you can simply erase the layer and start over.

Desaturating a selection

You'll use the Desaturate command to *desaturate,* or remove the color, from the pear selection. Saturation is the presence or absence of color in a selection. When you desaturate a selection within an image, you create a grayscale-like effect without affecting the colors in other parts of the image.

1 Choose Image > Adjust > Desaturate. The color is removed from the selection.

2 Choose Select > Deselect.

3 Choose File > Save to save your work.

Creating a layer and choosing a blending mode

Now you'll add a layer and specify a layer blending mode. By painting on a layer, you won't permanently alter the image. This makes it easy to change your mind and start again.

You use layer blending modes to determine how the pixels in a layer are blended with underlying pixels on other layers. By applying modes to individual layers, you can create myriad special effects.

1 In the Layers palette, click the New Layer button to add Layer 1 to the image. To rename the layer, double-click Layer 1, rename the layer **Paint**, and click OK.

Next to the New Layer button, you'll see the Trash button. Any time you want to throw your Painting layer away, you can drag the layer to the trash in the Layers palette.

Original

Clicking New Layer button to add layer

Now you'll choose a layer blending mode to determine how the pixels in this layer are blended with underlying pixels on the Background layer.

2 In the Layers palette, choose Color from the pop-up mode menu to the left of the Opacity slider.

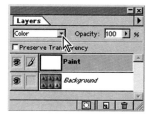

The Color mode lets you change the hue of a selection without affecting the highlights and shadows. This means you can apply a variety of color tints without changing the original highlights and shadows of the pears.

Applying painting effects

To begin painting, you must again load the selection that you created earlier.

1 Choose Select > Load Selection > Alpha 1. (Notice in the Load Selection dialog box that the color mode change you just made also was saved as a selection, called "Paint transparency.")

2 In the toolbox, double-click the paintbrush tool (✏) to display its Options palette. Set the Opacity to about 50%.

💡 *Change the paintbrush opacity by pressing a number on the keypad from 0 to 9 (where 1 is 10%, 9 is 90%, and 0 is 100%).*

3 In the Brushes palette, select a large, soft-edged brush. (To display the Brushes palette, choose Window > Show Brushes.)

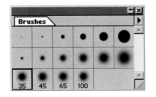

4 In the Swatches palette, click a yellow-green color that appeals to you for the foreground color. Paint the entire pear with the light yellow-green color. As you paint, you'll notice that the color of the pear changes to the color you selected.

Selecing yellow-green swatch   *Result*

5 Next, select a darker green from the Swatches palette. In the paintbrush Options palette, set the brush opacity to about 30%. Paint around the edges in the pear selection, avoiding the highlight area.

6 To add additional highlights to the pear, select a rose color from the Swatches palette, and select a smaller brush from the Brushes palette. In the Paintbrush Options palette, decrease the paint opacity to about 20%, and paint more highlights on the pear.

7 Choose Select > Deselect.

8 Choose File > Save to save your work.

Adding a gradient

Now you'll add a gradient to the other pear for a highlight effect. First you'll need to load the selection of the left pear you made earlier.

1 Choose Select > Load Selection, and select Alpha 2. Click OK. A selection border appears around the left pear in your image

2 In the Color palette, select red as the foreground color.

3 Click the background color swatch, and select yellow as the background color.

Selecting red as the foreground color   *Yellow selected as the background color*

4 Select the radial gradient tool (■) in the toolbox. (To select a hidden tool, position the pointer on the visible tool, and drag to highlight the tool you want.)

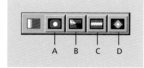

A. *Radial gradient*
B. *Angle gradient*
C. *Diamond gradient*
D. *Reflected gradient*

5 In the Radial Gradient Options palette, for Gradient, make sure that Foreground to Background is selected, so that the color blends from the foreground color (red) to the background color (yellow). Set the opacity to 40%.

6 Position the gradient tool near the pear's highlight, and drag toward the stem. (You can select other gradient tools and then drag to try out different effects.)

Applying radial gradient from   *Result*
pear's highlight to stem

7 Choose Select > Deselect.

8 When you've finished painting the set of pears, choose Layer > Merge Visible to merge the painting layer with the pear image and to keep the file size small. You'll continue the project by applying effects to the other pears in the image.

9 Choose File > Save to save your work.

Combining and moving selections

Before you begin to apply special effects to the next set of pairs, you'll combine the earlier selections you made. You'll also move the new combined selection so that you can use it with a different set of pears.

1 Select the zoom tool from the toolbox. Then hold down Alt (Windows) or Option (Mac OS) to select the zoom-out tool (Q).

2 Click the zoom-out tool as many times as necessary until both the top left pears and top middle pears are visible.

3 Choose Select > Load Selection, and select Alpha 1. Click OK.

4 Choose Select > Load Selection. Select Alpha 2, and click Add to Selection. Click OK. Now both pears are selected.

5 Using the rectangular marquee tool (⬚), drag the selection border to the right to position it over the middle pears in the top row.

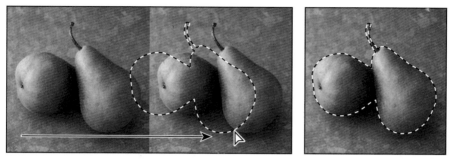

Alpha 1 and Alpha 2 selections combined, and then moved using marquee tool

Colorizing a selection

Now you will colorize the selected set of the pears. A colorized image has only one hue of color. In Adobe Photoshop, you colorize a selection or image with the Colorize option in the Hue/Saturation dialog box. You can use the Colorize option to add color to a grayscale image or to reduce the color values in an image to one hue.

1 Double-click the hand tool (✋) in the toolbox to fit the image in the window. The top middle pears should still be selected.

2 In the Layers palette, select the Background. You'll continue working on the Background rather than the Painting layer.

3 Choose Image > Adjust > Hue/Saturation.

The Hue/Saturation command lets you adjust the hue, saturation, and lightness of individual color components in an image according to the color wheel. The two color bars in the dialog box represent the colors in their order on the color wheel: red, yellow, green, cyan, blue, and magenta. Adjusting the hue, or color, represents a move around the color wheel. Adjusting the saturation, or purity of the color, represents a move across its radius.

4 Make sure that Preview is selected. Then select the Colorize option.

The upper color bar shows the color before the adjustment, the lower bar shows how the adjustment affects all of the hues at full saturation. The image takes on a reddish tint.

5 Enter **83** in the Hue text box, and **28** in the Saturation text box for a greenish color. You can use the sliders to adjust the Hue, Saturation, and Lightness, or you can type in numbers.

Decreasing the saturation lowers the intensity of the color.

6 Click OK to apply the changes.

7 To preview the changes without the selection border, choose View > Hide Edges.

8 Choose View > Show Edges, and then choose Select > Deselect to deselect everything.

9 Choose File > Save to save your work.

Using a grid

Before you adjust the next set of pears, you'll display a grid and use it to make a precise rectangular selection that you can repeat on the remaining sets of pears. A grid helps you lay out images or elements symmetrically. Selections, selection borders, and tools snap to the grid when they are dragged within 8 screen pixels of it.

1 Choose View > Show Grid. The grid with the default settings appears in the image window.

2 Choose File > Preferences > Guides & Grid.

You adjust the grid settings using the Preferences dialog box. You can set the grid to display as lines or as points, and you can change its spacing or color.

3 In the Grid section of the dialog box, for Color, choose Green. For Gridline Every, enter a value of **2**. For Subdivisions, enter a value of **1**. Click OK to apply the changes to the grid.

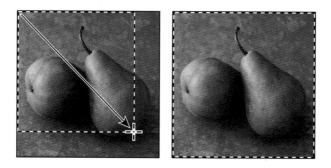

Setting grid option   *Result*

4 Select the zoom tool (⌕) in the toolbox, and zoom in on the pear image in the top right corner of the file.

5 Click the rectangle marquee tool (⬚) in the toolbox to select it. Then drag a selection border to select the top right set of pears. As you drag, the selection border snaps to the grid.

Next you'll set the rectangle marquee tool to a fixed size to make subsequent selections easier.

6 In the Marquee Options dialog box, choose Fixed Size from the Style pop-up menu. The width and height values match that of the selection border you just drew. The next time you use the marquee tool, the tool will draw a selection border of this size.

7 Choose View > Hide Grid to hide the grid.

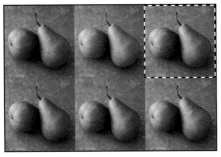

Set of pears selected using fixed-size marquee

Changing the color balance

Now you'll use an adjustment layer to adjust the color balance on this set of pears. You can apply any of the many color correction tools in Adobe Photoshop to an adjustment layer. (You can also apply color adjustments to a regular layer or to a channel.)

Making color adjustments to a channel or a regular layer permanently changes the pixels on that layer. With an adjustment layer, in contrast, your color and tonal changes reside only within the adjustment layer and do not alter any pixels. The effect is as if you were viewing the visible layers through the adjustment layer above them. This lets you try out color and tonal adjustments without permanently changing pixels in the image. (You can also use adjustment layers to affect multiple layers at once.)

1 Choose Layer > New > Adjustment Layer. For Type, choose Color Balance, and click OK.

The Color Balance command lets you change the mixture of colors in a color image and make general color corrections. When you adjust the color balance, you can keep the same tonal balance, as you'll do here. You can also focus changes on the shadows, midtones, or highlights.

2 In the Color Balance dialog box, enter these values: **+13, –14,** and **–38.** Click OK.

Notice that the adjustment layer thumbnail in the Layers palette resembles a mask. By making a selection and then adding an adjustment layer, the layer becomes a mask that applies the adjustment only to the selected area.

Adjustment layers act as layer masks, which can be edited repeatedly without permanently affecting the underlying image. You can double-click an adjustment layer to display the last settings used and adjust them repeatedly. Or you can delete an adjustment layer by dragging it to the Trash button at the bottom of the Layers palette.

3 Choose File > Save to save your work.

Applying filters

To conclude the project, you'll apply different styles of filters to the remaining pears. Because Adobe Photoshop includes so many different filters for creating special effects, the best way to learn about them is to try out different filters and filter options.

1 In the Layers palette, select the Background.

2 Using the rectangle marquee tool (⬚), click the lower left corner of the image to draw a selection border of the pears. The selection border matches the size of the last border you drew.

3 Choose Filter > Brush Strokes > Crosshatch. Adjust the settings as desired, using the Preview window to see the effect. Click OK.

Previewing and applying filters

To use a filter, you choose the appropriate submenu command from the Filter menu. These guidelines can help you in choosing filters:

•The last filter chosen appears at the top of the menu.

•Filters are applied to the active, visible layer.

•Filters cannot be applied to Bitmap-mode, indexed-color, or 16-bit per channel images.

•Some filters only work on RGB images.

•Some filters are processed entirely in RAM.

•Applying filters—especially to large images—can be time-consuming. Previewing effects can save time and prevent unintended results. Depending on the filter, you may have a preview window or the option to preview effects on the entire layer.

–From the Adobe Photoshop User Guide, Chapter 13

💡 *To save time when trying various filters, experiment on a small, representative part of your image or a low-resolution copy.*

You can fade the effect of a filter or of a color adjustment using the Fade command. The mode determines how the modified pixels in the selection appear in relation to the original pixels. The blending modes in the Fade dialog box are a subset of those available in the painting and editing tools Options palette.

Using filter shortcuts

Try any of these techniques to help save time when working with filters:

• To cancel a filter as it is being applied, press Esc or Command-(.) (period) (Mac OS only).

• To undo a filter, press Ctrl+Z (Windows) or Command+Z (Mac OS).

• To reapply the most recently used filter with its last values, press Ctrl+F (Windows) or Command+F (Mac OS).

• To display the dialog box for the last filter you applied, press Ctrl+Alt+F (Windows) or Command+Option+F (Mac OS).

–From the Adobe Photoshop User Guide, Chapter 13

---

4 Choose Filter > Fade Crosshatch to fade the filter effect. For mode, choose Multiply. Set the Opacity to 50% and click OK.

Crosshatch filter applied Fade command applied Result

5 Using the rectangle marquee tool, click the middle set of pears in the bottom row of the image to draw the fixed-size selection border. To adjust the position of the selection border, press the arrow keys to nudge it into place.

6 Choose Filter > Distort > Zigzag. For Amount, enter 4%; for Ridges, enter 9%; for style, select Pond Ripples. Click OK. The Zigzag filter distorts an image radially, creating ripples or ridges in an image.

7 Using the rectangle marquee tool, click to select the pears in the lower right corner of the bottom row.

8 Click the Default Colors icon in the toolbox to set the foreground and background colors to their defaults.

9 Choose Filter > Distort > Diffuse Glow. For Graininess, enter **6**; for Glow Amount, enter **6**; and for Clear Amount, enter **15**. Click OK. This filter adds white noise, or pixels, in the same color as the background color—to an image.

10 Choose File > Save to save your work; then close the file.

Tips for creating special effects

Try the following techniques to create special effects with filters. For illustrations of these techniques, see online Help.

Create edge effects. *You can use various techniques to treat the edges of an effect applied to only part of an image. To leave a distinct edge, simply apply the filter. For a soft edge, feather the edge, and then apply the filter. For a transparent effect, apply the filter, and then use the Fade command to adjust the selection's blending mode and opacity.*

Apply filters to layers. *You can apply filters to individual layers or to several layers in succession to build up an effect. For a filter to affect a layer, the layer must be visible and must contain pixels—for example, a neutral fill color.*

Apply filters to individual channels. *You can apply a filter to an individual channel, apply a different effect to each color channel, or apply the same filter but with different settings.*

Create backgrounds. *By applying effects to solid-color or grayscale shapes, you can generate a variety of backgrounds and textures. You might then blur these textures. Although some filters have little or no visible effect when applied to solid colors (for example, Glass), others produce interesting effects. You might try Add Noise, Chalk & Charcoal, Clouds, Conté Crayon, Craquelure, Difference Clouds, Glass, Grain, Graphic Pen, Halftone Pattern, Mezzotint, Mosaic Tiles, Note Paper, Patchwork, Pointillize, Reticulation, Rough Pastels, Sponge, Stained Glass, Texture Fill, Texturizer, and Underpainting.*

Combine multiple effects with masks or with duplicate images. *Using masks to create selection areas gives you more control over transitions from one effect to another. For example, you can filter the selection created with a mask. You can also use the history brush tool to paint a filter effect onto part of the image. First, apply the filter to an entire image. Next, step back in the History palette to the image state before applying the filter, and set the history brush source to the filtered state. Then, paint the image.*

Improve image quality and consistency. *You can disguise faults, alter or enhance, or make a series of images look related by applying the same effect to each. Use the Actions palette to record the process of modifying one image, and then use this action on the other images*

–From the Adobe Photoshop User Guide, Chapter 13

Improving performance with filters

Some filter effects can be memory intensive, especially when applied to a high-resolution image. You can use these techniques to improve performance:

• Try out filters and settings on a small portion of an image.

• Apply the effect to individual channels—for example, to each RGB channel—if the image is large and you're having problems with insufficient memory. (With some filters, effects vary if applied to the individual channel rather than the composite channel, especially if the filter randomly modifies pixels.)

• Experiment on a low-resolution copy of your file and note the filters and settings used. Then apply the filters and setting to the high-resolution original.

• Free up memory before running the filter by using the Purge command.

• Allocate more RAM to Photoshop. If necessary, exit from other applications to make more memory available to Photoshop.

• Try changing settings to improve the speed of memory-intensive filters, such as Lighting Effects, Cutout, Stained Glass, Chrome, Ripple, Spatter, Sprayed Strokes, and Glass filters. (For example, with the Stained Glass filter, increase cell size. With the Cutout filter, increase Edge Simplicity, or decrease Edge Fidelity, or both.)

• If you plan to print to a grayscale printer, convert a copy of the image to grayscale before applying filters. However, applying a filter to a color image and then converting to grayscale may not have the same effect as applying the filter to a grayscale version of the image.

This concludes the Special Effects lesson. Try out other filters to see how you can add different effects to your images.

▣   For detailed information on individual filters and a gallery of examples, see online Help.

Review questions

1 What is the purpose of saving selections?

2 Name a benefit of using a grid in your image.

3 Describe one way to isolate color adjustments to an image.

4 Describe one way to remove color from a selection or image for a grayscale effect.

Review answers

1 By saving a selection, you can create and reuse time-consuming selections and uniformly select artwork in an image. You can also combine selections or create new selections by adding to or subtracting from existing selections.

2 A grid helps you make precise, rectangular selections and lay out images symmetrically. Selections, selection borders, and tools snap to the grid when they are dragged within 8 screen pixels of it.

3 You can use adjustment layers to try out color changes before applying them permanently to a layer.

4 You can use the Desaturate command to desaturate, or remove the color, from a selection. Or you can use the Hue/Saturation command and adjust only the Saturation component. Photoshop also includes the sponge tool for removing color.

Lesson 10

Combining Illustrator Graphics and Photoshop Images

You can easily add a graphic created in a drawing program to an Adobe Photoshop file. This is an effective method for seeing how a line drawing looks applied to a photograph or for trying out Photoshop special effects on vector art. You can also export the resulting artwork for use in other graphics programs.

This lesson shows you how to do the following:

- Differentiate between bitmap and vector graphics.
- Place an Adobe Illustrator graphic in an Adobe Photoshop file.
- Scale the placed graphic.
- Distort a graphic to match the perspective of a photograph.
- Apply different blending modes to a graphic.
- Use the Export Transparent Image wizard to prepare a Photoshop image for use in an Illustrator file.

Combining artwork

You can combine Photoshop artwork with art from other graphics applications in a variety of ways for a wide range of creative results. Sharing artwork between applications allows you to combine line art with continuous-tone paintings and photographs. It also allows you to move between two types of computer graphics—bitmap images and vector graphics.

Bitmap versus vector graphics

Adobe Photoshop uses *bitmap images*, also called raster images, which are based on a grid of pixels. In working with bitmap images, you edit groups of pixels rather than objects or shapes. Because bitmap graphics can represent subtle gradations of shade and color, they are appropriate for continuous-tone images such as photographs or artwork created in painting programs. A disadvantage of bitmap graphics is that they lose definition and appear "jagged" when scaled up.

Vector graphics, also called draw graphics, are made up of shapes based on mathematical expressions and are created in drawing applications. These graphics consist of clear, smooth lines that retain their crispness when scaled. They are appropriate for illustrations, type, and graphics such as logos that may be scaled to different sizes.

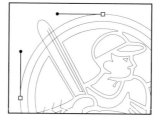

Logo drawn as vector art

Logo rasterized as bitmap art

In deciding whether to use Photoshop or a vector graphics program such as Illustrator for creating and combining graphics, consider both the elements of the image and how the image will be used. In general, use Photoshop for images that have the soft lines of painted or photographic art and for applying special effects to line art. Use Illustrator if you need to create art or type with clean lines that will look good at any magnification. In most cases, you will also want to use Illustrator for laying out a design, since Illustrator allows you more flexibility in working with type and with reselecting, moving, and altering images.

Project overview

To illustrate how you can combine vector art with bitmap images and work between applications, this lesson steps you through the process of creating a composite image. In this lesson, you will add a logo created in Adobe Illustrator to a photographic image in Adobe Photoshop and adjust the logo so that it blends with the photo. You will then save the resulting image so that it can be brought back into Illustrator for final layout as a print advertisement.

Logo drawn in Illustrator

Logo applied to image in Photoshop

Final layout in Illustrator

Getting started

Before beginning this lesson, delete the Adobe Photoshop Preferences file to restore the program's default settings. For step-by-step instructions, see "Restoring default preferences" on page 4. Then restart the Photoshop program.

Now you'll open the final Photoshop image for this project to see how the adjustments you'll make will affect the final artwork.

1 Choose File > Open. Locate and open the Lesson10 folder; then select End10.psd and click Open.

2 If you like, choose View > Zoom Out to make the image smaller, and leave it on your screen as you work. If you don't want to leave the image open, choose File > Close.

Now you'll open the start file, the photographic image to which you will add a logo.

3 Choose File > Open. Locate and open the Lesson10 folder, select Start10.psd, and click Open.

4 Choose File > Save As, type the name **Work10.psd**, and click Save.

Placing an Adobe Illustrator file

You can open an Adobe Illustrator file as a new Adobe Photoshop file, or you can use the Place or Paste commands to add an Illustrator file into an existing Photoshop file. When you open, place, or paste an Illustrator image, Photoshop *rasterizes* it so that it becomes a bitmap, or raster, image.

In this lesson, you will be using the Place command to add an Illustrator file to an existing Photoshop image. The advantage of the Place command is that it allows you to scale the image while it is still vector art, so that the scaling does not sacrifice image quality. With the Place command, a graphic is not rasterized until you press Enter (Windows) or Return (Mac OS). Alternatively, if you were to cut and paste a graphic from Illustrator into Photoshop, the image would come in already rasterized at the size it was in the Illustrator file. If you then scaled the graphic, it would lose image quality.

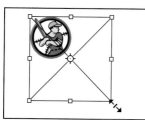 

Scaling placed Illustrator graphic *Result*

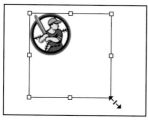 

Scaling pasted Illustrator graphic *Result*

1 With the photo of the gift box open, choose File > Place. Select the file Logo.ai located in the Lesson10 folder, and click Place. Notice that the logo appears with a bounding box around it and that Photoshop automatically creates a new Logo.ai layer for the image in the Layers palette.

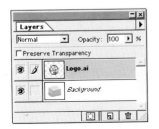

2 Hold down Shift, and drag a corner handle of the bounding box to scale the logo to fit the gift box. (Holding down Shift constrains the proportions of the logo.)

3 Position the pointer outside the bounding box (the pointer turns into a curved arrow), and drag to rotate the logo slightly counterclockwise.

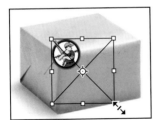

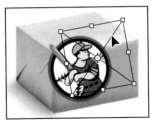

Scaling logo *Rotating logo* *Repositioning logo*

4 If necessary, position the pointer inside the bounding box so that you see a move pointer (▶), and drag to reposition the logo so that it fits within the borders of the box. Fine-tune with other rotation or scaling adjustments; then press Enter (Windows) or Return (Mac OS) to apply the changes and rasterize the logo.

Distorting the graphic to match the photograph

Your next step is to distort the logo so that it appears to wrap around the top and front of the box. To create this effect, you'll cut the logo in half, place each half on its own layer, and then apply the distortion to the logo's top half.

1 With the Logo.ai layer active, select the polygon lasso tool (🗇), and click the right front corner of the box top. Drag to the next corner, click, and then continue dragging around the box top, clicking at each corner. Complete the selection by crossing over the starting point.

Top half of box selected   *Selection placed on new layer*

2 Choose Layer > New > Layer Via Cut to cut the top half of the logo from the Logo.ai layer and place it on its own layer. Notice that a new layer, Layer 1, has appeared in the Layers palette. To see the artwork on the layer, turn off the other two layers by clicking the eye icon (👁) to the left of the layers in the Layers palette. Click again to turn all layers back on.

Now you're ready to distort the top of the logo.

3 Make sure that Layer 1 is active, and then choose Edit > Transform > Skew. A transformation bounding box appears around the top half of the logo.

4 Experiment by dragging the handles of the bounding box to distort the logo so that it matches the perspective of the box. In particular, try dragging the upper left handle in the direction of the back left corner of the box top.

Top half of logo distorted via Skew command   *Result*

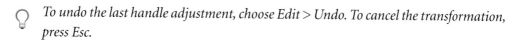
To undo the last handle adjustment, choose Edit > Undo. To cancel the transformation, press Esc.

5 When the logo appears to wrap around the top of the box, apply the transformation by pressing Enter (Windows) or Return (Mac OS).

Transforming objects in two dimensions

You can scale, rotate, skew, distort, and apply perspective to selected parts of an image, entire layers, paths, and selection borders. You can also rotate and flip part or all of a layer, an entire image, path, or selection border. Use the following guidelines when applying transformations:

• You can transform a linked layer. The transformation affects all the layers in the linking group.

• You cannot apply transformations to the background as a layer, or on 16-bit-per-channel images. You can, however, transform selections on the background.

• You can apply transformations to an alpha channel by first selecting it in the Channels palette.

• You can apply transformations to a layer mask by first selecting its thumbnail in the Layers palette.

Pixels are added or deleted during transformations. To calculate the color values of these pixels, Adobe Photoshop uses the interpolation method selected in the General Preferences dialog box. This option directly affects the speed and quality of the transformation. Bicubic interpolation, the default, is slowest but yields the best results.

–From the Adobe Photoshop User Guide, Chapter 10

Using blending modes on the graphic

Now you'll make the logo appear more integrated with the box by using different blending modes on each half of the logo. First you'll lighten the top half of the logo so that it matches the box top.

1 With Layer 1 still active in the Layers palette, change the opacity of the layer to 60% and make sure that Normal is selected for the blending mode. Changing the opacity of the layer lightens the top of the logo and makes it blend better with the highlights on the top of the box.

Normal mode for top half   *Multiply mode for bottom half*   *Result*
of logo   *of logo*

Next you'll darken the bottom half of the logo so that it blends with the shadow on the box front.

2 Click the Logo.ai layer in the Layers palette to make it active, change the opacity to 70%, and select Multiply from the blending mode menu. Using the Multiply blending mode on the layer darkens the bottom of the logo and makes it appear to be in shadow.

3 Choose File > Save.

Exporting the image

You'll now prepare the new composite image so that it can be placed back into Illustrator for its final layout. By default, when you export an Adobe Photoshop file to another program such as Illustrator, the entire image becomes opaque, including the background. In this project, the gift box in the Photoshop file is targeted for an Illustrator file with a colored background. Therefore, if you were to export the file without any adjustment, the white background around the box would appear as an opaque white area against the colored Illustrator background.

With the help of a Photoshop wizard, you can export a Photoshop image to Illustrator and hide, or clip, the background. Wizards are assistants available through the Help menu that guide you through common tasks in Photoshop. To hide the background around the box image, you will use the Export Transparent Image wizard, which identifies the desired portion of the photograph and makes everything outside it appear transparent when the image is exported.

Placed Photoshop file, exported with background

Placed Photoshop file, exported via Export Transparent Image

Before running the Export Transparent Image wizard, you must select the part of the image you want to make transparent. In the Work10.psd file, you will select the white background around the box.

1 In the Layers palette, click Background to make it active.

2 Select the polygon lasso tool, and draw a selection around the box. Then choose Select >Inverse to select the background around the box.

Selecting box with polygon lasso tool

Box selected

Background selected via Select > Inverse

You're now ready to run the wizard, which uses dialog boxes to step you through the process of exporting the file.

3 Choose Help > Export Transparent Image.

4 In the first dialog box, choose the second option, indicating that you have already selected the area of the image you want to make transparent. Then click Next.

5 In the next dialog box, choose Print and click Next.

6 In the third dialog box, accept the Photoshop EPS default file format and the default filename, and click Save.

7 In the EPS Options dialog box, for Preview choose the option TIFF (8 bits/pixel) for Windows or the option Macintosh (8 bits/pixel) for Mac OS, and click OK.

Note: If you place an EPS file with a TIFF preview into Adobe Illustrator, the transparency created by the wizard won't display properly. This display affects the on-screen preview only; when the image prints to a PostScript® printer, the areas designated for transparency in the wizard will in fact be transparent.

8 In the final dialog box, click Finish.

Note that you now have two files open on your desktop: Work10.psd and Export Wizard-1.eps (Windows) or Export Assistant-1 (Mac OS). Because you are finished with the Work10.psd file, you can close it. Be careful not to save the file, however, since the Export Transparent Image wizard flattened the file's layers as one of the steps in preparing the file for export. If you save this version of the file, you will lose the original file's separate layers.

9 With the Work10.psd file active, choose File > Close.

10 In the dialog box, click the Don't Save option.

The final step in preparing the Photoshop file for export to a print color publication is to change the image to CMYK color mode so that it will be printed correctly in four-color process inks. You can use the Mode command to change the image's color mode.

For more information on color modes, see "Choosing a Color Mode" in online Help or Chapter 4 in the Adobe Photoshop User Guide.

11 With the Export Wizard-1.eps (Windows) or Export Assistant-1 (Mac OS) window active, choose Image > Mode > CMYK Color.

12 Choose File > Save.

For an illustration of the finished artwork, see the color signature.

The box-and-logo image is now fully composed and ready for placement in the Adobe Illustrator layout. If you have a copy of Illustrator, you can also try placing the exported image in the Mailer.ai file located in the Lesson10 folder.

Exploring on your own

Now that you've learned the basic steps involved in combining an Illustrator graphic with a Photoshop image, you can try applying the logo to a new Photoshop image.

1 Locate and open the Lesson10 folder. Then select Cap.psd or Cup.psd, and click Open.

2 Choose File > Place. Select the Logo.ai file, and click Place.

Now try out techniques presented here to blend the graphic with the Photoshop image.

Review questions

1 What is the difference between bitmap images and vector graphics?

2 What is the advantage of using the Place command to add an Illustrator file to a Photoshop image?

3 How can you export an image from Photoshop into Illustrator without also exporting its opaque background?

Review answers

1 Bitmap or raster images are based on a grid of pixels and are appropriate for continuous-tone images such as photographs or artwork created in painting programs. Vector graphics are made up of shapes based on mathematical expressions and are appropriate for illustrations, type, and drawings that require clear, smooth lines.

2 The Place command allows you to scale the image while it is still vector art, so that the scaling does not sacrifice image quality.

3 You can use the Export Transparent Image wizard, which hides, or clips, the background. You simply identify the part of the image you want to clip, and the wizard makes this area transparent when the image is exported.

Lesson 11

Preparing Images for Web Publication

The file formats and compression options you choose for images to be distributed on the World Wide Web are determined by the image type. For example, a full-color image is saved with a different file format than a flat-color image. When preparing images for distribution on the Web, the goal is to create the smallest file possible that still maintains the integrity of the image.

This lesson shows you how to do the following:

• Determine which file formats and compression options are appropriate for publishing specific types of images on the Web.

• Prepare four types of images for distribution on the Web.

• Use the Actions palette to record a series of commands, and then run the action list on a series of files to prepare them for Web distribution.

Restoring default preferences

Before starting this lesson, delete the Adobe Photoshop Preferences file to restore the program's default palettes and command settings. For step-by-step instructions about how to delete the preferences file, see "Restoring default preferences" on page 4. After you've deleted the preferences file, restart Adobe Photoshop.

Preparing images for the Web

This lesson shows you how to use Photoshop to prepare four different types of images for distribution on the World Wide Web—a grayscale image, a flat-color image, a full-color image, and an image containing a gradient. It is not intended to show you how to serve images to the Web.

For optimal file compression and image quality, use Adobe ImageReady to prepare your Web images. Adobe ImageReady gives you greater control over the compression and color settings of images. For more information, see "Optimizing Images for Web Publication."

When preparing images for distribution on the Web, keep in mind that the smaller the image, the faster the download time. Of course, it's also important that your image look good, so the trick is in maintaining the quality of the image while keeping the file size at a minimum.

For future reference, the following table shows which file formats and color modes should be used when preparing specific types of images for online distribution. *Flat-color images* refer to images with areas of repetitive, solid color, such as line art, logos, and illustrations with type. *Full-color images* refer to images that contain broad color range and continuous tones, such as photographs and images with flesh tones.

Image	Color mode	File format
Flat-color	Indexed Color	GIF
Full-color (continuous-tone)	RGB or Grayscale	JPEG
Gradient	RGB or Grayscale	JPEG
Grayscale	Grayscale	Export GIF89a
Black or white	Bitmap	Export GIF89a

Turning off image previews

One of the ways you can reduce the size of images for the Web is to turn off the Image Preview option in the Preferences dialog box. Turning off the Image Preview option saves files without a preview icon.

1 Choose File > Preferences > Saving Files.

2 Choose Never Save from the Image Previews menu; then click OK.

Note: If you throw away your Preferences file, you will have to reselect the Image Preview option.

Color display options

Each image mode in Adobe Photoshop uses a color lookup table, or color palette, to store the colors used in the image. When you're working with a display system that supports 8-bit color (or fewer colors), the monitor displays only 256 different colors at a time. For example, a 24-bit RGB image can display 16.7 million colors in any image at a time. However, if the monitor can display only 256 of the 16.7 million colors, Adobe Photoshop uses a technique called dithering to mix pixels of available colors and thus simulate colors not currently available.

By default, Adobe Photoshop uses pattern dithering, which can result in a distinctive pattern of darker or lighter areas in the image. In contrast, diffusion dithering eliminates this distinctive patterning by using the surrounding pixels in the mix of pixel color. But diffusion dithering can cause visual inconsistencies when only part of a screen is redrawn as you scroll, edit, or paint. Keep in mind that dithering effects only appear on-screen, not in print.

–From the Adobe Photoshop User Guide, Chapter 4

Preparing a flat-color image for the Web

For best results, flat-color images should be converted to Indexed Color mode, and then saved as GIF files. Flat-color images appear best on the Web without any *dithering—* mixing colors to approximate those not present in the image.

You'll prepare a flat-color image of a map.

1 Choose File > Open. Locate and open the Lesson11 folder, select the Africa.psd file, and then click Open.

Notice that the image uses a limited range of colors in flat, repetitive patterns.

2 Choose File > Save As, name the file **Africa2.psd**, choose Photoshop for the format, and click Save.

Note the file size of the image before continuing.

You'll start by converting the RGB image to Indexed Color mode. Indexed Color mode produces an 8-bit image, which uses a *color palette* to display up to 256 colors (or shades of gray). By reducing the color range of the flat-color image, you can conserve file size without losing image quality.

3 Choose Image > Mode > Indexed Color to convert the RGB image to Indexed Color.

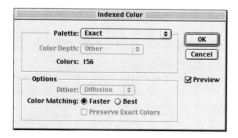

The Palette menu in the Indexed Color dialog box lets you select a color palette option, which determines the colors used to display your image. If the original image has more than 256 colors, all but 256 of the colors are removed from the image. If the original image contains fewer than 256 colors, the palette defaults to Exact and the number of colors in the image appears in the dialog box.

You select from these Palette options:

• The Exact option uses exactly the same colors for the palette as those that appear in the RGB image. No dithering option is available for the Exact palette, because all the colors in the image are present in the palette. The Exact option is available only if 256 or fewer colors are used in the RGB image.

• The System (Windows or Mac OS) option builds a color table using the color table of the system you select. It is an 8-bit palette, capable of displaying 256 colors.

- The Web option consists of the 216 colors that are shared in common by the Windows and Macintosh system palettes. Using the Web palette ensures that the colors in the image will display consistently between browsers on different platforms. This is also a good palette to choose if you plan to display more than one image on a page—for example, side-by-side images—because the images will be composed of the same colors.

- The Uniform option builds a palette using an evenly spaced sampling of colors from the RGB spectrum.

- The Adaptive option builds a color table using the colors from your image. If you're displaying one image at a time, choose the Adaptive palette option.

- The Custom option lets you build a color table by editing individual colors in the table or by loading a previously saved color table.

4 For Palette, select Web.

The Color Depth menu lets you select how many colors you want to use to display the image. This option is only active when you select the Uniform or Adaptive palette.

5 For Dither, select None. (Dithering makes the flat color look spotted.)

Note: When the Dither option is set to None, all colors in the image shift to the nearest corresponding colors in the palette. Keep this in mind when designing your flat-color images.

6 Click OK to apply the color mode change to the map image.

7 If desired, choose Edit > Undo. Then choose Image > Mode > Indexed Color again, and choose different palette and dither settings.

For example, try using the Adaptive palette with a Diffusion dither setting, and observe the effects on the image. When you are finished experimenting, return to using the Web palette with a dither of None.

8 Choose File > Save As. Name the file **Africa.gif**, for format choose CompuServe GIF, and then click Save.

The GIF Options dialog box appears, letting you specify the appearance of the image as it is downloaded:

- The Normal option displays the image only after it has been downloaded completely from the server.

• The Interlaced option displays a low-resolution proxy of the image as it is being downloaded. The image gradually increases in detail until the downloading is complete. Selecting the Interlaced option increases the file size.

9 For Row Order, select Normal; then click OK.

10 Choose File > Close; do not save changes.

Now you'll see how the file size of the GIF image differs from the original image.

11 Check the file size of the original image:

• In Windows, use Windows Explorer to select Africa.gif in the file list, and choose File > Properties.

• In Mac OS, return to the desktop, select Africa.gif in the file list, and choose File > Get Info.

For the most accurate file size, note the value enclosed in parentheses next to Size.

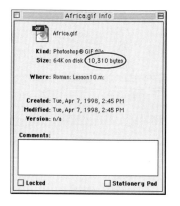

12 Repeat step 11 to check the file size for Africa2.psd. Close the Properties or Get Info dialog box when you are finished.

Preparing a grayscale image for the Web

Grayscale images should be converted to RGB mode and then exported using the GIF89a Export module. Converting a grayscale image to RGB mode lets you select the number of colors (in this case, shades of gray) you want to use to display the image.

1 In Photoshop, choose File > Open. Locate and open the Lesson11 folder, select the Hands.psd file, and then click Open.

First, you'll convert the hands image to RGB color mode.

2 Choose Image > Mode > RGB Color.

Now that you've converted the grayscale image to RGB, you can use the GIF89a Export module to select the number of grays you want the image to display.

3 Choose File > Export > GIF89a Export.

Note: If the GIF89a dialog box doesn't appear, make sure that the GIF89a Export module is installed in the Plug-Ins folder, and then restart Adobe Photoshop.

When you export an RGB image to GIF89a format, the image is converted to 8-bit Indexed Color mode.

4 In the GIF89a Export dialog box, deselect Interlaced to minimize the file size.

You don't need to use interlacing because the file you're working with is small enough to download quickly.

5 Click Preview to see a preview of the final image.

6 Click OK to return to the GIF89a Export dialog box.

When working with grayscale images, you can usually use fewer than 256 shades of gray without significantly affecting the display quality of the image. Reducing the number of grays used to display a grayscale image reduces the file size, thus speeding download time on the Web.

7 To reduce the number of grays used to display the image, select Adaptive from the Palette menu, and enter **32** for Colors.

8 Click Preview to display a preview of the hands image again using 32 shades of gray instead of the default 256 shades. You'll notice that there isn't much difference.

9 Experiment by selecting different values from the Colors menu and then clicking Preview to see how the image is affected. Try to use the fewest shades of gray that can still represent the detail in the hands image.

10 When you're finished experimenting, click OK to close the GIF89a Export dialog box. A dialog box appears, letting you save the image.

11 Name the file **Hands2.gif**, and click Save to save the image.

12 To see the difference between the original file and the GIF file you just saved, choose File > Open, open the Hands2.gif file, and align it next to the original file.

13 Choose File > Close to close both files, and do not save changes.

Preparing a full-color image

Full-color images such as photographs should be saved as JPEG files. The compression option you use determines how the color information in the image is preserved and the overall size of the file.

You'll save two copies of an identical RGB image as JPEG files using two different compression options. After you've saved the images, you'll close and then reopen them to compare the differences in file size and image quality.

1 Choose File > Open. Locate and open the Lesson11 folder, select the Giraffe.psd file, and then click Open.

2 Choose File > Save a Copy. In the Save a Copy dialog box, name the file **Giralow.jpg**. For the format, choose JPEG, and then click Save.

Now you'll experiment with JPEG compression settings.

3 In the JPEG Options dialog box, drag the slider to the left to small file to select the Low quality compression.

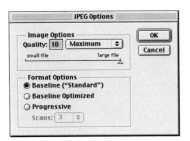

The Format Options let you specify the type of JPEG file to save:

• The Baseline ("Standard") option uses the JPEG format that is recognizable to most Web browsers.

• The Baseline Optimized option optimizes the color quality of the image and can produce a slightly smaller file size. However, this format is not supported by all Web browsers.

• The Progressive option causes the image to display gradually as it is downloaded—in a series of scans that show increasing details of the image. This option increases the file size and is not supported by all Web browsers.

4 For Format Options, select Baseline ("Standard"). Click OK.

5 Choose File > Close to close the Giralow.jpg file.

6 With the Giraffe.psd file still open, repeat step 2, but this time, save the file as **Girahi.jpg**.

7 In the JPEG Options dialog box, drag the slider all the way to the right to Large File to select Maximum quality compression. Click OK.

8 Choose File > Close to close the Girahi.jpg file.

Now you'll compare the size and quality of the two images. Before you open the files, you'll check their size.

9 In Windows Explorer (Windows) or on the desktop (Mac OS), select the Giralow.jpg image in the file list. Choose File > Properties (Windows) or File > Get Info (Mac OS), and note the size value in parentheses.

10 Repeat step 7 to check the size of the Girahi.jpg image. Close the Properties or Get Info dialog box when you are finished.

11 Return to Adobe Photoshop and choose File > Open to open both the Giralow.jpg image and the Girahi.jpg file. Compare the differences between the quality of the images.

You'll probably notice some image degradation in the Giralow.jpg image—such as banding patterns in the sky and fuzziness around the edges of the giraffe. In general, your choice of JPEG options will depend on your image size and quality needs.

12 Close both the open files, and do not save changes.

Preparing an image containing a gradient

Images containing gradients should be saved to JPEG format. The JPEG format preserves the continuous tone of a gradient image and produces a smaller file than the GIF format with an Adaptive palette. Saving a gradient to GIF format may cause banding in the gradient.

Now you'll work with an image containing a gradient.

1 Choose File > Open. Locate and open the Lesson11 folder, select the Economy.psd file, and then click Open.

2 Choose Image > Duplicate, name the copy **Gradlow.jpg**, and click OK.

3 Repeat step 2, this time naming the copy **Gradhi.jpg**, and click OK.

You'll select two different compression options for these images.

4 Close the original Economy.psd file.

5 Align the Gradlow.jpg and Gradhi.jpg images side by side.

6 Click the Gradlow.jpg window to make it active; then choose File > Save As. For the format, choose JPEG, and click Save.

7 In the JPEG Options dialog box, drag the slider to the left to select small file/Low, and then click OK.

8 Click the Gradhi.jpg window to make it active; then choose File > Save As. For the format, choose JPEG, and then click Save.

9 In the JPEG Options dialog box, drag the slider to the right to select large file/Maximum, and click OK.

10 Before continuing, close both images. You must reopen them to compare the difference in image quality.

11 Choose File > Open. In the Lesson11 folder, open the Gradhi.jpg and Gradlow.jpg images, and align them side by side.

Compare the quality of the gradient in both images. You'll notice that the quality of the gradient saved with large file/Maximum compression is significantly better than the image saved with small file/Low compression.

Select the Medium, High, or Maximum compression options for images containing gradients; these options preserve most of the color information in the gradient.

12 Close the files, and do not save changes.

Saving an image with transparency

You can create transparent areas in an image using the GIF89a Export module. To define areas as transparent, you must first convert the image to Indexed Color mode.

You'll define the edges of an image as transparent to create a soft-edged effect around the image.

1 Choose File > Open, locate the Lesson11 folder. Then select the Zebra.psd file from the list of files, and click Open.

2 Choose Image > Mode > Indexed Color. For Palette, choose Web, and for Dither, choose Diffusion; then click OK.

3 Before continuing, select the zoom tool in the toolbox, and zoom in on a corner of the zebra image.

Notice the khaki green area outside the scalloped edges of the image. This gray area is the area you'll define as transparent, so that only the scalloped edges are visible when the image is opened in a Web browser.

4 Choose File > Export > GIF89a Export.

The GIF89a Export dialog box shows a preview of the image and a color table representing the colors used in the image.

5 Double-click the hand tool (within the GIF89a Export dialog box) to see the entire image in the preview area.

One way to define background transparency is by loading an existing alpha channel. In this case, we've created an alpha channel that masks the image, showing only the outside border.

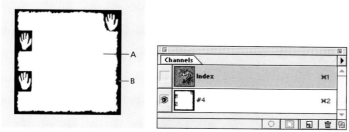

A. Mask B. Border

6 In the GIF89a Export dialog box, choose 4 from the Transparency From menu to load the selection mask.

Notice that the border now appears as a gray area in the preview. This gray color represents the transparency preview color, indicating areas of the image that will appear transparent in a Web browser. The mask you loaded restricts the transparency only to the border area.

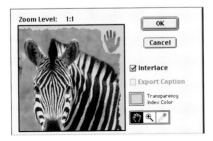

Now, you'll change the transparency preview color to preview how the image will look when placed against the background color of your Web page. Remember that this transparency color affects the preview only; in the final image, the border is filled with transparency, not color.

7 Click the Transparency Preview Color (Windows) or the Transparency Index Color (Mac OS) swatch.

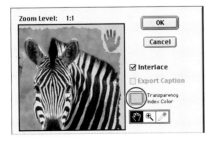

8 Select a color that matches the background color of your Web page. (For this example, try selecting a color that isn't present in the image so that the result is obvious.) Click OK.

The image is displayed on the background color with the transparency settings.

9 Click OK to close the GIF89a Export dialog box. The Save dialog box appears.

10 Enter a filename with a .gif extension, and click Save to save the image.

The image appears to be unaffected by the transparency settings—you won't see the transparent areas around the border of the image until you open it in a Web browser.

11 Choose File > Close to close the file. If prompted, do not save changes to the file.

Using the Actions palette to automate tasks

The Actions palette lets you automate repetitive tasks by recording and then playing back a series of commands on a single file or on a series of files in the same folder. Each set of commands is called an *action*.

Action

Although this lesson won't show you all the ways you can use Actions, you'll get a basic understanding of how the Actions palette works.

Creating and recording actions

When you create an action, Photoshop records the commands (including any specified values) and tools you use, in the order you use them.

The following guidelines can help you in designing actions:

•Most, but not all, commands can be recorded. However, you can allow for commands that cannot be recorded.

•The gradient, marquee, crop, polygon, lasso, line, move, magic wand, paint bucket, and type tools, and the Paths, Channels, Layers, and History palettes can be recorded.

•Actions created in Photoshop 4 are compatible with this version of Photoshop, but not vice versa.

•You can record the Play command listed on the Actions palette menu, and record the Batch command listed in the File > Automate menu to cause one action to play another.

•Modal operations and tools, and any tools that record position, use the units currently specified for the ruler. A modal operation or tool is one that requires you to press Enter or Return to apply its effect, such as the transformation commands or the crop tool. Tools that record position include the gradient, magic wand, lasso, marquee, and path tools.

• *When recording an action, keep in mind that playback results depend on such variables as the current background and foreground colors, and on file and program settings, such as the image color mode, resolution, and active layer. For example, a 3-pixel Gaussian blur won't create the same effect on a 72-ppi file as on a 144-ppi file. Likewise, Color Balance won't work on a grayscale file.*

• *Because Photoshop executes the commands as you record them, it's a good idea to record a complicated action using a copy of a file, and then play the action on the original.*

• *Until you specifically save a set of actions with the Save Actions command, actions are automatically saved in the file Actions Palette.psp (Windows) or Actions Palette (Mac OS) located in the Adobe Photoshop Settings folder within the Photoshop folder.*

–From the Adobe Photoshop User Guide, Chapter 16

For complete information about how the Actions palette works, see "Automating Tasks" in online Help or Chapter 16 of the Adobe Photoshop User Guide.

Saving filename extensions

Before you create an action, you'll instruct Photoshop to save images with three-character filename extensions. Filename extensions indicate a file's format and are necessary for files you want to use or transfer to a Windows system.

1 Choose File > Preferences > Saving Files.

2 Specify an extension option:

• In Windows, for File Extension, choose Use Lower Case. You cannot turn off filename extensions in Windows.

• In Mac OS, for Append File Extension, choose Always. Then select Use Lower Case.

Filename extensions help you keep track of files that are automatically saved using actions.

3 Click OK.

Recording actions

When you create an action, Photoshop records the commands you choose, in the order you choose them. Not all commands and functions can be recorded, but you can insert nonrecordable commands using the Insert Menu Item command in the Actions palette.

In this lesson, you'll create an action for a series of files, called a *batch process*. Let's assume the following scenario: You have four images, originally prepared for print, that you now want to prepare for distribution on the Web. You will automate the tasks of changing the pixel dimensions, color mode, and file format of the images.

1 Choose File > Open, locate and open the Lesson11 folder, and then open the folder named Images within the Lesson11 folder. Select the Crocodil.psd image from the list of files, and click Open.

You must have a file open to record an action.

2 Click the Actions palette tab. (If the Actions palette is hidden, choose Window > Show Actions.)

3 Choose New Action from the Actions palette menu.

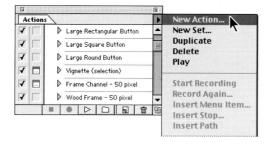

4 In the Actions dialog box, type the name **Web Specs**, and click Record. The Action name appears at the bottom of the actions list in the palette.

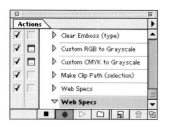

At the bottom of the Actions palette, the Record icon becomes red, indicating that recording has begun.

5 Choose Image > Image Size. For Pixel Dimensions, enter **100** in the Width and Height text boxes. All of the images in the batch process will be resized to these dimensions.

6 Click OK to continue. Notice that the Image Size command appears in the Actions palette.

7 Choose Image > Mode > Indexed Color. Choose Web from the Palette menu, and then click OK to continue. Now the Convert Mode command appears in the Actions palette.

8 Choose File > Save As, and choose CompuServe GIF for the format. Notice that the extension .gif is automatically appended to the filename. Locate and select the NewImage folder inside the Lesson11 folder, and click Save.

9 Select Interlaced, and click OK.

At this point, you've recorded all the commands you need for the Web action.

10 Stop recording in either of the following ways:

• Click the Stop button at the bottom of the Actions palette to stop recording.

• Choose Stop Recording from the Actions menu.

Before you play back the action on the remainder of the files, take a moment to look at the Actions palette.

In the Actions palette, click the triangle next to the Image Size command. The command is expanded to show all the parameters you set for the Image Size command.

Click the triangle next to the Save command. Notice that the save location and file format are recorded, but not the filename.

11 Choose File > Close to close the Crocodil.psd file before continuing. Do not save changes.

Playing back an action

Once you've recorded an action, you can play it back on a single file or on a folder of files. You use the batch feature to play back an action on a folder of files. In this lesson, you'll run your newly created action on the four files you want to prepare for Web publication.

For information about all of the playback options you can use with actions, see "Automating Tasks" in online Help or Chapter 16 in the Adobe Photoshop User Guide.

Note: You can also exclude commands that you don't want to apply when playing an action, or pause a command to display its dialog box as the action is playing.

1 Choose File > Automate > Batch. The Batch dialog box appears.

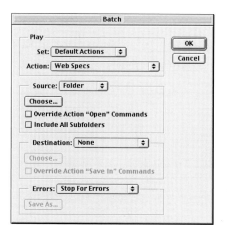

2 For Action, choose Web Specs.

3 For Source, choose Folder and then click Choose to select the folder containing the files you want to batch-process:

• In Windows, locate and double-click the Images folder inside the Lesson11 folder. Then click OK.

• In Mac OS, locate and highlight the Images folder inside the Lesson11 folder. Then click the Select "Images" button.

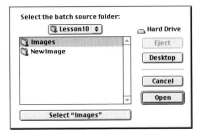

4 Click OK to begin executing the action. Each of the images in the Images folder is opened; and the size, resolution, and color mode of each image is edited, based on the parameters you set while recording the action. Each image is changed to GIF format and saved as a modified copy in the NewImage destination folder.

5 If desired, open the NewImage folder after you've played the Web Specs action to see how the images were adjusted.

You've completed this lesson. Now take a few minutes to review what you've learned and to think about ways you might use these techniques in your own work.

Batch processing

The Batch command lets you play an action on a folder of files and subfolders. If you have a digital camera or a scanner with a document feeder, you can also import and process multiple images with a single action. Your scanner or digital camera may need an acquire plug-in module that supports actions. (If the third-party plug-in wasn't written to import multiple documents at a time, it may not work during batch-processing or if used as part of an action. Contact the plug-in's manufacturer for further information.)

When batch-processing files, you can leave all the files open, close and save the changes to the original files, or save modified versions of the files to a new location (leaving the originals unchanged). If you are batch-processing a folder of files, copy all the desired files to the same level of a folder before starting the batch. If you are saving the processed files to a new location, you may want to create a new folder for the processed files before starting the batch.

For better batch performance, reduce the number of saved history states and deselect the Automatically Create First Snapshot option in the History palette.

–From the Adobe Photoshop User Guide, Chapter 16

Review questions

1 What determines the file format you should use when saving images for Web publication?

2 What is the benefit of selecting the Web palette when preparing images for publication on the World Wide Web?

3 How could you use actions in your own work to expedite repetitive tasks?

4 What is the first step you must perform when creating an action?

Review answers

1 The type of image you're working with determines the file format you should use to save an image for publication on the Web.

2 Selecting the Web palette ensures that your images are displayed using the same color palette, regardless of the platform on which the image is displayed.

3 You might create an action to change the mode, the size, and the resolution of a batch of images, or you might create an action to assign a frequently used command to a function key.

4 You should choose New Action from the Actions palette menu. This ensures that you are creating a new action, and not appending commands to an existing action.

Lesson 12

Preparing Images for Two-Color Printing

Not every commercially printed publication requires four-color reproduction. Printing in two colors using a grayscale image and spot color can be an effective and inexpensive alternative. In this lesson, you'll learn how to use Photoshop to prepare full-color images for two-color printing.

In this lesson, you'll learn how to do the following:

- Use the Channel Mixer command to convert a color image to monochrome and improve its overall quality.

- Adjust the tonal range of the image by assigning black and white points.

- Sharpen the image with the Unsharp Mask filter.

- Convert a color image to grayscale.

- Add spot color to selected areas of the image.

Printing in color

Color publications are expensive to print commercially because they require four passes through the press—one for each of the four process colors used to create the full-color effect. The colors in the publication must be separated into cyan, magenta, yellow, and black plates for the press, which also adds to the expense.

Printing images in two colors can be a much less costly yet effective approach for many projects, even if they begin with an image in full color. With Photoshop, you can convert color to grayscale without sacrificing image quality. You can also add a second spot color for accent, and Photoshop will create the two-color separations needed for the printing process.

Note: Spot color is intended for images that will be printed to film during the printing process. The spot color techniques covered in this lesson are not appropriate for color images printed to desktop printers or for images designed for electronic distribution.

Using channels and the Channels palette

Channels in Adobe Photoshop are used for storing information and play an important role in this lesson. As you learned in Lesson 5, "Masks and Channels," *color channels* store the color information for an image, and *alpha channels* store selections or masks that let you edit specific parts of an image. In addition, *spot color channels* let you specify color separations for printing an image with spot color inks.

In this lesson, you'll use all three types of channels. You'll learn to mix color channels to improve the quality of an image. You'll select areas of the image by loading a selection from an alpha channel. And you'll use a spot color channel to add a second color to the image.

Getting started

Before beginning this lesson, delete the Adobe Photoshop Preferences file to restore the program's default settings. For step-by-step instructions, see "Restoring default prefer-ences" on page 4. Then restart the Photoshop program.

Now you'll open the final Photoshop image for this lesson to see what you'll create.

1 Choose File > Open. Locate, and open the Lesson12 folder. Then select End12.psd, and click Open.

An image of a construction foreman is displayed.

2 If you like, choose View > Zoom Out to make the image smaller, and leave it on your screen as you work. If you don't want to leave the image open, choose File > Close.

Now you'll open the start file for the lesson.

3 Choose File > Open, locate and select Start12.psd in the Lesson12 folder, and then click Open.

4 Choose View > Hide Guides.

5 Choose File > Save As, type the name **Work12.psd**, and click Save.

About channels and file size

Color information channels are created automatically when you open a new image. The image's color mode (and not its number of layers) determines the number of color channels created. For example, an RGB image has three default channels: one for each of the red, green, and blue colors plus a composite channel used for editing the image.

Alpha channels store selections as 8-bit grayscale images and are added to the color channels in an image. You use alpha channels to create and store masks, which let you manipulate, isolate, and protect specific parts of an image. An image can have up to 24 channels, including all color and alpha channels. In addition, spot color channels can be added to an image to let you specify additional plates for printing with spot color inks.

The file size required for a channel depends on the pixel information in the channel. For example, if the image has no alpha channels, duplicating a color channel in an RGB image increases the file size by about one-third, in a CMYK image by about one-fourth. Each alpha channel and spot color channel also adds to the file size.

Certain file formats compress channel information and can save space, including the TIFF and Photoshop formats. The size of a file, including alpha channels and layers, appears as the second (right) value in the lower left corner of the window when the Document Size command is chosen.

–From the Adobe Photoshop User Guide, Chapter 10

Mixing color channels

Sometimes it's possible to improve the quality of an image by blending two or more color channels. For instance, one channel in an image may look particularly strong but would look even better if you could add some detail from another channel. In Photoshop, you can blend color channels with the Channel Mixer command in either RGB mode (for on-screen display) or CMYK mode (for printing).

Note: For more information on color modes, see Lesson 13, "Ensuring and Printing Accurate Color."

In this lesson, you'll use the Channel Mixer command to improve the quality of an RGB image that you'll then convert to grayscale mode. But first, you'll use the Channels palette to view the different channels in the image.

1 Choose Window > Show Channels, click the Channels tab, and drag the palette off the Layers and Paths palette. Place the Channels palette on your screen where you can easily access it.

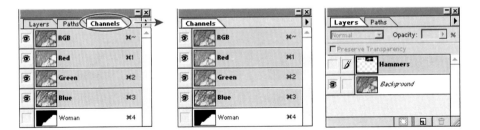

Because the image is in RGB mode, the Channels palette displays the image's red, green, and blue channels. Notice that all the color channels are currently visible, including the RGB channel, which is a composite of the separate red, green, and blue channels. To see the individual channels, you can use the palette's eye icons.

2 Click the eye icons to turn off all color channels in the Channels palette except the red channel. The colors in the Work12 image change to shades of gray.

Red channel

3 Drag the eye icon from the red channel to the green channel and then to the blue channel. Notice how the monochrome image in the Work12 window changes with each channel. The green channel shows the best overall contrast and the best detail in the woman's face, while the blue channel shows good contrast in the framework behind the woman.

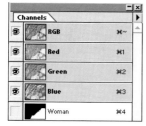 

Green channel *Blue channel*

4 In the Channels palette, click the eye icon column for the composite RGB channel to display all the color channels in the image.

All channels displayed *RGB image*

You'll now use the Channel Mixer command to improve the image in this lesson. Specifically, you'll divide the image into two areas, the woman and the framework, and mix different amounts of source channels in each selection.

For illustrations of the image before and after mixing channels, see figures 12-1 and 12-2 in the color signature.

About the Channel Mixer

The Channel Mixer command lets you modify a color channel using a mix of the current color channels. With this command, you can do the following:

- *Make creative color adjustments not easily done with the other color adjustment tools.*
- *Create high-quality grayscale images by choosing the percentage contribution from each color channel.*
- *Create high-quality sepia-tone or other tinted images.*
- *Convert images to and from some alternative color spaces, such as YCrCb.*
- *Swap or duplicate channels.*

–From the Adobe Photoshop User Guide, Chapter 10

Mixing the woman's image

First you'll select the woman's image by loading a premade selection.

1 In the Layers palette, make sure that the background is active.

2 Choose Select > Load Selection. In the dialog box, select Woman from the Channel menu to load a selection that outlines the image of the woman. Click OK.

Now you'll mix the green and blue channels to improve the selection's contrast. You'll use green as the base channel because it has the best overall contrast for the image.

3 Choose Image > Adjust > Channel Mixer.

4 At the top of the Channel Mixer dialog box, choose Green for the Output Channel. Notice that the Source Channel for Green changes to 100%.

5 At the bottom of the dialog box, select the Monochrome option to change the image to shades of gray. This option gives you an idea of how the selection will look in Grayscale mode, so that you can more accurately adjust the selection's tonal range.

The resulting image is a little flat. You can bring out the contrast and improve the highlights by blending in some of the blue channel.

6 Drag the slider for the Blue Source Channel to 10%.

Selection loaded   *Channel Mixer dialog with 10% blue*

7 Click OK.

Mixing the framework's image

Next you'll select the framework, convert this part of the image to monochrome, and again mix channels to improve the contrast and detail.

1 Choose Select > Inverse to select the framework behind the woman.

2 Choose Image > Adjust > Channel Mixer.

3 In the Channel Mixer dialog box, again choose Green for the Output Channel, and select the Monochrome option.

This time the resulting image is dark and lacks contrast. You can improve the image again by blending in some of the blue channel.

4 Drag the slider for the Blue Source Channel to 27%.

Inverse of selection   *Channel Mixer dialog with 27% blue*

5 Click OK.

6 Choose Select > Deselect.

Both the woman and the framework now show better contrast and detail. But the image is still an RGB color image (one that contains only gray values). To convert the image to Grayscale mode, you will use the Grayscale command.

7 Choose Image > Mode > Grayscale. When prompted, select Don't Flatten to keep the image's two layers intact. (You'll use the second layer later in this lesson.) The image converts to grayscale mode, and the color channels in the Channels palette are replaced by a single Black channel.

8 Choose File > Save.

Assigning values to the black and white points

You can further improve the quality of the image by adjusting the black and white limits of its tonal range. In Lesson 6, "Photo Retouching," you learned to use the sliders on the Levels command histogram to adjust the range. In this lesson, you'll control the range more accurately by using the Levels command eyedropper to assign specific values to the darkest and lightest points.

1 Choose Image > Adjust > Levels.

2 In the Levels dialog box, double-click the white eyedropper tool to open the color picker for the white point.

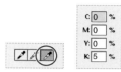

3 Enter **0, 0, 0,** and **5** in the CMYK text boxes, and click OK. These values generally produce the best results when printing the white points (highlights) of a grayscale image onto white paper.

4 Next double-click the black eyedropper tool in the Levels dialog box to open the color picker for the black point.

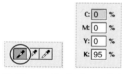

5 Enter **0, 0, 0,** and **95** in the CMYK text boxes, and click OK. These values generally produce the best results when printing the black points (shadows) of a grayscale image onto white paper.

Now that you've defined the values for the black and white points, you'll use the Levels command eyedropper to assign the values to the darkest and lightest areas in the image.

6 Reselect the black eyedropper tool, and position it in the darkest area of the framework behind the woman's elbow. Click to assign this area the values you set in step 5.

7 Next click the white eyedropper tool in the Levels dialog box, position the tool in the lightest area of the woman's collar, and click to assign this area the values you set in step 3.

Black eyedropper selecting
darkest area behind elbow

White eyedropper selecting
lightest area in collar

8 Click OK to close the dialog box, and apply the changes.

Assigning the black and white points shifts the image's histogram to produce a more evenly distributed tonal range.

Original   *Result*

9 Choose File > Save.

Sharpening the image

By applying the Unsharp Mask filter to the image, you can create the illusion of a more focused image.

1 Choose Filter > Sharpen > Unsharp Mask. Make sure that the Preview option is selected so that you can view the effect before you apply it. To get a better view, you can place the pointer within the preview window and drag to see different parts of the image (we focused on the woman's face). You can also change the magnification of the preview image with the plus and minus buttons located below the window.

2 Drag the Amount slider until the image is as sharp as you want (we used 57%), and make sure that the Radius is set to 1 pixel.

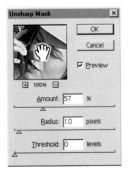

3 Click OK to apply the Unsharp Mask filter to the image.

Setting up for spot color

Spot colors, also called *custom colors*, are premixed inks that are used instead of, or in addition to, the cyan, magenta, yellow, and black process color inks. Each spot color requires its own color separation or printing plate. Graphic designers use spot colors to specify colors that would be difficult or impossible to achieve by combining the four process inks.

You'll now add spot color to the image in this lesson by creating a spot color channel.

1 In the Channels palette, choose New Spot Channel from the pop-up menu at the top right corner of the palette.

2 In the New Spot Channel dialog box, click the color box, and select Custom from the color picker.

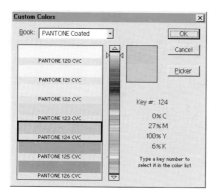

3 In the Custom Colors dialog box, type **124** for the Pantone custom color 124. (Because there is no text box for the number, you must type it quickly.) Then click OK.

4 In the next dialog box, enter **100%** for Solidity. The solidity setting lets you simulate on-screen the ink solidity of the printed spot color. Inks range from transparent (0% solidity) to opaque (100% solidity). The Solidity option affects the on-screen preview only and has no effect on the printed output.

5 Click OK to create the spot color channel. A new spot color channel named PANTONE 124 CVC has been added to the Channels palette.

6 Choose File > Save.

Using spot channels

Spot channels let you add and preview spot colors in an image. The following guidelines can help you in using spot channels:

• If you need spot color graphics that have crisp edges and knock out the underlying image, consider creating the additional artwork in a page-layout or illustration application.

• You can create new spot channels or convert an existing alpha channel to a spot channel.

• Like alpha channels, spot channels can be edited or deleted at any time.

• Spot colors can't be applied to individual layers.

• Spot colors are overprinted on top of the fully composited image.

• If you print an image that includes spot color channels to a composite printer, the spot colors print out as extra pages.

• You can merge spot channels with color channels, splitting the spot color into its color channel components. Merging spot channels lets you print a single-page proof of your spot color image on a desktop printer.

• The names of the spot colors print on the separations.

• Each spot channel is overprinted in the order in which it appears in the Channels palette.

• You cannot move spot colors above a default channel in the Channels palette except in Multichannel mode.

–From the Adobe Photoshop User Guide, Chapter 10

Adding spot color

You can add spot color to selected areas of an image in different ways with varying effects. For instance, you can apply spot color to part of a grayscale image so that the selection prints in the spot color rather than in the base ink. Because spot colors in Photoshop print over the top of a fully composited image, you may also need to remove the base color in an image when adding spot color to it. If you do not remove the base color, it may show through the semitransparent spot color ink used in the printing process.

You can also use spot color to add solid and screened blocks of color to an image. By screening the spot color, you can create the illusion of adding an extra, lighter color to the printed piece.

Removing a grayscale area and adding spot color

You'll begin your work in spot color by changing the framework behind the woman to the color. You must first select the framework, remove it from the grayscale image, and then add the selection to the spot color channel.

1 In the Channels palette, click the Black channel to make it active.

2 Choose Select > Load Selection. In the dialog box, select Woman from the Channel menu and also select the Invert option.

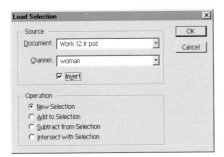

3 Click OK to load a selection of the framework behind the woman.

4 Choose Edit > Cut to cut the selection from the image.

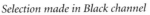

Black channel active   *Selection made in Black channel*   *Selection cut from Black channel*

5 In the Channels palette, click the PANTONE 124 CVC channel to make it active.

6 Choose Edit > Paste to paste the framework selection into the spot color channel. In the Work12 window, the framework reappears in the Pantone color.

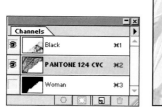

Selection pasted into spot color channel

7 Choose Select > Deselect.

Removing spot color from a grayscale area

Now you'll remove some spot color where it overlaps the grayscale area of a second layer of the image.

1 In the Layers palette, click the eye icon column for the Hammers layer to make it visible. (Click just the eye icon column. Do not make the layer itself active.)

Notice that the spot color of the framework overlaps part of the Hammers layer. You'll remove this overlap by making a new selection and cutting it from the spot color channel.

2 Choose View > Show Guides.

3 In the toolbox, select the rectangular marquee tool (⌑), and make a selection across the top of the image to the depth of the first horizontal guide.

4 Make sure that the spot channel in the Channels palette is still active, and press Delete to remove the rectangular selection from the channel. In the Work12 window, the spot color disappears from the hammers image.

Making selection

Selection cut from spot color channel

5 Choose Select > Deselect.

6 Choose File > Save.

Adding solid and screened areas of spot color

Next you'll vary the effect of adding spot color by adding a solid block of the color and then a block of the color screened to 50%. The two areas will appear to be different colors even though you have used the same Pantone custom color on the same color separation.

First you'll make a selection for the solid block of color and fill the selection using a keyboard shortcut.

1 With the rectangular marquee tool still selected, make a selection in the upper right corner of the image bounded by the two guides.

2 Hold down Alt (Windows) or Option (Mac OS), and press Delete to fill the selection with the foreground color. Because you are in the PANTONE 124 CVC channel, the foreground color is Pantone 124 and fills the square with solid color.

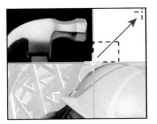

Making selection for spot color   Selection filled with solid color

Now you can add a lighter block of spot color to the image.

3 Make a rectangular selection directly below the horizontal hammer and bounded by the guides.

4 In the Color palette, move the color slider to 20% to set the value for the new block of color.

5 Again hold down Alt/Option and press Delete to fill the selection with a 20% screen of Pantone 124.

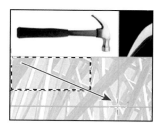
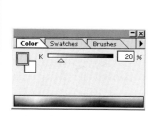
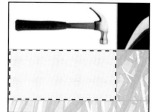

Making selection   *Color value set to 20%*   *Selection filled with 20% color*

6 Choose Select > Deselect.

7 Choose View > Hide Guides.

8 Choose File > Save.

Adding spot color to text

Text in an image can also appear in spot color. There are different methods for creating this effect, but the most straightforward is to add the text directly to the spot color channel. Note that text in a spot channel behaves differently from text created on a type layer. Spot channel text is uneditable. Once you create the type, you cannot change its specifications, and once you deselect the type, you cannot reposition it.

You will now add text to the spot color channel and place the text in the light block of spot color.

1 In the Color palette, return the color slider to 100%.

2 Select the type tool (T) in the toolbox, and click the image in the light block of color.

3 In the Type Tool dialog box, choose Helvetica Bold from the Font menus, and enter **66** for the point size in the Size text box.

4 Type **work** in the large text box at the bottom of the dialog box.

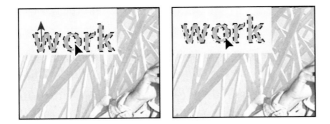

5 Click OK. The text appears in solid Pantone 124 where you first clicked the image.

6 Select the move tool (✥) in the toolbox, and drag the text so that it is centered in the light block of color.

7 Choose Select > Deselect.

8 Choose File > Save.

You are now finished preparing the image for two-color printing. To see how the color separations for the printed piece will look, try alternately hiding and displaying the two color channels in the Channels palette.

9 Click the eye icon for the Black channel in the Channels palette. The Black channel is hidden, and the image window changes to just the areas of the image that will print in the spot color.

10 Redisplay the Black channel by clicking its eye icon column. Then hide the PANTONE 124 CVC channel by clicking its eye icon. Just the grayscale areas of the image appear in the image window.

11 Click the eye icon column for the PANTONE 124 CVC channel to display both channels.

Final image   *Black channel*   *PANTONE 124 CVC channel*

If you have a printer available, you can also try printing the image. You'll find it prints on two sheets of paper—one representing the color separation for the spot color and one for the grayscale areas of the image.

Review questions

1 What are the three types of channels in Photoshop and how are they used?

2 How can you improve the quality of a color image that has been converted to grayscale?

3 How do you assign specific values to the black and white points in an image?

4 How do you set up a spot color channel?

5 How do you add spot color to a specific area in a grayscale image?

6 How can you apply spot color to text?

Review answers

1 Channels in Photoshop are used for storing information. Color channels store the color information for an image, alpha channels store selections or masks for editing specific parts of an image, and spot color channels create color separations for printing an image with spot color inks.

2 You can use the Color Mixer command to blend color channels to bring out the contrast and detail in an image. You can extend the tonal range of the image by adjusting its black and white points. You can also sharpen the image by applying the Unsharp Mask filter.

3 You assign specific values with the Levels command black and white eyedropper tools.

4 You set up a spot color channel by choosing New Spot Channel from the pop-up menu on the Channels palette and by specifying a color from the Custom color picker in the New Spot Channel dialog box.

5 With the Black channel active, you select the area, cut it from the Black channel, and paste it into the spot color channel.

6 You can add the text to the spot color channel. However, text created in this way is not editable and cannot be repositioned once it is deselected.

Lesson 13

Ensuring and Printing Accurate Color

Reproducing color accurately begins with calibrating your monitor to ensure a consistent display of on-screen color. It includes defining the color space in which to edit and display RGB images, and in which to edit, display, and print CMYK images to ensure a close match between on-screen and printed colors.

In this lesson, you'll learn to do the following:

- Calibrate your monitor so that it displays color accurately.
- Define RGB, grayscale, and CMYK color spaces for displaying, editing, and printing images.
- Create a color separation, the process by which the colors in an RGB image are distributed to the four process ink colors: cyan, magenta, yellow, and black.
- Understand how images are prepared for printing on-press.
- Prepare an image for printing on a PostScript CMYK printer.

Reproducing colors

Colors on a monitor are displayed using combinations of red, green, and blue light (called RGB), while printed colors are typically created using a combination of four ink colors—cyan, magenta, yellow and black (called CMYK—with the letter K representing black). These four inks are called *process colors* because they are the standard inks used in the four-color printing process.

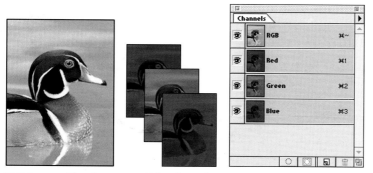

RGB image with red, green, and blue channels

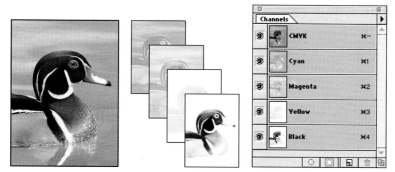

CMYK image with cyan, magenta, yellow, and black channels

For color samples of channels in both RGB and CMYK images, see figures 13-1 and 13–2 in the color signature.

Not suprisingly, because the RGB and CMYK color models use very different methods to display colors, they each have a slightly different range of colors, or *gamut*, that they can reproduce. For example, because RGB uses light to produce color, its gamut includes neon colors, such as you'd see in a neon sign. On the other hand, printing inks excel at reproducing certain colors, such as some pastels and pure black, that can lie outside of the RGB gamut. For an illustration of the RGB and CMYK gamuts, see figures 13–3, 13–4, and 13-5 in the color signature.

But not all RGB and CMYK gamuts are alike. Each model of monitor and printer is different, and so each displays a slightly different gamut. For example, one brand of monitor may produce slightly brighter blues than another. The *color space* for a device is defined by the gamut it can represent. Just as RGB and CMYK are different color spaces, so each model of monitor and output device can have a different color space.

RGB model

A large percentage of the visible spectrum can be represented by mixing red, green, and blue (RGB) colored light in various proportions and intensities. Where the colors overlap, they create cyan, magenta, and yellow.

Because the RGB colors combine to create white, they are also called additive colors. Adding all colors together creates white—that is, all light is reflected back to the eye. Additive colors are used for lighting, video, and monitors. Your monitor, for example, creates color by emitting light through red, green, and blue phosphors.

CMYK model

The CMYK model is based on the light-absorbing quality of ink printed on paper. As white light strikes translucent inks, part of the spectrum is absorbed and part is reflected back to your eyes.

In theory, pure cyan (C), magenta (M), and yellow (Y) pigments should combine to absorb all color and produce black. For this reason these colors are called subtractive colors. Because all printing inks contain some impurities, these three inks actually produce a muddy brown and must be combined with black (K) ink to produce a true black. (K is used instead of B to avoid confusion with blue.) Combining these inks to reproduce color is called four-color process printing.

The subtractive (CMY) and additive (RGB) colors are complementary colors. Each pair of subtractive colors creates an additive color, and vice versa.

–From the Adobe Photoshop User Guide, Chapter 4

Color management

Color management is the process of maintaining consistent, accurate color across these color spaces—that is, as an image is displayed on different monitors, converted between RGB and CMYK modes, opened in different software applications, and printed from different output devices.

Using ICC profiles to manage color

One way Photoshop can help you manage color is by using International color consortium (ICC) profiles. An ICC profile describes color spaces, whether it's the particular RGB color space for your monitor, the RGB color space in which you want to edit images, or the CMYK color space of the color laser printer you've selected. Although you do not have to use ICC profiles, they are becoming a standard in the graphics industry, and can help you more easily reproduce colors accurately across different platforms, devices, and ICC-compliant applications (such as Adobe Illustrator and Adobe PageMaker).

In this lesson, you'll choose which monitor, RGB, and CMYK ICC profiles to use. Once you specify the profiles, Photoshop can embed them into your image files. Photoshop (and any other application that can use ICC profiles) can then interpret the ICC profiles in the image file to automatically manage color issues for that image.

For more information on embedding ICC profiles, see "Reproducing Color Accurately" in online Help or Chapter 5 in the Adobe Photoshop User's Guide.

Getting started

Before beginning this lesson, delete the Adobe Photoshop Preferences file to restore the program's default settings. For step-by-step instructions, see "Restoring default preferences" on page 4. Then restart the Photoshop program.

Calibrating your monitor

Based on a variety of factors, such as changes in lighting, the temperature of the monitor, and the phosphors used to display the color, colors may vary from monitor to monitor. Calibrating your monitor serves two main purposes—to display colors accurately on-screen, and to ensure that the colors you see on the screen are the closest possible match to what comes out of the printer.

In this part of the lesson, you will learn to calibrate your monitor using the Adobe Gamma utility. This utility lets you calibrate the contrast and brightness, gamma (midtones), color balance, and white point of your monitor. This helps eliminate any color cast (for example, many monitors add a green tint to colors), make grays as neutral as possible, and make colors in the same image consistent on all monitors that have been similarly calibrated. The utility then saves these settings as an ICC profile for your monitor that defines your monitor's particular RGB color space.

This process only needs to be done once, unless you change monitors, the controls on your monitor, or the lighting conditions under which you view the monitor.

1 Make sure your monitor has been turned on for at least a half hour. This helps stabilize the monitor's display.

2 Set the room lighting at the level you plan to use when viewing Photoshop images.

3 Turn off any desktop patterns and change the background color on your monitor to a light gray. This prevents the background color from interfering with your color perception and helps you adjust the display to a neutral gray. (If you need more information on how to do this, see the manual for your operating system.)

4 Open the Goodies/Calibration folder inside the Photoshop folder.

5 Start the utility Adobe Gamma.

The initial dialog box presents you with two choices: Step By Step and Control Panel. Step By Step contains the same options as the Control Panel version, but walks you through each option.

6 Select Step By Step and click Next.

Because you'll be changing the settings anyway, for this example you won't load a different profile to serve as a starting point for calibrating your monitor.

7 Click Next.

8 Follow the calibration instructions that appear on the screen. If you are uncertain whether to change an option, leave it at its default setting.

9 When the last set of instructions appears indicating you have completed the Adobe Gamma Wizard, enter a filename in the File Name text box, click Finish, and then click Save.

Defining the RGB color space for images

In the previous part of this lesson, you calibrated your monitor, defining the RGB color space for it. In this part of the lesson, you'll choose the RGB color space in which to edit RGB images. Photoshop lets you define the color space in which you work on RGB images separately from the RGB color space of the monitor that displays them. This is because a monitor can display only a subset of all possible RGB colors. Rather than restrict you to editing images using only the range of colors your particular monitor can display, you can choose from a set of more generalized RGB color spaces. Your images can then contain colors that might be displayable on another monitor or RGB device, even if they aren't displayable on yours.

In this part of the lesson, you'll use the RGB Setup dialog box to define the RGB color space to use for editing RGB images. As with the Adobe Gamma utility, the RGB Setup dialog box saves the settings you specify as an ICC profile.

1 Choose File > Color Settings > RGB Setup. The ICC profile for your monitor is listed in the bottom of the dialog box.

2 Select Display Using Monitor Compensation to display images using the monitor's RGB color space.

This option does not affect the color information in images, only the way images look on the screen, and provides a more accurate display. Leaving this option deselected displays images directly to the monitor, with no compensation, and can make screen updates faster but less accurate. It is usually a good idea to leave this option selected.

3 For RGB, choose different RGB color spaces from the menu.

Notice that the Gamma, White Point, and Primaries settings listed in the dialog box change to reflect the different values for each RGB color space you choose.

4 When you are through experimenting, choose SMPTE-240 M as the color space.

This color space encompasses more of the printable (CMYK) color gamut than the other color spaces. Because this lesson assumes that you will be printing the file, SMPTE-240 M is a reasonable choice.

The color space you choose depends on what you intend to do with the image. For example, the default color space, sRGB represents the color space that can be displayed by the hypothetical "average" personal computer monitor. The sRGB color space is endorsed by a wide variety of hardware and software manufacturers and is becoming the default color space for many scanners, low-end printers, and software applications. This means it's a good choice if you are creating images to be viewed on the Web.

▣ For more information on the individual color spaces available, see "Reproducing Color Accurately" in online Help or Chapter 5 of the Adobe Photoshop User Guide.

5 Click OK.

Defining the CMYK color space for images and printing

Similarly to the way you defined the RGB color space for working with RGB images, you'll now define the CMYK color space for editing and printing CMYK images. Photoshop uses the information you enter in the CMYK Setup dialog box when you convert images between RGB and CMYK modes, and to give you an accurate preview on the screen of what an image will look like when printed.

There are several ways to describe the CMYK color space. In this lesson, you'll choose an ICC profile that describes the printer you plan to use. Photoshop can then map the colors in your image to the range of colors the printer can print.

▣ For information on other methods of describing the CMYK color space, see "Reproducing Color Accurately" in online Help or Chapter 5 in the Adobe Photoshop User Guide.

1 Choose File > Color Settings > CMYK Setup.

The CMYK Setup dialog box appears showing the options you can choose from if you want to describe how a particular ink, printer, and paper work together.

To make the process easier, you'll choose from an existing ICC printer profile instead.

2 For CMYK Model, select ICC.

For this exercise, you'll use the default CMYK settings. When you're doing your own work, you'll probably change the values in this dialog box depending on the device you're printing to and the requirements of the individual project.

3 For Profile, choose the printer profile you want to use.

For this lesson, you don't have to print the image, so you can choose any printer profile you want.

Note: If you want to print the image and the printer you want to use is not listed in the Profile menu, contact your printer manufacturer for the appropriate printer profile or create one using third-party printer profiling software. Alternatively, you can create a printer profile using the Olé No Moire CMYK image included with the Adobe Photoshop software. For more information, see the Read Me file that accompanies the Olé No Moire file.

4 For Engine, choose Built-in to use Photoshop's built-in ICC profile interpreter.

5 For Intent, choose Perceptual (Images).

This option maintain the relative color values among the original pixels as they are mapped to the printer's CMYK gamut. This method preserves the relationship between colors, although the color values themselves may change. Unless you are experienced with color and need to select a different option, you should use this option when choosing the Intent.

6 Select Black Point Compensation.

This option makes Photoshop convert the darkest neutral color of the source's color space to the darkest neutral color of the destination's color space rather than to black when converting colors. For example, if you were converting an image from RGB mode to CMYK mode, selecting this option would convert the darkest neutral color in the image's RGB color space to the equivalent in the CMYK color space.

7 Click OK.

Compensating for dot gain in grayscale images

Dot gain is the tendency of the dots of ink to spread and print larger than they should on the press, creating darker tones or color than expected. Different printers and papers have different dot gains.

If your grayscale images will be viewed only on-screen, you don't need to compensate for dot gain. However, for this lesson, we're assuming you're setting up your images for printing, and so you should apply the same dot gain values you used for CMYK output. The Grayscale Setup dialog box lets you specify whether grayscale images behave as RGB images or black ink.

1 Choose File > Color Settings > Grayscale Setup.

2 For Grayscale Behavior, select Black Ink to use the dot gain settings specified as part of the ICC profile you chose in the CMYK Setup dialog box.

3 Click OK.

Preparing images for print

The first step in preparing an image for print is to make any color and tonal adjustments to the image. To try making tonal adjustments on your own, see Lesson 12, "Preparing Images for Two-Color Printing."

For more information, see "Making Color and Tonal Adjustments" in online Help or Chapter 6 in the Adobe Photoshop User Guide.

The most common way to output images is to produce a negative image on film, and then transfer the image to a printing plate that will be run on a press.

To print a continuous-tone image, the image must be broken down into a series of dots. These dots are created when you apply a *halftone screen* to the image. The dots in a halftone screen control how much ink is deposited at a specific location. The varying size and density of the dots create the optical illusion of variations of gray or continuous color in the image.

A printed color image consists of four separate halftone screens—one each for cyan, magenta, yellow, and black (the four process ink colors). You can also add extra custom colors, called spot colors. To create a spot color yourself, see Lesson 12, "Preparing Images for Two-Color Printing."

Preparing a color separation in Adobe Photoshop

In Adobe Photoshop, preparing a color separation consists of the following process:

• Entering settings in the CMYK Setup dialog box to specify the properties of the printer you will use and to control how the CMYK plates are generated.

• Converting the image from RGB mode to CMYK mode to apply the CMYK Setup values to the image and to separate the colors in the image onto the four process color plates.

• Setting the line screen at which the image will be printed, either in Photoshop or in the page-layout program from which you're going to print.

Separating an RGB image

You've already calibrated your monitor, and specified the working RGB color space and the CMYK color space. Now you're ready to convert your RGB image to CMYK to separate the colors in the RGB image onto the four process color plates, one each for cyan, magenta, yellow, and black.

When you convert an RGB image to CMYK mode, the settings in the CMYK Setup dialog box are applied to the image.

1 Choose File > Open. Locate and open the Lesson13 folder, select Start13.psd, and click Open.

A sample RGB image is displayed.

2 With the Start13.psd image selected, choose Image > Duplicate.

3 Enter the name **CMYK.psd**, and then click OK to create a duplicate of the original file.

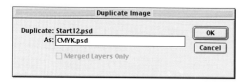

4 Align the images side by side so you can see both of them on your screen.

5 Make sure that the CMYK.psd image is the active window; then choose Image > Mode > CMYK Color.

When you choose the CMYK mode, the image now consists of four channels (cyan, magenta, yellow, and black). You'll notice a difference between the colors in the RGB image and the CMYK image. This is natural when converting RGB colors to CMYK colors, because they have different gamuts.

You have successfully completed the process of preparing a file for color separation and printing.

Strategies for successful printing

The rest of this lesson provides tips and techniques to help you successfully print your images.

Working in RGB mode

One strategy for creating color separations is to work in RGB mode, set the CMYK Setup options to compensate for conditions on-press, and then convert the image to CMYK mode. During the conversion, Adobe Photoshop applies the CMYK Setup settings to the image, which alters the pixel values in the image to compensate for the separation preferences.

Working in RGB mode is faster than working in CMYK mode because RGB files are smaller. In addition, some filters and options are available only for RGB images.

Working in CMYK mode

Another strategy for creating color separations is to work in CMYK mode. You can print a color proof to check colors in the image. If you used an ICC printer profile to specify the settings in the CMYK Setup dialog box and the color proof doesn't match the on-screen preview, you can verify that the printer is calibrated correctly or adjust the image and reprint color proofs until the proof looks the way you want.

For information on making color adjustments to an image, see "Making Color and Tonal Adjustments" in online Help or Chapter 6 in the Adobe Photoshop User Guide.

Note: Keep in mind that even though you may have calibrated your system to create a close match between the on-screen and printed colors, you are still displaying CMYK data on an RGB monitor, and slight discrepancies in color may occur.

When you work in CMYK mode, the CMYK Setup settings affect the way the image is displayed on the monitor. But because you are not converting this CMYK data to RGB mode, any changes affect only the on-screen image—the actual pixel values are not altered. For example, if the ICC profile you chose in the CMYK Setup dialog box specifies an expected dot gain of 30% while your image is in CMYK mode, the image becomes darker on-screen to approximate the dot gain, but the actual pixel values in the image are not changed. (In contrast, setting separation options on the same file while in RGB mode and then converting to CMYK mode *will* affect the actual pixel values in the image.)

Displaying individual channels

Each channel in an image provides information about that image's color values. RGB images are composed of three channels: one each for red, green, and blue. CMYK images are composed of four channels: one each for cyan, magenta, yellow, and black. You can view the individual channels in an image using the Channels palette.

By default, the individual channels are shown in grayscale, to more clearly show the intensity of the RGB phosphors or CMYK inks for that channel. Only the composite image is shown in color. You'll change this temporarily so that you can get an idea of how colo in the individual channels blend together to make the final range of colors in the composite channel.

1 Choose File > Preferences > Display & Cursors.

2 In the Display section of the dialog box, select Color Channels in Color; then click OK.

3 Make the Start13.psd window the active window; then choose Window > Show Channels to display the Channels palette.

Notice that the colors in the RGB image are distributed in the red, green, and blue channels (the composite channel at the top of the palette shows the combined channels).

RGB image and channels

For a color illustration of the RGB channels, see figure 13-1 in the color signature.

4 In the Channels palette, click in the far left column of one or more of the individual channels (red, green, or blue) to display and hide the channels and see how they blend to create the composite image.

5 Click the RGB composite channel at the top of the Channels palette to return to the composite view.

6 Now click the CMYK.psd window to make it active.

The Channels palette now shows the distribution of the colors in the image in the cyan, magenta, yellow, and black channels. The color in each channel represents the percentage of ink used on each of the printing plates.

CMYK image and channels

For a color illustration of the CMYK image and channels, see figure 13-2 in the color signature.

7 To see how each plate contributes to the overall color of the final image, click in the far left column for each of the four process colors in the Channels palette.

Although viewing the individual channels in color is helpful for seeing how the channels blend to make up a range of colors in the image, relying on these color channel previews can be misleading for making color or tonal corrections to the image. For example, yellow in the CMYK image shows up lighter on a monitor than it does in print. So now you'll return the channel previews to grayscale.

8 Choose File > Preferences > Display and Cursors.

9 Deselect Color Channels in Color; then click OK.

10 Close the Start13.psd file and the CMYK.psd file without saving your changes.

Identifying out-of-gamut colors

Most scanned photographs contain RGB colors within the CMYK gamut, and changing the image to CMYK mode converts all the colors with relatively little substitution. Images that are created or altered digitally, however, often contain RGB colors that are outside the CMYK gamut—for example, neon-colored logos and lights.

Note: Out-of-gamut colors are identified by an exclamation point next to the color swatch in the Colors palette, the Color Picker, and the Info palette.

Before you convert an image from RGB mode to CMYK mode, you can preview the CMYK color values while still in RGB mode.

1 Choose File > Open. Locate and open the Lesson13 folder, then select Start13.psd and click Open.

2 Choose Image > Duplicate, enter the name **CMYK.psd**, and click OK to duplicate the image.

3 Align the images side by side.

4 With the CMYK.psd window active, choose View >Preview > CMYK.

Notice the difference in the two images, particularly in the intensity of the blue areas of the image. At this point, the CMYK.psd image is still in RGB mode, and is just a preview of what it would look like in CMYK mode.

5 With the CMYK.psd window still active, Choose View > Preview > CMYK again to turn off the CMYK preview.

Note: If you plan to continue editing an RGB image, turn off the CMYK preview to improve system performance.

Next, you'll identify the out-of-gamut colors in the image.

6 Choose View > Gamut Warning. Adobe Photoshop builds a color conversion table and displays a neutral gray where the colors are out-of-gamut.

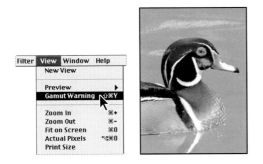

Note: You can change the gamut warning color to distinguish it from the colors in the image by choosing File > Preferences > Transparency & Gamut and then selecting a new color from the Color Picker.

7 To bring the colors into the CMYK color gamut, choose Image > Mode > CMYK Color.

The gamut warning color is removed and the out-of-gamut RGB colors are converted to the CMYK gamut (using the Separation Setup and Printing Inks settings you entered.)

Note: You can also adjust the gamut using Photoshop's color-correction tools, such as the Curves command.

For more information, see "Making Color and Tonal Adjustments" in online Help or Chapter 6 in the Adobe Photoshop User Guide.

8 Choose File > Save to save the CMYK.psd image.

9 Keep both images open on your screen.

Previewing a printed image

Because of the discrepancy between the display resolution and the image resolution, the size of an image on-screen may not accurately represent its printed size. You can preview the print size of a printed image using the Print Size command.

With the image CMYK.psd still active, choose View > Print Size. The image appears in its printed size.

Important: In Adobe Photoshop, images always print from the center of the page. You cannot change the position of the image on the page to print it in a different location unless you export the file to a page- layout program.

Selecting print options

To select printing options, you make choices in the File Info and Page Setup dialog boxes, and then choose Options from the Print dialog box. The next few sections introduce you to some of the printing options.

For information on all the print options, see "Printing" in online Help or Chapter 15 in the Adobe Photoshop User Guide.

Entering file information

Photoshop supports the information standard developed by the Newspaper Association of America and the International Press Telecommunications Council to identify trans-mitted text and images.

In Windows, you can add file information to files saved in Photoshop, TIFF, and JPEG formats. In Mac OS, you can add file information to files saved in any format.

1 Choose File > File Info.

2 In the File Info dialog box, type a description of the file in the Caption text box.

Note: To print a caption when you print an image, choose File > Page Setup and click the Caption option.

3 Enter your name in the Caption Writer text box.

4 Enter any special instructions you may have for printing the image in the Special Instructions text box.

5 For Section, choose Origin. In the origin section, enter information that you or others can refer to later, including an address, date, and other data.

6 Click the Today button to enter today's date in the date box.

Other types of file information you can record include the following:

• Keywords for use with image browser applications

• Categories for use with the Associated Press regional registry

• Credits for copyrighted images

7 Click OK to attach the information to the file.

For complete information about all the File Info sections, see "Saving and Exporting Images" in online Help or Chapter 14 in the Adobe Photoshop User Guide.

Specifying settings for different image types

The type of image you're printing, and the type of output you want, determine the selections you make in the Page Setup and Print dialog boxes.

The Page Setup dialog box lets you set up print labels, crop marks, calibration bars, registration marks, and negatives. You can also print emulsion-side down, and use interpolation (for PostScript Level 2 printers).

Printing

When you're ready to print your image, use the following guidelines for best results:

• Set the parameters for the halftone screen.

• Print a *color composite*, often called a color *comp*. A color composite is a single print that combines the red, green, and blue channels of an RGB image (or the cyan, magenta, yellow, and black channels of a CMYK image). This indicates what the final printed image will look like.

• Print separations to make sure the image separates correctly.

• Print to film.

Printing a halftone

To specify the halftone screen when you print an image, you use the Halftone Screen option in the Page Setup dialog box. The results of using a halftone screen appear only in the printed copy; you cannot see the halftone screen on-screen.

You use one halftone screen to print a grayscale image. You use four halftone screens (one for each process color) to print color separations. In this example, you'll be adjusting the screen frequency and dot shape to produce a halftone screen for a grayscale image.

The *screen frequency* controls the density of dots on the screen. Since the dots are arranged in lines on the screen, the common measurement for screen frequency is lines per inch (lpi). The higher the screen frequency, the finer the image produced (depending on the line screen capability of the printer). Magazines, for example, tend to use fine screens of 133 lpi and higher because they are usually printed on coated paper stock on high-quality presses. Newspapers, which are usually printed on lower-quality paper stock, tend to use lower screen frequencies, such as 85-lpi screens.

The *screen angle* used to create halftones of grayscale images is generally 45°. For best results with color separations, select the Auto option in the Halftone Screens dialog box (choose Page Setup > Screens > Halftone Screens). You can also specify an angle for each of the color screens. Setting the screens at different angles ensures that the dots placed by the four screens blend to look like continuous color and do not produce moiré patterns.

Diamond-shaped dots are most commonly used in halftone screens. In Adobe Photoshop, however, you can also choose round, elliptical, linear, square, and cross-shaped dots.

1 Make sure the Start13.psd file is open on your desktop.

2 Select Start13.psd to make it the active window.

3 Choose Image > Mode > Grayscale; then click OK to discard the color information.

4 Choose File > Page Setup and choose Adobe Photoshop 5.0.

5 Click Screen.

6 In the Halftone Screen dialog box, deselect the Use Printer's Default Screen checkbox to enter another number.

7 For Frequency, enter **133** in the Frequency text box, and make sure that the unit of measurement is set to lines/inch.

8 Leave the screen angle at the default setting of 45°.

9 For Shape, choose Ellipse.

10 Click OK, and click OK again in the Page Setup dialog box.

11 To print the image, choose File > Print. (If you don't have a printer, skip this step.)

12 Look at the printed output to see the shape of the halftone dots (in this case, Ellipse).

13 Choose File > Close, and do not save changes.

🔲 For more information about printing halftones, see "Printing" in online help, Chapter 15 in the Adobe Photoshop User Guide, or talk with your print service bureau.

Converting the color space of images while printing

Photoshop has several color management features to help you print a composite image on a printer.

To convert the color space of an image while printing:

1. Choose File > Print.

2. In Mac OS, choose Adobe Photoshop 5.0 from the dialog box menu.

3. For Space, choose a color space profile:

•Grayscale, RGB Color, CMYK Color, or Lab Color to have Photoshop convert the image to the specified color mode before the file data is sent to the printer. If you choose a profile other than the image's current mode, Photoshop uses the conversion settings you specify in the Color Settings dialog boxes.

•Any other option (except Separations) to match the file data to the color space of the specified profile or output device.

4. Select Printer Color Management to instruct the printer to convert the file data to the printer's color space; for PostScript printers, the option changes to PostScript Color Management. Select this option only if you are printing to an RGB-based printer or if you have not already converted the file to the printer's color space.

Only PostScript Level 3 printers support PostScript Color Management for images using CMYK color space. To print a CMYK image using PostScript Color Management on a Level 2 printer, go back to step 2 and choose Lab Color.

–From the Adobe Photoshop User Guide, Chapter 15

Printing separations

By default, a CMYK image prints as a single document. To print the file as four separations, you need to select the Separations option in the Print dialog box. Otherwise, the CMYK image prints as a single, composite image.

In this optional part of the lesson, you can print the file.

1 If the file CMYK.psd is not still open, choose File > Open. In the Lesson13 folder, select CMYK.psd and click Open.

2 Choose File > Print.

3 Do one of the following:

• In Windows, for Space, choose Separations (at the bottom of the dialog box).

• In Mac OS, choose Adobe Photoshop® 5.0. For Space, choose Separations.

4 Click Print. (If you don't have a printer, skip this step.)

5 Choose File > Close, and do not save changes.

This completes your introduction to producing color separations and printing using Adobe Photoshop.

For information about all of the color management and printing options, see "Reproducing Color Accurately" and "Printing" in online Help, or chapters 5 and 15 in the Adobe Photoshop User Guide.

Review questions

1 What steps should you follow to reproduce color accurately?

2 What is a gamut?

3 What is an ICC profile?

4 What is a color separation? How does a CMYK image differ from an RGB image?

5 What steps should you follow when preparing an image for print?

Review answers

1 Calibrate your monitor, and then specify the RGB and CMYK color spaces if you will be working with these types of images. If you will be working with grayscale images, enter settings for the Grayscale Setup dialog box as well.

2 The range of colors that can be reproduced by a color model. For example, the RGB and CMYK color models have different gamuts.

3 An ICC profile is a description of a device's color space, such as the CMYK color space of a particular printer. Applications such as Photoshop can interpret ICC profiles in an image to maintain consistent color across different applications, platforms, and devices.

4 A color separation is created when an image is converted to CMYK mode. The colors in the CMYK image are separated in the four process color channels: cyan, magenta, yellow, and black. An RGB image has three color channels: red, green, and blue.

5 You prepare an image for print by following the steps for reproducing color accurately, and then you convert the image from RGB mode to CMYK mode to build a color separation.

ImageReady Tour

Adobe ImageReady 1.0

Adobe ImageReady software simplifies many of the tasks of preparing graphics for the World Wide Web. It's the perfect complement to Adobe Photoshop and Adobe Illustrator. With ImageReady you can do the following:

• Save files in common Web formats.

• Interactively optimize them for quick downloads.

• Preview and fix problems caused by browser dither or platform screen gamma differences.

• Use the power of layers to create Web animations.

• Automate and batch process graphics for your Web pages.

The tutorials in this section of the book will introduce you to this powerful software from Adobe Systems.

A Quick Tour of Adobe ImageReady

This interactive tour of Adobe ImageReady, excerpted from the Adobe ImageReady User Guide, provides an overview of key features of the program. More detailed instructions on how to use the features in this tour are provided in the individual lessons that follow.

Optimizing images for the Web

You work in ImageReady interactively—trying various image quality settings and evaluating the resulting images and file sizes. You see the trade-off in image quality as you make adjustments, so you can quickly choose the appropriate settings for your needs.

ImageReady can optimize files for the Web in common file formats: GIF, JPEG, PNG-8, and PNG-24. The format you choose for an image depends on the type of image: Full-color photographs generally yield the best results when saved as JPEG files. JPEG and PNG-24 compression can preserve the broad color and tonal range in photographic images better than other compression formats can, and JPEG files will generally be smaller than PNG-24 files.

GIF and PNG are usually the best file formats for illustrations with areas of solid color. GIF and PNG formats compress files by reducing repetitive areas, such as large areas of solid color. The more repetition in an image, the more the image can be compressed.

Saving a photograph as a JPEG

You'll begin the tour by optimizing a photographic image as a JPEG and comparing the results of various file settings.

1 Start ImageReady.

You work in ImageReady by opening an original image, then making changes to the image, setting compression options, and viewing the optimized image, with compression and color settings applied.

You choose file format and compression settings in the Optimize palette. By default, the Optimize palette appears in the upper-right side of your screen.

2 Choose File > Open, and select the Hammer.psd file from the IRTour folder.

3 If the Optimize palette is not showing, choose Window > Show Optimize.

4 In the Optimize palette, choose JPEG from the file format pop-up menu, and then choose Maximum from the Quality pop-up menu.

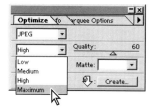

At the top of the image window, notice the tabs for Original and Optimized. The tabs let you toggle between the original and optimized images, making it easy for you to compare image quality and refine the optimized image.

5 In the image window, click the Optimized tab to view the optimized image. ImageReady takes a moment to generate an optimized image based on the settings.

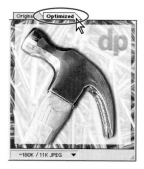

6 Toggle between the original and optimized images. With the Maximum quality setting selected in step 4, you probably won't see much difference in image quality between your original and the JPEG. However, the file size is significantly decreased in the optimized image.

7 At the bottom of the image window, make sure that Original/Optimized File Size is selected in the Image Info pop-up menu. The number on the left is the original file size, and the number on the right is the optimized file size.

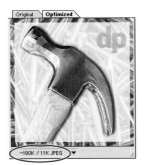

Optimized file size

You'll try another quality setting and check the Optimized file size again shortly, but first you'll create a duplicate of the Optimized image on your screen.

8 Press Alt (Windows) or Option (Mac OS), and drag the Optimized tab from the image window to create a duplicate.

ImageReady generates a duplicate of the Optimized image, named Hammer.psd copy. You can position the duplicate image window so you can see both the original and duplicate image windows, and use the duplicate as a reference while you try other settings in the Optimize palette.

9 In the Hammer.psd image window, select the Optimized tab.

10 In the Optimize palette, drag the Quality slider to 10 to create a smaller (more compressed) JPEG file of the optimized image.

ImageReady regenerates the optimized image.

11 Click in the Hammer.psd copy image window, and select the Optimized tab. ImageReady generates the optimized image.

12 Select View > Zoom In in the Hammer.psd Optimized image window and in the Hammer.psd copy Optimized image window. Repeat if necessary until you can clearly see a difference between the two images.

13 Compare the quality and file size of the Hammer.psd and Hammer.psd copy images. Also compare the two optimized images to the original Hammer.psd image.

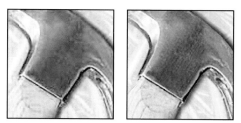

Image size 6.7K and 11K

14 Double-click the zoom tool in the toolbox to return the view to actual size in both image windows.

15 With the Hammer.psd Optimized image window active, choose File > Close, and close the image without saving.

16 With the Hammer.psd copy Optimized image window active, choose File > Save Optimized As, and name the optimized image file Hammer2.jpg. (ImageReady adds the extension specified by the Optimize palette, in this case .jpg.)

Note: Be sure not to delete the filename extension when saving optimized images. The extension is needed by browsers and other applications to identify the file format.

17 Close Hammer.psd copy without saving it by clicking the close box in the upper left corner of the image window, or by choosing File > Close.

18 Choose File > Close to close the file.

Now you're ready to optimize an illustration.

Saving an illustration as a GIF

In this lesson you'll optimize a flat-color illustration as a GIF and compare different color settings for the file.

1 Choose File > Open, and select Logo.psd from the IRTour folder.

2 In the Optimize palette, choose GIF from the file format pop-up menu and Web from the color palette menu.

Options in the Optimize palette change depending on the file format you choose.

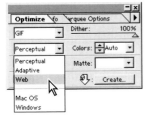

The Web palette consists of the 216 colors common to the Windows and Macintosh system palettes.

3 At the top of the image window, click the Optimized tab. ImageReady takes a moment to generate the optimized image.

The Optimized Colors palette displays the colors included in the GIF, based on the color palette you choose for the optimized image.

4 If the Optimized Colors palette is not visible, choose Window > Show Optimized Colors.

You can see the Web palette colors that are used in this image in the Optimized Colors palette. Notice at the bottom of the color table that not all 216 Web colors are showing. ImageReady drops colors from the palette that are not used in the image. You can also selectively reduce the number of colors in an image, as you'll do later in this lesson.

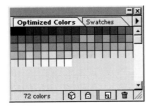

5 Select the zoom tool ($\mathbb{Q}$) and click on the gradient in the image.

Look at the gradient parts of the optimized image. Notice how the gradient has separated into bands of color. At the top of the image window, click the Original tab and then the Optimized tab to toggle between the original and optimized images and better see the image degradation in the gradient.

6 Double-click the zoom tool in the toolbox to return the view to actual size.

Now try the image's adaptive palette.

7 Make sure that the Optimized image is visible. In the Optimize palette, choose Adaptive from the color palette pop-up menu.

ImageReady regenerates the optimized image and loads the image's adaptive palette into the color table.

8 Select the zoom tool (🔍) and click in the image to magnify the view.

9 Check the gradient in this image, and toggle between the optimized and original images. The gradient should look better with the adaptive palette than with the Web palette. The Adaptive palette creates a custom palette based on the colors that occur most frequently in the image and can represent small gradations in color better than the Web palette can.

Image optimized with Web palette; and with
Adaptive palette

Most designers create images for the Web using 24-bit color, or millions of colors. When those images are viewed in a Web browser on an 8-bit color system (256 colors), the browser uses *dithering* to simulate the colors not in the palette. The Browser Dither feature allows you to preview how the image will be dithered by a browser using 8-bit color.

10 Double-click the zoom tool to return the view to actual size.

11 With the optimized image displayed, choose View > Browser Dither.

12 Look at the dither pattern on the text in the logo.

Image displayed with 24-bit color with no dithering; and with 8-bit color, simulating browser dither

Dithering often creates an acceptable simulation of colors, but in this image, the dithering in the text is too conspicuous. In ImageReady, you can prevent selected colors from dithering in a browser by shifting the colors to the nearest colors in the Web palette.

13 Click the Original image tab to view the original image. Then select the eyedropper tool (✐), and click on the text to select the green color.

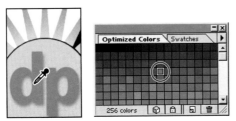

Selecting color in Original image; and color selected in Optimized Colors palette

The color is selected in the Optimized Colors palette, indicated by a white border around the color swatch. You may have to scroll down in the Optimized Colors palette to see the selected color.

14 Click the Web Shift button (◉) in the Optimized Colors palette.

A small diamond appears in the center of the selected color, indicating that the color has been Web-shifted.

15 At the top of the image window, select the Optimized tab.

Note that the text is no longer dithered.

16 Choose View > Browser Dither to turn off the browser dither preview and continue editing the image.

You can reduce the number of colors in a GIF to further reduce file size. When you reduce the number of colors, ImageReady eliminates the least-used colors in the image.

17 Make sure that Original/Optimized File Size is selected in one of the Image Info pop-up menus at the bottom of the image window. Then check the optimized image's file size.

18 Choose 64 from the Colors menu in the Optimize palette.

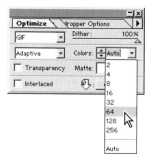

19 Check the optimized image's file size in the Image Info pop-up menu again.

20 Try other color settings until you find one that yields an acceptable image with the fewest number of colors.

Once you've created the optimized image in ImageReady, you can easily preview the image in a Web browser.

21 Choose File > Preview In, and choose a browser from the submenu. When you install ImageReady, all browsers on your system are added to the Preview In submenu.

You can add other browsers to the submenu after ImageReady is installed, by placing a shortcut (Windows) or an alias (Mac OS) for the browser in the Preview In folder in the Helpers folder, located in the ImageReady application folder.

ImageReady launches your browser if it is not running, and displays the image, with information about the image's Optimize palette settings, size, and HTML tag.

22 Return to ImageReady.

Now you are ready to save the optimized image as a GIF file.

23 In ImageReady, choose File > Save Optimized As, and name the file **Logo2.gif**. (ImageReady adds the .gif extension.) Click Save to save the file.

Keep the Logo.psd file open. You'll use it for the next lesson.

Automating image optimization

You can streamline the image optimization process by saving Optimize palette settings and automatically applying the settings to single images or batches of images. To automate Optimize palette settings, you create a *droplet*, a small application that you can save and use repeatedly.

Now you'll create a droplet from the Optimize palette settings used to create the GIF in the previous section.

1 Click the Create button in the Optimize palette.

2 Use the default name for the droplet. Save the droplet to the desktop, and click Save.

Note: You can also create a droplet by dragging the script icon ($) to the desktop or a folder. In this case ImageReady names the droplet with a brief summary of the Optimize palette settings. You can rename the droplet as you would any desktop icon.

You can view a detailed list of a droplet's settings in the droplet window.

3 Navigate to the droplet on the desktop and double-click the droplet icon to launch it.

4 In the droplet window, click the triangle next to Save as GIF89a to view the list of the Optimize palette settings saved with the droplet.

5 Close the droplet window without saving it.

Now you'll use the droplet to compress and save a batch of images.

6 Locate the Batch folder in the IRTour folder and open the folder to view its contents. The folder should contain the files Button1.psd, Button2.psd, Button3.psd, and Button4.psd.

7 Drag the Batch folder onto the droplet icon.

Progress bars in the Batch Progress dialog box indicate that the files in the Batch folder are being compressed and saved.

8 Open the Batch folder again to view its contents. The folder now contains Button1.gif, Button2.gif, Button3.gif, and Button4.gif, the GIF files created by the droplet.

9 Open the four new GIF files to view the optimized images, and close the files when you have finished.

You can save droplets on your desktop or in a folder for future use. If you drag a file or files onto a droplet when ImageReady is not running, the droplet launches ImageReady and applies the droplet settings to the files.

Note: You cannot activate a droplet by dragging the droplet icon onto a file or folder.

10 Choose File > Close to close the Logo.psd file.

Creating an animated GIF file

It's easy to create animated GIFs using ImageReady. An animated GIF is a sequence of images, or frames. Each frame differs slightly from the preceding frame, creating the illusion of movement when the frames are viewed in quick succession.

You start with a single image and create a sequence of animation frames, applying changes to frames to create the appearance of movement in the animation file. When you save the file, ImageReady places all the frames in a single GIF file.

Beginning a new animation

1 Choose File > Open, and select LogoAnim.psd from the IRTour folder.

You'll create the animation frames while in Original image mode. When the frames are complete, you'll set GIF compression options to complete the animated GIF.

2 Choose Window > Show Animation if the Animation palette is not visible.

The Animation palette displays a a thumbnail of a single frame containing the LogoAnim.psd image. You can choose from three sizes for the thumbnail.

3 In the Animation palette menu, choose Thumbnail Size.

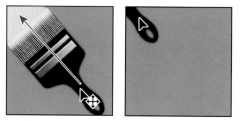

4 In the Thumbnail Size (Animation) dialog box, select the mid-sized thumbnail option. Then click OK.

5 Choose Window > Show Layers if the Layers palette is not visible.

The Layers palette displays the layers contained in the current frame. Each layer is a separate element, equivalent to an animation cel. You apply changes to the layers in each frame to create animation effects.

Tweening frames to adjust layer position

You use *tweening* to quickly create a series of frames that vary in layer opacity or position, to create animation effects such as fading in or out, or moving an element across a frame.

In this section you'll adjust the position of a selected layer and use the Tween command to create new frames.

1 Select the Paintbrush layer in the Layers palette.

2 Select the move tool (⊹) in the toolbox. Then, in the image window, move the paintbrush up and to the left, so only the brush handle shows in the upper left corner of the image.

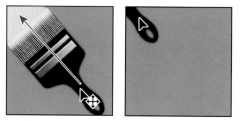

Moving paintbrush to upper left corner with move tool

3 Click the New Frame icon (⊡) in the Animation palette.

4 Select the move tool, and move the paintbrush down and to the right in the image window, so that only the paint swath shows in the image.

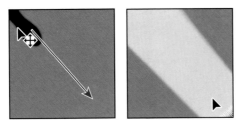

Moving paintbrush to lower right corner with move tool

5 Select Tween from the Animation palette options menu.

6 In the Tween dialog box, type **3** in the Frames to Add text box. Choose Previous Frame from the Tween With pop-up menu. Select Position, if it is not selected, and deselect Opacity. Then click OK.

ImageReady generates three new frames between the first and last frames, with the Paintbrush layer moving successively farther down and to the right in each frame.

Now you're ready to preview the animation in ImageReady.

7 Click the Play button (▷) in the Animation palette.

8 When you have finished viewing the animation, click the Stop button (☐).

Tweening frames to adjust layer opacity

In this section, you'll adjust the opacity of a selected layer and use the Tween command to create new frames.

1 Click the last frame in the animation to select it, if it is not already selected. (A black border around the frame indicates that it is selected.)

2 Click the New Frame button (🖬) in the Animation palette.

3 In the Layers palette, click in the column to the far left of the Logo layer. An eye icon (👁) appears in the column.

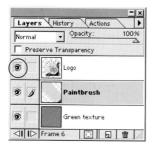

You click in the eye column to hide or show a layer. The eye icon indicates that the layer is visible in the image.

4 Click the Logo layer to select it. The layer is highlighted when selected, and a brush icon (✏) appears to the left of the layer, indicating that you can edit the layer.

5 Move the Opacity slider to 1% opacity. (1% is the lowest value for opacity, and creates a transparent layer.)

6 In the Animation palette, click the New Frame button.

7 In the layers palette, move the Opacity slider to 100%. The Logo layer appears in the new frame in the Animation palette.

8 Select Tween from the Animation palette options menu.

9 In the Tween dialog box, choose Previous Frame from the Tween with pop-up menu. (The dialog box still displays 3 in the Frames to Add text box.) Select Opacity, if it is not selected, and deselect Position. Then click OK.

ImageReady generates three new frames between the last frame and the previous frame, with the Logo layer increasing in opacity from 1% to 100%.

You'll preview the animation in a moment.

Setting delay and saving an animation

You can specify delay time for individual frames or for the entire animation. By default, all frames are set to a delay time of 0 seconds.

1 In the Animation palette menu, choose Set Delay For All Frames.

2 Enter **.15** in the Seconds text box. Then click OK.

3 Click the Play button (▷) to view the animation again with the new delay time. When you are finished viewing, click the Stop button (□).

4 In the Optimized palette, select GIF from the file format menu and Adaptive from the color palette menu.

5 Click the Optimize tab at the top of the image window.

ImageReady takes a moment to render the optimized image with the compression settings.

6 Click on a few frames in the Animation palette to view the frames with the compression settings, and note the Optimized image file size at the bottom of the image window. (The Optimized file size is for the entire animated GIF, not for individual frames.)

As when optimizing a photograph or illustration, you can preview optimization settings with an animated GIF and adjust settings to achieve the desired image quality and file size.

You can reduce the number of colors in the image to reduce the file size.

7 In the Optimize palette, choose 64 from the Colors menu.

ImageReady takes a moment to regenerate the optimized image.

8 Click on a few frames in the Animation palette to view the frames with the new number of colors, and note the reduced Optimized file size in the Image Info menu.

9 Choose File > Save Optimized As. Name the file **LogoAnim2.gif**. (ImageReady adds the extension .gif.)

You can also preview the animation in a browser.

10 Choose Preview In, and select a browser from the submenu.

The animation is displayed in your Web browser.

11 Return to ImageReady.

12 Close the LogoAnim.psd file without saving it.

Adding text to an image

With ImageReady you can add horizontal or vertical type to an image, and specify the font, style, color, tracking, leading, kerning, and alignment.

You add type to an image using the horizontal or vertical type tool. Once you have created type, you can return to the type to edit its contents, attributes, and orientation.

You'll add type to the file Order.psd to create an order button and adjust the style and formatting of the type.

1 Choose File > Open, and select the Order.psd file in the IRTour folder.

2 Select the horizontal type tool (**T**) in the toolbox. The pointer changes to an I-beam.

3 Click in the image to set an insertion point for the type.

Clicking in the image displays the Type Tool dialog box, where you enter type and select type attributes.

4 Choose a font from the Font menu.

5 Choose a point size from the type size menu. We used 42.

6 Select the center alignment option (≡) to center-align the text.

7 Choose Other from the Color pop-up menu, or just click the color swatch.

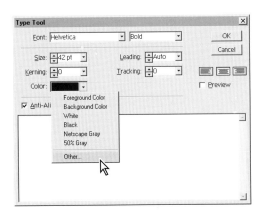

8 Choose a color for the type from the color picker. Then click OK.

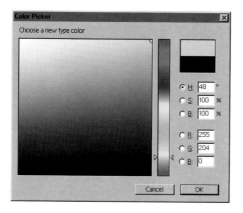

9 In the text area of the Type Tool dialog box, type "ORDER NOW" on two lines. To preview type attributes in the image, make sure Preview is selected in the Type Tool dialog box. Then click OK.

When you add type to an image, ImageReady creates a new layer to contain the type. You can transform type layers using the Transform commands in the Edit menu. You can continue to edit type after transforming the type layer, until the type layer has been flattened or merged with another layer.

10 Choose Window > Show Layers if the Layers palette is not visible, and make sure the type layer is selected in the Layers palette.

11 Select the move tool (▸₊) in the toolbox. Position the move tool over the text, and drag the text to be centered on top of the button.

Dragging text onto button with move tool

12 Choose Edit > Transform > Rotate.

A bounding box with handles appears around the text.

13 Position the cursor outside the bounding box, and rotate the text layer approximately 45° counterclockwise. Then press Enter (Windows) or Return (Mac OS).

Rotating text with Rotate command.

14 Choose Window > Show Type to view the Type palette if it's not already visible.

The Type palette provides a second way, in addition to the Type Tool dialog box, to set type attributes.

15 Select a new font from the Font pop-up menu, and a new size from the type size menu, if necessary.

16 Choose File > Close, and click Yes (Windows) or Save (Mac OS) to save and close the file.

Automating a series of tasks

ImageReady provides two ways of automating tasks. Earlier in the tour, in the section "Automating image optimization," you used a droplet to automate Optimize palette settings.

You can also automate a series of steps and commands by adding them as *actions* in the Actions palette, and then applying those actions to a single image or a batch of images. Actions can include a combination of steps such as adjusting, editing, compressing, and saving. You can create a droplet from the Actions palette, just as you can from the Optimize palette, to save the actions for later use.

Now you'll edit an image and create actions based on the editing steps, to apply to a batch of images.

Using the History palette to create actions

As you work in ImageReady, changes you make to an image are recorded as steps in the History palette. One way to automate tasks in ImageReady is to copy steps from the History palette to the Actions palette. (You can also use the History palette to undo changes applied to an image.)

[?] For more information on the History palette and reverting to previous states of an image, see "Reverting to any stage of the image" on page 131 in the Adobe ImageReady User Guide, or in online Help.

Now you'll display the History palette, so you can view steps as they are recorded in the palette while you work. By default, the Actions palette, History palette, and Layers palette are grouped in one palette.

Click the History palette tab to view the History palette. (If you cannot see the History palette tab, choose Window > Show History.)

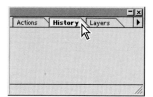

Editing the original image

First you'll open an image and make some adjustments to create a color effect. The changes you make to the original image are recorded in the History palette, and can be used to create actions in the Actions palette.

1 Choose File > Open, and select the Nuts.psd file from the IRTour folder.

2 Choose Image > Adjust > Auto Contrast.

Notice that the Auto Contrast command is recorded in the History palette.

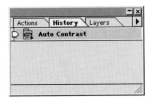

3 Choose Image > Image Size.

4 Make sure Constrain Proportions is selected. Then enter **50** in the Percent text box, and click OK.

Note that the Resize Image command is recorded in the History palette.

5 Choose Filter > Sharpen > Unsharp Mask.

6 Enter **75** in the Amount text box, or use the slider to set Amount to 75%. Make sure Radius is set to 1.0 and Threshold to 0 (the default values). Then click OK.

7 Choose Image > Adjust > Hue/Saturation.

8 Select Colorize.

9 Enter **45** in the Hue text box and **40** in the Saturation text box, or use the sliders to set the values. Then click OK.

Note that the Unsharp Mask and Hue/Sat Adjustment commands now appear in the History palette.

Creating actions in the Actions palette

Now you're ready to display the Actions palette and copy steps from the History palette to the Actions palette.

1 Click the Actions palette tab to view the Actions palette. (If you cannot see the Actions palette tab, choose Window > Show Actions.)

2 Drag the Actions palette tab onto the desktop to create a new location for the palette.

Separating palettes

3 Choose New Action from the Actions palette menu.

4 Name the action **Edit**. Then click Record.

5 Drag each of the four items in the History palette onto the last step of the Edit action in the Actions palette, to add the items to the end of the Edit action. (The items must appear in the same order in which they were originally performed on the Nuts.psd image.)

The items from the History palette become steps in the Edit action.

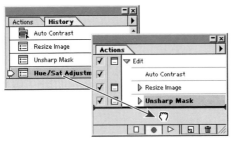

Items recorded in History palette; and moved to
Actions palette

6 Click the Stop button (□) to stop recording.

7 Close Nuts.psd without saving it by clicking the close box in the upper left corner of the image window, or by choosing File > Close.

Notice that the History palette is cleared. Items in the History palette are deleted when you close an image file, or when you open another image file without closing the first file.

8 Click the *modal control* icon (▭) to the left of the Edit action in the Actions palette. The modal control icons in the action disappear, indicating that modal controls are turned off.

Modal controls allow you to turn on or off controls for commands in actions. When modal controls are turned on, ImageReady pauses when playing back actions to allow you to specify different values in dialog boxes for each image you process. When modal controls are turned off, ImageReady plays back actions using the values specified when you recorded the action. This enables you to batch-process images without attending to each image individually.

Adding Optimize palette settings to the Actions palette

Now you'll choose Optimize palette settings for the original image, and save the settings as an action in the Actions palette.

1 Open Nuts.psd again. In the Optimize palette, select JPEG from the file format menu, and select Medium from the Quality menu.

2 Drag the script icon ($) from the Optimize palette onto the last step of the Edit action in the Actions palette.

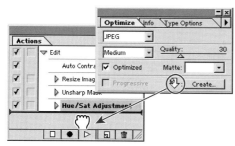

Script button in Optimize palette clicked to create droplet,
and dragged to Actions palette

Applying actions to a batch of images

Now you're ready to create a droplet from the actions, and apply the actions to a batch of images.

1 Click the Edit action in the Actions palette to select it.

2 Choose Create Droplet from the Actions palette menu.

3 Name the Actions droplet **Colorize**. Include the extension .exe (Windows only). Save the droplet to the desktop, and click Save.

Now you'll apply the Colorize droplet to a batch of images.

4 Open the IRTour folder and select the files Nuts.psd, Nails.psd, Screws.psd, and Washers.psd. Make sure the Actions droplet is visible. Then drag the four files onto the droplet. The droplet icon highlights when the droplet is activated.

The droplet performs the recorded actions. When the actions are completed, the compressed files appear in the IRTour folder as JPEG files.

5 Open the JPEG files to view them. Then choose File > Close to close each of the files.

Congratulations! You've completed the Adobe ImageReady tour. You're now ready to use ImageReady to create your own graphics for the World Wide Web or multimedia use.

See the Adobe ImageReady User Guide or online Help for detailed information on using the features in ImageReady.

Lesson 1

Optimizing Images for Web Publication

Adobe ImageReady lets you optimize the display and file size of your images for effective Web publishing results. In general, the file size of an image should be small enough to allow reasonable download times from a Web server, but large enough to represent desired colors and details in the image. You should also check and adjust how the image will display on different monitors and platforms.

In this lesson, you'll learn how to do the following:

• Optimize an image in GIF format and adjust the optimization settings to achieve the desired balance between file size and image quality.

• Adjust the amount of dithering applied to the image.

• Define a transparent background for the image.

• Create a hypertext image map and export the image as an HTML file.

Optimizing images with Adobe ImageReady

Adobe ImageReady gives you an effective range of controls for compressing the file size of an image while optimizing its online display quality. Compression options vary according to the file format used to save the image.

• The GIF format is effective at compressing solid-color images and images with areas of repetitive color (line art, logos, illustrations with type). This format uses a palette of up to 256 colors to represent the image, and supports background transparency.

• The JPEG format is designed to preserve the broad color range and subtle brightness variations of continuous-tone images (photographs, images with gradients). This format can represent images using millions of colors.

• The PNG format is effective at compressing solid-color images and provides sophisticated transparency support. The PNG-8 format uses a 256-color palette to represent an image; the PNG-24 format supports 24-bit color (millions of colors). However, many older browser applications do not support PNG files.

In this lesson, you'll learn how to optimize and save images in GIF format for distribution on the World Wide Web. You'll work with a set of images designed to be used on a fictitious Web site for Southwest travel.

Getting started

Before beginning this lesson, delete the Adobe ImageReady Preferences file to restore the program's default settings. For step-by-step instructions, see "Restoring default preferences" on page 4. Then restart the ImageReady program.

Optimizing a GIF image

In this part of the lesson, you'll optimize a flat-color image in GIF format and compare the results of different palette and dither settings.

Choosing optimization settings

The Optimize palette lets you specify the file format and compression settings for the optimized image. ImageReady updates the optimized image as you edit, letting you interactively preview the effects of different settings.

1 Choose File > Open. Locate and open the Less01IR folder, select Desert.psd, and then click Open.

This image was created by scanning a photograph into Adobe Photoshop, and then modifying the details to produce a hand-drawn appearance. Notice the many areas of solid color in the image.

2 In the Optimize palette, choose GIF from the file format pop-up menu.

The GIF format represents an image using a color palette, which can contain up to 256 colors. You choose the type of color palette based on the display needs of your image.

• The Perceptual palette gives priority to colors that appear most commonly in the image and are more sensitive to the human eye. This palette usually produces images with the greatest color integrity.

• The Adaptive palette samples colors from the portion of the RGB spectrum that appears most commonly in the image. For example, an image containing predominantly blue hues produces a palette consisting mostly of shades of blue.

• The Web palette consists of the 216 colors that are shared in common by the Windows and Macintosh system palettes. When displaying images, a browser application will use a 16-bit or 24-bit color table (thousands or millions of colors) if the monitor display is set to one of these modes; otherwise, the browser will use the default 8-bit system palette. While 8-bit monitors are uncommon for Web designers' systems, they are found on many Web users' systems.

• The Windows System or Macintosh System palette uses the system's default 8-bit (256-color) palette, which is based on a uniform sampling of RGB colors.

3 Choose Perceptual from the palette pop-up menu. (Perceptual is the default palette option.) In the image window, click the Optimized tab to view the optimized image. ImageReady takes a moment to build the optimized image.

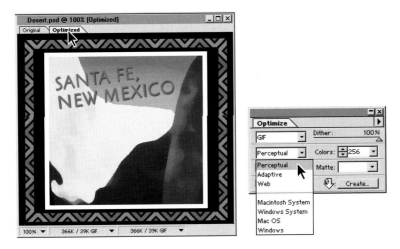

The bar at the bottom of the image window displays the view magnification and other useful file information about the original and optimized versions of the image. You can display two sets of file values simultaneously.

Look at the first file value box. The value on the left represents the file size of the original image; the value on the right represents the file size of the optimized image.

4 Position the pointer over the triangle in the second file value box, hold down the mouse, and choose Size/Download Time (28.8Kbps).

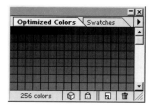

This option displays the projected download time of the optimized image using a 28.8Kbps modem.

5 If the Optimized Colors palette is not showing, choose Window > Show Optimized Colors.

This palette shows the colors that comprise the Perceptual palette for the desert image. The total number of colors appears at the bottom of the palette. You can resize the palette or use the scroll bar to view all the colors. You can also change how the colors are arranged in the palette.

6 Choose Sort By Hue from the Optimized Colors palette menu.

Now you'll observe how a different palette option affects the image.

7 In the Optimize palette, choose Web for the palette.

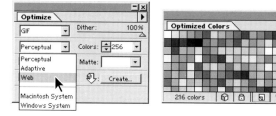

Notice the color changes in the image and in the Optimized Colors palette, which updates to reflect the Web palette.

Experiment with different palette options and notice the effects on the image and on the Optimized Colors palette.

> ### Prioritizing colors for an adaptive or perceptual palette
>
> *ImageReady allows you to give priority to selected colors in an image when generating an adaptive or perceptual palette. You make a selection to indicate important colors in an image. When you rebuild the color palette using the Rebuild Optimized Colors command, ImageReady assigns more colors in the palette to the selected colors. To prioritize colors, follow these steps:*
>
> *•Make a selection in the image using the selection tools or the Select menu commands.*
>
> *•Choose Rebuild Optimized Colors from the Optimized Colors palette menu.*
>
> –From the Adobe ImageReady User Guide, Chapter 4

Reducing the color palette

To compress the file size further, you can decrease the total number of colors included in the Optimized Colors palette. A reduced range of colors will often preserve good image quality while dramatically reducing the file space required to store extra colors.

1 In the Optimize palette, choose the Perceptual palette option.

2 Hold down Alt (Windows) or Option (Mac OS), and drag the Optimized tab out of the image window to create a duplicate of the optimized image.

The optimized desert image is duplicated as a new original image, Desert.psd copy. You'll experiment with reducing the color palette for this new image, comparing the results with the first 256-color image.

3 If needed, drag the bar at the top of the Desert.psd copy window until you can view both windows side by side. Then click the Optimized tab in the Desert.psd copy window to build the optimized image.

Before reducing the color palette, you'll lock the green color in the border pattern to ensure that the color does not drop from the reduced palette.

4 Select the eyedropper tool ( ), and click in the green area of the border to sample the color in that area.

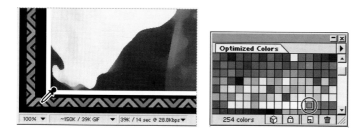

The green color appears highlighted, or selected, in the Optimized Colors palette.

5 Click the Lock button ( ) at the bottom of the Optimized Colors palette to lock the selected color. A small square appears in the lower right corner of the green color, indicating that the color is locked.

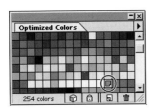

6 In the Optimize palette, for Colors, choose 128 to reduce the total number of colors by half. Notice that the locked color remains in the palette after the reduction.

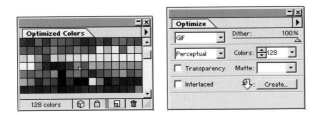

Compare the 128-color image with the first 256-color version. You'll notice that there isn't much difference in quality.

7 Experiment with reducing the color palette to different values and comparing the image results. Note that significant image degradation starts to occur when the palette is reduced to 32 colors.

For the best file compression of a GIF image, try to use the fewest number of colors that will still display the quality you need.

For an illustration of the image set to different palette values, see figure IR1-1 in the color signature.

8 When you have finished experimenting, set the colors to 32 in the Optimize palette.

9 Click the bar at the top of the Desert.psd window to make the image active. Then choose File > Close, and do not save changes.

If you have a browser application installed on your computer, you can view an online gallery of images optimized with different file format and palette settings. Start your browser application and open Gallery.htm in the Gallery folder inside the Less01IR folder. Close the file when you have finished viewing it, and return to Adobe ImageReady.

Controlling dither

You may have noticed that certain areas of the desert image appear mottled or spotty when optimized with different color palettes and numbers of colors. This spotty appearance results from *dithering,* the technique used to simulate the appearance of colors that are not included in the color palette. For example, a blue color and a yellow color may dither in a mosaic pattern to produce the illusion of a green color that does not appear in the color palette. ImageReady automatically determines the pattern used to dither colors.

Note: *To fine-tune and improve the appearance of dithered colors, you can create your own dither patterns using the Dither Box filter.*

For more information, see "Optimizing Images" in online Help or Chapter 4 in the Adobe ImageReady User Guide.

When optimizing images, keep in mind the two kinds of dithering that can occur:

• *Application dither* occurs when Adobe ImageReady attempts to simulate colors that appear in the original image but not in the optimized color palette you specify. You can control the amount of application dither by dragging the Dither slider in the Optimize palette.

• *Browser dither* occurs when a Web browser using an 8-bit (256-color) display simulates colors that appear in the optimized image's color palette but not in the system palette used by the browser. Browser dither can occur in addition to application dither. You can control the amount of browser dither by Web-shifting selected colors in the Optimized Colors palette.

In Adobe ImageReady you can view application dither directly in the optimized image window. You can also preview the additional browser dither that will appear in the final image when viewed in a browser using an 8-bit display.

Controlling application dither

The Dither slider lets you control the range of colors that ImageReady simulates by dithering. Dithering creates the appearance of more colors and detail, but can also increase the file size of the image. For optimal compression, use the lowest percentage of application dither that provides the color detail you require.

The Desert.psd copy image should be open. Make sure that the optimized image view is displayed, and that the Optimize palette is set to GIF format, Perceptual palette, and 32 colors.

1 If needed, in the Optimize palette, drag the Dither slider to 100%.

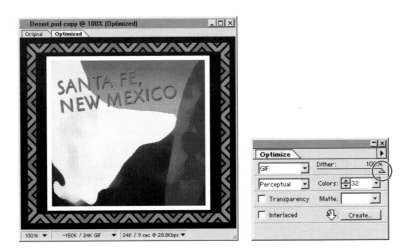

With 100% dither, ImageReady tries to simulate most of the colors and tonalities that appeared in the original image. Notice the speckled pattern that appears in the blue sky and along the red mountain as a result of the dithering.

2 Now drag the Dither slider to 0%.

ImageReady minimizes the amount of dither in the image, resulting in a coarser, banded appearance.

For an illustration of the effects of different dither percentages on the image, see figure IR1-2 in the color signature.

3 Experiment with different dither percentages, observing the effects on the image. When you are finished experimenting, set the dither to 75%.

4 Choose File > Save Optimized As. Name the file Desert1.gif, and click Save.

Previewing and minimizing browser dither

As you learned earlier, images undergo a process of dithering when displayed in a Web browser using an 8-bit display, as the browser simulates colors that do not occur in the 8-bit system palette. ImageReady lets you preview how an optimized image will look when dithered in a Web browser.

To protect a color from browser dither, you can Web-shift the color, converting the color to its nearest equivalent in the Web palette. Because the Web palette includes the subset of colors that appear both in the Windows and the Macintosh system palettes, Web palette colors will display without dithering in browsers on any platform.

1 With the optimized Desert.psd copy image open, choose View > Browser Dither. A check mark appears next to the command when it is toggled on, letting you preview the effects of browser dithering on the optimized image.

Notice that browser dither occurs throughout the image. If you don't see the dithering right away, turn off the browser dither preview and then turn it back on to observe the effects. You can quickly toggle the browser dither preview off and on by pressing Shift+Ctrl+Y (Windows) or Shift+Command+Y (Mac OS).

Next, you'll Web-shift one of the blue sky colors to reduce the amount of browser dither in that area.

2 Select the eyedropper tool (🖋), and click in the sky to sample a blue color. The sampled color appears selected in the Optimized Colors palette.

3 Click the Web Shift button (🎲) at the bottom of the Optimized Colors palette.

A small diamond appears in the center of the selected color, indicating that it has been shifted to its nearest Web-palette equivalent.

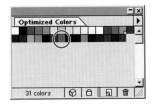

If desired, use the eyedropper tool to sample other colors in the image, and Web-shift them.

4 Choose File > Save Optimized. Then choose File > Close to close the original image without saving changes.

Specifying background transparency

Background transparency lets you place a non-rectangular graphic object against the background of a Web page; the areas outside the borders of the object are defined as transparent, letting the Web background color show through. You can specify background transparency for GIF and PNG images.

Making transparent and matted images

By specifying different Transparency and Matte options in the Optimize palette, you can create various types of background transparency in a GIF image.

Transparency on, Matte set to None *You can create hard-edged transparency in a GIF, in which all fully or partially transparent pixels in the original image are fully transparent in the optimized image. This feature prevents the halo effect that can result when an image with partially transparent pixels, such as those at the edges of an anti-aliased image, is placed on a Web page. However, hard-edged transparency can cause jagged edges in the image.*

Transparency on, Matte set to Web background color *You can choose to preserve fully transparent pixels as transparent, and matte only the partially transparent pixels, such as those at the edge of an anti-aliased image. When the image is placed on a Web page, the Web background color shows through the transparent pixels, and the edges of the image blend with the background color. This feature prevents the halo effect that results when an anti-aliased image is placed on a background color that differs from the image's original background. This feature also prevents the jagged edges that result with GIF hard-edged transparency.*

Transparency off, Matte set to Web background color *You can choose to blend all transparent pixels with the matte color. Fully transparent pixels are filled with the matte color, and partially transparent pixels are blended with the matte color.*

–From the Adobe ImageReady User Guide, Chapter 4

Creating transparency

In this part of the lesson, you'll optimize a logo image in GIF format and specify transparency options.

1 Choose File > Open, locate and select the Logo.psd file in the Less01IR folder, and click Open.

This logo image was created against a transparent background in Adobe Photoshop.

Note: You can use the magic eraser tool in Adobe ImageReady to convert a solid-colored background quickly to transparency.

🛈 For more information, see "Painting" in online Help or Chapter 10 in the Adobe ImageReady User Guide.

2 Select the zoom tool (🔍) and drag over the text area of the image as shown in the illustration.

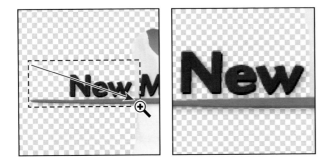

Notice the feathering along the edges of the text and the aquamarine underline. Double-click the zoom tool in the toolbox to return to 100% magnification.

3 In the Optimize palette, choose the GIF format with the Adaptive palette option. For colors, choose Auto to automatically reduce the colors in the palette to only those colors used in the image.

4 In the Optimize palette, select Transparency. For Matte, choose No Matte. Then click the Optimized tab in the image window to view the effects on the optimized image.

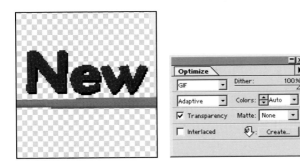

Selecting the Transparency option converts areas in the original image with less than 50% opacity to background transparency in the optimized image.

To view the transparency you've just defined, you'll preview the image in a Web browser.

5 Choose File > Preview In, and choose the desired browser application from the submenu.

Note: To use the Preview In command, you must have a browser application installed on your system. When you install Adobe ImageReady, the installer automatically creates shortcuts to your browser programs and places these shortcuts in the Preview In submenu. If you install a new browser program after installing ImageReady, you must create a new shortcut and place it in the Helpers\Preview In folder inside the ImageReady application folder.

If it is not already open, the browser application launches and displays the optimized image in the top left corner of the page. In addition, the browser displays the pixel dimensions, file size, file format, and optimization settings for the image, along with the HTML code used to create the preview.

Notice that the logo displays with sharp, unfeathered edges against the browser background color.

To smooth the transition between transparent and non-transparent areas in the logo, you'll specify a matte color.

6 Return to ImageReady. In the Optimize palette, for Matte, choose White. The semitransparent pixels along the logo's edges are blended with white to preserve a feathered appearance.

Note: When specifying a matte, be sure to choose a color that matches the background color you plan to use in your final Web page. If the matte color doesn't match the Web background color, a halo will appear around the edges of the image.

7 Choose File > Preview In, and choose a browser from the submenu to preview the revised background transparency.

Notice that the logo now displays with soft, feathered edges.

Trimming extra background areas

Although the background of the logo image contains transparent pixels that do not display, these pixels still take up file space, adding to the size of the image. You can trim away unneeded background areas to improve the layout of the image and optimize the file size.

1 Return to ImageReady, and choose Image > Trim.

The Trim command lets you crop your image, according to the transparency or pixel color of the extra border area.

2 Select Transparent Pixels and click OK.

ImageReady trims the extra transparent areas from the image.

3 Choose File > Save Optimized As. Name the file Logo1.gif, and click Save. Then choose File > Close to close the original image without saving changes.

Creating an image map

1 An *image map* is an image file that contains multiple hypertext links to other files on the Web. Different areas, or *hot spots,* of the image map link to different files. Adobe ImageReady creates client-side image maps that are fast to navigate. Unlike server-side image maps, client-side image maps are interpreted directly by the browser application and do not require a reference file on the Web server.

In this part of the lesson, you'll create an image map from an existing image. You define hot spots by placing each area on a separate layer.

2 Choose File > Open, locate and select the Map.psd file in the Less01IR folder, and click Open.

You'll make this collage image into a graphical table of contents linking to different areas of the Southwest travel Web site. In order to define an image map, you must be working in the optimized image.

3 In the Optimize palette, choose JPEG for the format and Medium for the quality. In the image window, click the Optimize tab to build the optimized image.

4 If the Layers palette is not already showing, choose Window > Show Layers.

Notice that the icons in the image reside on separate layers.

5 In the Layers palette, double-click the compass layer.

The Layer Options dialog box appears, letting you specify various settings for the compass layer.

6 Select Use Layer as Image Map. For Shape, choose Circle.

The Shape option determines the boundary of the hot spot area.

7 The URL option lets you specify the target file for the hot spot link. You can link to another file in your Web site, or to a different location on the Web. For the purposes of this lesson, you'll link your hot spots to the Adobe Systems home page.

8 For URL, enter **http://www.adobe.com**, and click OK.

The URL you entered appears below the compass layer name in the Layers palette.

9 Repeat steps 4 through 6 for the bell and wagon wheel layers, entering the following settings:

• For the bell layer, choose Polygon for the shape. For URL, enter **http://www.adobe.com**.

• For the wagon wheel layer, choose Circle for the shape. For URL, enter **http://www.adobe.com**.

Previewing and adjusting the cross-platform gamma range

Now you'll check to see if the brightness of your image is compatible across monitors on different platforms. Windows monitors generally display a darker midtone brightness, or *gamma*, than do Macintosh monitors. Be sure to preview and, if necessary, adjust the cross-platform brightness of your image before publishing it on the Web.

1 Choose View > Mac Gamma or View > Windows Gamma to preview how the image will appear across platforms.

An image created on a Windows system will appear lighter on a Macintosh monitor. An image created on a Macintosh system will appear darker on a Windows monitor.

2 Choose Image > Adjust > Gamma.

The Gamma dialog box appears, letting you automatically correct the image's gamma for cross-platform viewing.

3 Click the Windows to Macintosh button or the Macintosh to Windows button, and click OK.

4 Choose File > Save Optimized As. Name the image **Map1.jpg**, and click Save.

Now you'll preview your image map in a Web browser.

5 Choose File > Preview In, and choose a browser from the submenu. Move the pointer over the compass, bell, and wagon wheel, and notice that these elements contain hypertext links. If you have a modem and an Internet connection, you can click the hotspots to open the destination URL.

6 Return to Adobe ImageReady.

Creating the HTML file

When you export an image as an HTML file, ImageReady automatically generates the basic HTML tags needed to display your image on a Web page.

1 Make sure the optimized version of the image is displayed, and choose File > Export > Save HTML.

Note: You can also create an HTML file automatically when you save an optimized image by selecting Save HTML File in the Save Optimized As dialog box.

2 Name the file **Map1.html**, and click Save.

3 Choose File > Close to close the image without saving changes.

If desired, you can use your Web browser to open and view Map1.html. You can also open the file in a word-processing or HTML-editing program to make your own revisions to the HTML code.

Review questions

1 What is a color palette?

2 When does browser dither occur, and how can you minimize the amount of browser dither in an image?

3 What is the purpose of assigning matte color to a GIF image?

4 Summarize the procedure for creating an image map.

Review answers

1 A color palette is a table that contains the colors used to represent a GIF or PNG image. The GIF format supports different types of color palettes (Perceptual, Adaptive, Web, System), which can contain up to 256 colors. ImageReady lets you adjust the composition and number of colors in a color palette.

2 Browser dither occurs when a Web browser simulates colors that appear in the image's color palette but not in the browser's display system. To protect a color from browser dither, you can select the color in the Optimized Colors palette, and then click the Web Shift button at the bottom of the palette to shift the color to its closest equivalent in the Web palette. Alternatively, you can protect your entire image from browser dither by choosing the Web palette option in the Optimize palette.

3 By specifying a matte color, you can blend partially transparent pixels in an image with the background color of your Web page. Matting lets you create GIF images with feathered or anti-aliased edges that blend smoothly into the background color of your Web page.

4 To create an image map, you first place the hotspot areas of the image on separate layers. While in Optimized image view, double-click each hotspot layer in the Layers palette to open the Layer Options dialog box; then select Use Layer As Image Map, specify the shape and target URL for the hotspot, and click OK. Finally, save the optimized image, and create an HTML file that references the optimized image.

Lesson 2

Creating Animated Images

To add dynamic content to your Web page, use Adobe ImageReady to create animated GIF images. Compact in file size, animated GIFs display and play in most Web browsers. Adobe ImageReady provides an easy and convenient way to create imaginative animations.

In this lesson, you'll learn to do the following:

• Use the Layers palette in conjunction with the Animation palette to create animation sequences.

• Preview animations in ImageReady and in a Web browser.

• Open and edit an existing animated GIF image.

Creating animations in Adobe ImageReady

You compose animations by using the Animation palette to create animation frames and the Layers palette to define the image state associated with each frame. When creating an animation sequence, it's best to remain in Original image view—this saves ImageReady from having to re-optimize the image as you edit the frame contents.

In this lesson, you'll work with a set of images designed to appear on the Web page of a fresh juice company.

About layer-based animation

When creating an animation in ImageReady, the layers in the image function as separate elements that can be moved and changed in each frame.

You can make changes in layers that affect individual frames, groups of frames, or an entire animation. Changes you make to a layer using layer palette commands and options affect only the current frame in which the changes are made. Changes you make to a layer using ImageReady painting and editing tools, color and tone adjustment commands, filters, and type affect every frame in which the layer is included.

–From the Adobe ImageReady User Guide, Chapter 5

If you have a browser application installed on your computer, you can preview the finished animations. Start your browser application and open Jus.htm in the Jus folder inside the Less02IR folder. Close the file when you have finished viewing it, and return to Adobe ImageReady.

Getting started

Before beginning this lesson, delete the Adobe ImageReady Preferences file to restore the program's default settings. For step-by-step instructions, see "Restoring default preferences" on page 4. Then restart the ImageReady program.

Creating simple motion

You'll start by animating the construction of a text logo.

Using layers to create animation frames

In this part of the lesson, you'll adjust the position and opacity of layers in an image to create the starting and ending frames of an animation sequence.

1 Choose File > Open, locate and select the Logoa.psd file inside the Less02IR folder, and click Open.

The logo consists of four different components that reside on separate layers. In the Layers palette, notice that all the layers are currently visible. Visible layers appear with eye icons in the palette.

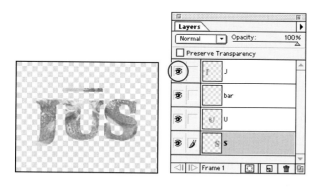

To define an animation, you use the Layers palette in conjunction with the Animation palette. The Animation palette lets you compose the content and order of animation frames.

2 Choose Window > Show Animation.

The Animation palette opens with a single default frame that reflects the current state of the layers in the image. The frame is selected, or outlined by a border, indicating that you can change its content by editing layers.

You'll compose animation frames that show the letters of the logo appearing and moving into place from different areas. The current image state reflects how you want the logo to appear at the end of the animation.

3 Click the New Frame button (🖫) at the bottom of the Animation palette to create a new animation frame.

Now you'll show the components of the logo text in different starting positions.

4 In the Layers palette, select the J layer.

5 With frame 2 selected in the Animation palette, select the move tool (✛). Hold down Shift to constrain the movement, and drag the J in the image to the left, repositioning it at the left edge of the image. Then lower the opacity of the J layer to 20%.

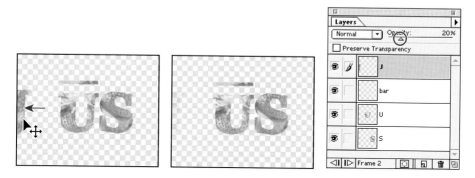

6 Now select the S layer in the Layers palette. Use the move tool to Shift-drag the S to the right edge of the image. Then lower the opacity of the S layer to 20%.

Repeat this step to select, move, and change the opacity of the bar layer and the U layer, as follows:

• Move the bar to the top edge of the image, and lower the opacity to 20%.

• Move the U to the bottom edge of the image, and lower the opacity to 20%.

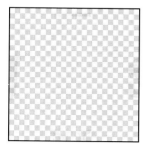

In the Animation palette, notice that frame 2 has updated to reflect the current image state. To make frame 2 the starting state of your animation, you'll switch the order of the two frames.

7 In the Animation palette, drag frame 2 to the left, releasing the mouse when the black bar appears to the left of frame 1.

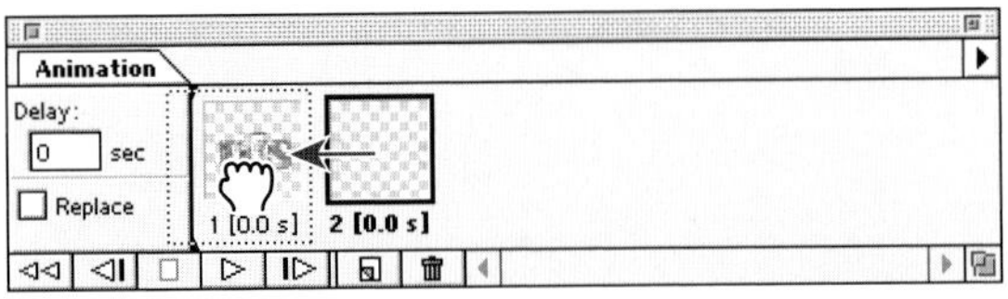

Tweening the position and opacity of layers

To finish the animation sequence, you'll add frames that represent transitional images states between the two existing frames. When you change the position or opacity of any layer between two animation frames, you can instruct ImageReady to *tween*, or automatically create intermediate frames.

1 In the Animation palette, make sure that frame 1 is selected; then choose Tween from the palette menu.

2 For Frame to Add, enter **4**; for Tween With, choose Next Frame. Select the Position and Opacity options, and click OK.

ImageReady creates four new transitional frames based on the opacity and position settings of the layers in the original two frames.

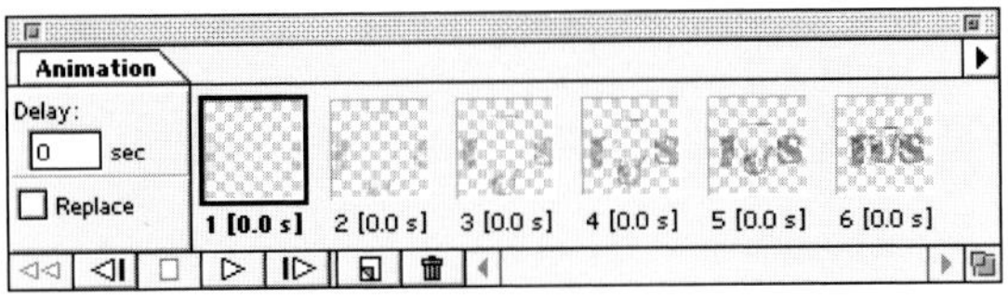

3 Choose Play Options from the Animation palette menu. Select Once (the default option), and click OK.

4 Click the Play button (▷) at the bottom of the Animation palette to preview your animation in ImageReady.

Managing transparency in animations

Next, you'll optimize the image in GIF format with background transparency and preview your animation in a Web browser. Remember that only the GIF format supports animated images.

Using layer transparency in an animation

You can use layer transparency in animation frames to reposition or edit elements and create the appearance of movement. With layer transparency you can create the appearance of a single element in a scene moving or fading in and out over a still background, or the appearance of several elements moving independently.

Using layer transparency can create unwanted effects in an animation. Previous frames can appear through the transparent areas in the current frame, causing an overlapping effect in which multiple views of a layer are visible at once. In ImageReady, you can prevent this effect by using the Replace option. When the Replace option is selected, each frame in the animation is fully discarded from the display before the new frame is displayed. Only a single frame is displayed at any time.

–From the Adobe ImageReady User Guide, Chapter 5

1 In the Optimize palette, choose GIF for the format, Perceptual for the palette, and Auto for the number of colors. Select Transparency to preserve the background transparency of the original image, and set the matte color to White.

2 In the image window, click the Optimized tab to build the optimized image.

Notice the Optimized file size at the bottom of the image window. Adding animation frames to an image also adds to the file size. To reduce the file size of your animated GIF images, try experimenting with different palette and color settings, as described in ImageReady Lesson 1, "Optimizing Images for Web Publication."

3 Choose File > Preview In, and choose a browser application from the submenu.

Note: *To use the Preview In command, you must have a browser application installed on your system.*

Notice that leftover remnants from previous frames appear in the browser window as the animation is being played. This ghosting effect is caused by previous frames showing through the transparent areas of the current frame.

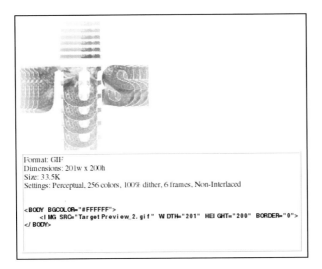

4 Return to the ImageReady program. In the Animation palette, select frame 1, and then select Replace.

When you turn on the Replace option, ImageReady clears the selected frame before the next frame is played, eliminating the danger of displaying leftover remnants.

5 Repeat step 4 to turn on the Replace option for each frame in the sequence.

6 Choose File > Preview In, and choose a browser from the submenu to preview your revised animation. Notice that the animation now plays correctly.

7 Return to ImageReady.

8 Choose File > Save Optimized As, name the image **Logo1.gif**, and click Save.

Navigating animation frames

You can use a number of techniques to preview and scroll through your animation frames.

1 Use the following navigation controls to practice moving through the frames of the logo text animation.

• You can select a frame by clicking its thumbnail in the Animation palette. The image and the Layers palette update to reflect the state of the selected frame.

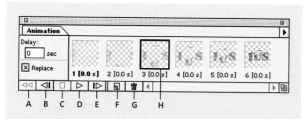

A. Rewind button B. Backward button C. Stop button
D. Play button E. Forward button F. New Frame button
G. Trash H. Selected frame

• The Forward and Backward buttons at the bottom of the Animation palette let you move forward and backward through the frame sequence. The First Frame button lets you select the first frame in the sequence.

• The Forward and Backward buttons at the bottom of the Layers palette let you move forward and backward through the frame sequence. These controls are especially convenient when you want to quickly edit the layers for a succession of frames.

A. Forward button
B. Backward button

2 When you are finished practicing, choose File > Close, and close the original image without saving changes.

Creating a transition between image states

Now you'll animate layer opacity to create the illusion of an image fading gradually into
a different state.

1 Choose File > Open, locate and select the Logob.psd file inside the Less02IR folder, and
click Open.

The logo image contains two layers that represent different background styles. A photographic background of an orange tree currently appears in the image.

2 In the Layers palette, click in the eye column next to the photo layer to hide the layer.
The illustration layer is now visible in the image, showing a version of the background
tree that looks more hand-drawn.

You'll create an animation that shows the background transitioning from the photo style
to the illustration style.

3 In the Layers palette, click in the eye column to make the photo layer visible. Eye icons
should appear next to both the photo and illustration layers. The photo background
appears in the image, defining the starting state of the animation.

Now you'll define the ending state of the animation.

4 Click the New Frame button (⬚) at the bottom of the Animation palette.

5 In the Layers palette, click in the eye column to hide the photo layer.

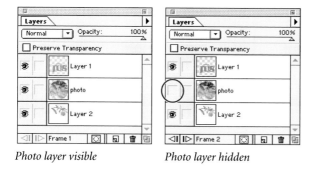

Photo layer visible   *Photo layer hidden*

6 Choose Tween from the Animation palette menu. For Frames to Add, enter **4**; for Tween With, choose Previous Frame. Deselect Position, select Opacity, and click OK.

ImageReady adds four transitional frames with intermediate opacities. When tweening the frames, ImageReady treats the hidden photo layer as a 1% opaque layer.

7 From the Animation palette menu, choose Play Options. Select Once (the default option) and click OK.

8 Play the animation sequence.

Although you can preview animations in ImageReady, the timing of this preview may not be accurate. This is because ImageReady takes a moment to build the composition of each frame during playback. For a more accurate preview, play your animation in a Web browser.

9 Choose File > Preview In, and choose the desired browser application from the submenu.

10 When you are finished previewing the animation, return to ImageReady.

11 Choose File > Save Optimized As, name the image **Logo2.gif**, and click Save. ImageReady saves the animation as a GIF using the settings in the Optimize palette. Remember that you can change the palette and color settings in the Optimize palette to reduce file size.

12 Choose File > Close to close the original image without saving changes.

Creating a two-step animation

You can create a simple two-step animation by toggling the visibility of two layers. For example, you can make an animated character alternate between different expressions, or make an object move back and forth in a simple pattern. In this part of the lesson, you'll animate the shaking of a cartoon juice blender.

1 Choose File > Open, locate and select the Blender.psd file inside the Less02IR folder, and click Open.

The blender image consists of several layers. You'll create animation frames that alternate between hiding and showing two layers representing different positions of the blender pitcher.

An eye icon should appear in the Layers palette next to Layer 1, indicating that this is the only visible layer in the image.

2 Click the New Frame button (🖼) at the bottom of the Animation palette.

3 In the Layers palette, click in the eye column next to Layer 2 to display this layer in the image. Since Layer 2 sits above Layer 1 in the stacking order, there is no need to hide Layer 1.

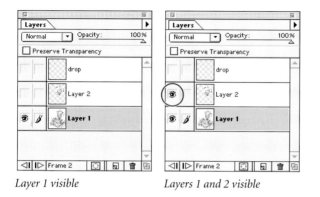

Layer 1 visible   Layers 1 and 2 visible

4 From the Animation palette menu, choose Play Options. Select Forever and click OK.

5 Click the Play button (▷) at the bottom of the palette to preview the animation. Click the Stop button (□) to stop the animation.

Now you'll preview the animation in a Web browser.

6 Choose File > Preview In, and choose a browser program from the submenu. (You can also press Ctrl+Alt+P (Windows) or Command+Option+P (Mac OS) to launch a browser preview quickly.)

When you are finished previewing the animation, close the browser window, and return to Adobe ImageReady.

7 Choose File > Save Optimized As, name the image **Blender1.gif**, and click Save.

Rotating and moving an object

Now you'll animate a different element in the blender image, adding to the existing animation. By successively copying and transforming a layer, you can make an object move or fall in a realistic trajectory.

Creating transformed layers

You'll start by creating layers that simulate the path of a juice drop falling from the top of the blender as the blender shakes.

Before adding layers to an image that already contains an animation, it's a good idea to create a new frame first. This step helps to protect your existing frames from unwanted changes.

1 In the Animation palette, select frame 2. Then click the New Frame button (▣) to create a new frame after frame 2.

2 In the Layers palette, make the drop layer visible.

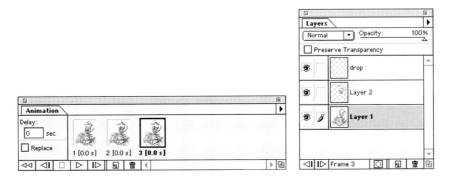

Notice the small juice drop that appears at the top left edge of the blender in the image.

3 Select the drop layer in the Layers palette. Drag the layer name to the New Layer button (▣) to duplicate the layer.

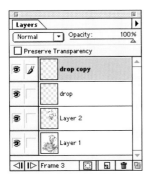

4 With the drop copy layer selected, choose Edit > Free Transform.

The transformation bounding box appears around the drop copy layer.

5 Position the pointer outside the bounding box (the pointer becomes a curved double arrow (↰)) and drag to rotate the drop counterclockwise. Then position the pointer inside the bounding box (the pointer becomes an arrowhead (►)) and drag to reposition the drop as shown in the illustration. (You may need to zoom in on the drop to see the pointer change to an arrow.) Press Enter (Windows) or Return (Mac OS) to apply the transformation.

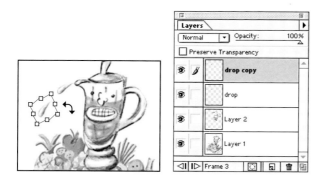

6 Now drag the drop copy layer to the New Layer button (⬚) to duplicate the layer.

7 With the drop copy 2 layer selected, choose Edit > Free Transform. Rotate and reposition the layer as shown in the illustration. Press Enter/Return to apply the transformation.

You should now have two copied and transformed drop layers.

8 Choose File > Save Original As, name the image **Blender1.psd**, and click Save to save a copy of the original image with the layers you've just created.

Creating simultaneous animations

Now you'll define the falling drop animation by successively hiding and showing the layers you've just created. You'll also build in the shaking blender animation as the drop falls.

1 In the Animation palette, make sure that frame 3 is selected. In the Layers palette, make the drop layer and Layer 1 visible, and hide all other layers.

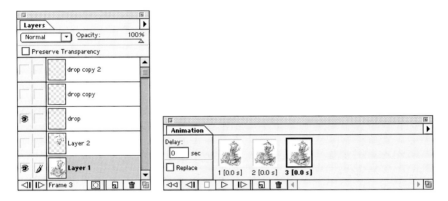

Now you'll add a frame that continues the shaking of the blender while the drop falls.

2 Click the New Frame button (🖹) at the bottom of the Animation palette.

3 In the Layers palette, make Layer 2 visible.

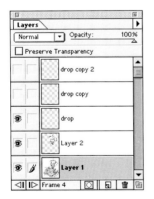

Continue to use the Animation and Layers palettes to create the following frames:

• For frame 5, make drop copy and Layer 1 the visible layers.

- For frame 6, make drop copy, Layer 2, and Layer 1 the visible layers.

- For frame 7, make drop copy 2 and Layer 1 the visible layers.

- For frame 8, make drop copy 2, Layer 2, and Layer 1 the visible layers.

4 Choose Set Delay For All Frames from the Animation palette menu. Enter **0.05** for the delay, and click OK.

When you specify a time delay in the Set Delay For All Frames dialog box, the specified delay is applied to all the frames in the palette, as indicated by the value that appears enclosed in brackets below each frame thumbnail.

5 Choose Play Options from the Animation palette menu. Select Forever and click OK.

6 Click the Play button at the bottom of the Animation palette to view your animation.

The juice drop should fall as the blender shakes. Click the Stop button (☐) to stop the animation.

7 Choose File > Save Optimized As. Name the image **Blender1.gif**, click Save, and replace the existing file. Then choose File > Close to close the original image without saving changes.

Creating a montage sequence

In this part of the lesson, you'll create a quickly changing sequence, or *montage,* of fruit images. You create montage effects by hiding and showing layers in succession.

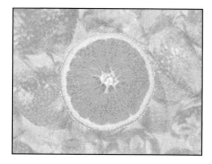

Setting the montage order

You'll work with an image that contains a number of layers showing different fruit images.

1 Choose File > Open, locate and select the Fruit.psd file inside the Less02IR folder, and click Open.

2 In the Layers palette, choose Make Frames From Layers from the palette menu.

The layers in the image appear as individual frames in the Animation palette.

3 Choose Set Delay For All Frames from the Animation palette menu. Enter **0.25** for the delay, and click OK.

4 Click the Play button (▷) to view the sequence of images. Click the Stop button (□) to stop the animation.

Now you'll reorder the animation frames so that the lemons appear first in the sequence.

5 In the Animation palette, click to select the frame containing the lemons. Then drag the selected frame to the left until a double line appears before frame 1, and release the mouse.

The lemons frame is now the first frame in the sequence.

6 Click the Play button (▷) to view the revised montage.

7 Choose File > Save Optimized As. Name the image **Fruit1.gif**, and click Save.

Smoothing the transition between frames

Now you'll enhance your newly assembled montage by adding intermediate frames that smooth the transition between the strawberries and the orange.

1 In the Animation palette, select the frame containing the strawberries. The image window and the Layers palette update to reflect the contents of the frame.

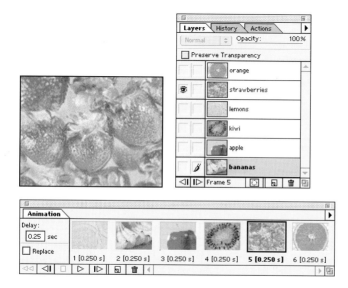

2 Click the New Frame button (🖫) at the bottom of the Animation palette to create a new frame after the strawberries frame.

3 In the Layers palette, select the strawberries layer, and drag the Opacity slider to 1%.

4 Choose Tween from the Animation palette menu. For Frames to Add, enter **4**; for Tween With, choose Previous Frame. Deselect Position, select Opacity, and click OK.

5 Click the Play button to view the new montage.

If desired, you can add transitional opacities between the other fruit images in the sequence.

Making an object grow in size

For the grand conclusion to the fruit montage, you'll animate the orange swelling from a small to a large size.

First you'll copy and resize the orange layer several times.

1 In the Animation palette, select the frame containing the orange.

2 In the Layers palette, drag the orange layer to the New Layer button (🖹) to create a duplicate layer. Repeat this step to create three more duplicates of the orange layer.

3 Click the Link icon next to the orange layer and the orange layer copies to unlink the layers.

4 Double-click the orange copy layer to display the Layer Options dialog box. For name, enter **orange 20%**. Then click OK.

Repeat this step for the other duplicate layers, renaming the layers **orange 40%, orange 60%,** and **orange 80%.**

5 Select and make visible the orange 20% layer. Hide the other orange layers.

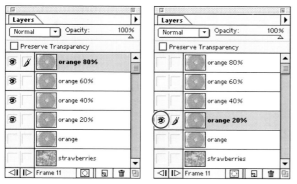

Renaming layers　　　*Making orange 20% layer visible*

6 Choose Edit > Transform > Numeric. For Percent, enter **20**. Make sure that Constrain Proportions is selected, and click OK.

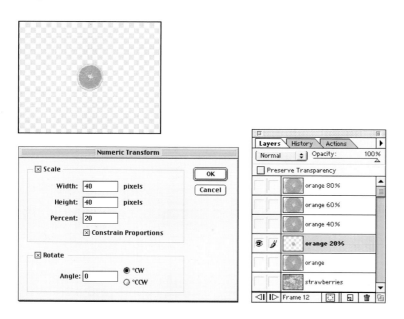

7 Click the New Frame button in the Animation palette to create a new frame. Select and make visible the orange 40% layer and hide the orange 20% layer. Choose Edit > Transform > Numeric, and resize the layer to 40%.

Repeat this step to create frames containing the orange 60% and orange 80% layers resized to their respective percentages, hiding the previous layer with each step.

8 Play your animation.

9 Choose File > Save Optimized. ImageReady saves the animation as a GIF using the current settings in the Optimize palette.

10 Choose File > Close to close the original image without saving changes.

Using advanced layer features to create animations

In this part of the lesson, you'll learn some animation tricks that can be created through the use of advanced layer features, such as layer masks and clipping groups.

You'll work with versions of the logo image that you saw at the beginning of the lesson.

Using layer masks to create animations

First you'll use a layer mask to create the illusion of juice filling slowly to the top of the "U" in the logo text.

1 Choose File > Open, locate and select the Logoc.psd file inside the Less02IR folder, and click Open.

2 In the Layers palette, hide the photo layer and leave the text layer and the juice layer visible.

The juice layer contains a layer mask, as indicated by the grayscale thumbnail that appears to the right of the layer thumbnail in the palette. The layer mask is U-shaped, restricting the orange juice to appear only through the "U" in the logo text.

The orange juice should currently fill to the brim of the "U." Next, you'll move the juice layer to define another frame that shows the "U" empty of juice.

3 Click the New Frame button (🖪) at the bottom of the Animation palette to create a second frame. In the Layers palette, click to turn off the link icon between the layer and layer mask thumbnails.

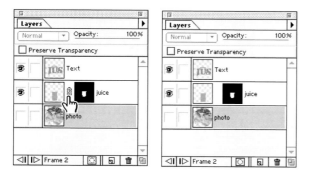

Turning off the link icon lets you move the layer independent of its layer mask.

4 Select the move tool (▶₊).

5 Click the layer thumbnail for the juice mask layer to select the layer.

6 Position the move tool over the orange color in the image, and drag to reposition the layer below the curve of the "U."

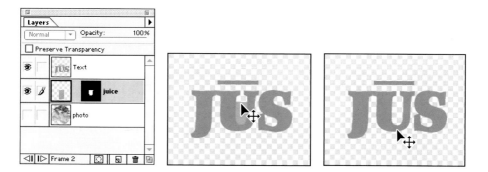

7 In the Animation palette, drag to reverse the order of frames 1 and 2.

Since you have defined the two frames by repositioning a single layer, you can generate intermediate frames automatically using the Tween command.

8 Choose Tween from the Animation palette menu. For Frames to Add, enter **5**; for Tween With, choose Next Frame. Select Position, deselect Opacity, and click OK.

9 Make the photo layer visible in frame 1 and frame 2.

10 Choose Play Options from the Animation palette menu, select once, and click OK.

11 Select frame 1, and play the animation.

12 Choose File > Save Optimized As, name the file **Logo3.gif**, and click Save. Then choose File > Close to close the original file without saving changes.

Using clipping groups to create animations

Now you'll create the effect of strawberries shaking inside the logo text.

1 Choose File > Open, locate and select the Logod.psd file inside the Less02IR folder, and click Open.

2 In the Layers palette, make the strawberries and text layers visible.

To make the strawberries appear only through the shape of the logo text, you'll create a clipping group.

3 Select the strawberries layer. Then choose Layer > Group with Previous.

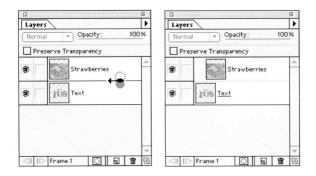

Notice that the strawberries now appear masked by the logo text. The thumbnail for the strawberries layer is indented, indicating that the layer is grouped with the layer that precedes it.

4 Click the New Frame button at the bottom of the Animation palette.

For the second animation frame, you'll reposition the strawberries layer slightly.

5 Select the strawberries layer in the Layers palette. Then select the move tool in the toolbox.

6 In the image, drag the strawberries layer slightly to the right or use the arrow keys to move the layer.

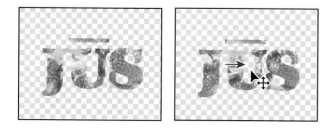

7 Choose Play Options from the Animation palette menu, select Forever, and click OK.

8 Play the animation.

The strawberries should shake from side to side inside the logo text. Click the Stop button to stop the animation.

9 Choose File > Save Optimized As, name the file **Logo4.gif**, and click Save. ImageReady saves the animation as a GIF using the current settings in the Optimize palette.

10 Choose File > Close to close the original image without saving changes.

Review questions

1 In what instances can you tween animation frames?

2 When should you use the Replace option?

3 How do you edit an existing animation frame?

Review answers

1 You can instruct Adobe ImageReady to tween intermediate frames between any two frames, to change layer opacity or position or add new layers to a sequence of frames.

2 When you change the position or opacity of a layer between two frames, you can instruct Adobe ImageReady to tween intermediate frames.

3 You should select the Replace option for all frames that contain background transparency. The Replace option redraws each frame completely as it is played, to prevent the appearance of unwanted ghost patterns from previous frames. Remember that you must select Replace for each frame in order to affect the entire animation sequence.

4 To edit an existing animation frame, you first select the frame, either by clicking the frame thumbnail in the Animation palette, or navigating to the desired frame using the controls at the bottom of the Animation palette or Layers palette. Then edit the layers in the image to update the contents of the selected frame.

Index

Production Notes

This book was created electronically using Adobe FrameMaker®. Art was produced using Adobe Illustrator, Adobe ImageReady, and Adobe Photoshop. The Minion® and Frutiger® families of typefaces are used throughout the book.

Photography

Photographic images intended for use with tutorials only.

Adobe Image Club ObjectGear: ImageReady Lesson 1 (hotel desk bell, compass, wagon wheel)

Adobe Image Library: Lesson 8 (tulips, sunflower, winter, leaves); Lesson 12 (framing, woman on phone); Lesson 13 (duck); Lesson 11 (giraffe); ImageReady Lesson 2 (bananas, kiwi, lemons, apple, strawberries)

CMCD Inc.: Lesson 12 (hammer)

Dean Dapkus: Lesson 5 (Venice)

Julieanne Kost: Lesson 1 (roller skater); Lesson 2 (vegetables); Lesson 5 (egret); Lesson 7 (cat mask); Lesson 9 (pears); Lesson 11 (zebra, hands, warthog, elephant, hippos, crocodile); ImageReady Tour (all photos); ImageReady Lesson 1 (oranges)

Leon Sobon: Lesson 10 (grapes)

Lisa Milosevich: Image Ready Lesson 1 (desert scene)

PhotoDisc, Inc.: Lesson 10 (box, cap, cup); Lesson 3 (keyboard, clock, bearing, gauge) All PhotoDisc images: ©1997 PhotoDisc, Inc., 2013 Fourth Ave., Seattle, WA 98121, 1-800-528-3472, www.photodisc.com.